SOYBEANS AND POWER

SOYBEANS AND POWER

Genetically Modified Crops, Environmental Politics, and Social Movements in Argentina

Pablo Lapegna

OXFORD
UNIVERSITY PRESS

OXFORD
UNIVERSITY PRESS

Oxford University Press is a department of the University of Oxford. It furthers the University's objective of excellence in research, scholarship, and education by publishing worldwide. Oxford is a registered trade mark of Oxford University Press in the UK and certain other countries.

Published in the United States of America by Oxford University Press
198 Madison Avenue, New York, NY 10016, United States of America.

Library of Congress Cataloging-in-Publication Data
Names: Lapegna, Pablo, author.
Title: Soybeans and power : genetically modified crops, environmental politics, and social movements in Argentina / Pablo Lapegna.
Description: New York : Oxford University Press, 2016. | Series: Global and comparative ethnography | Includes bibliographical references and index.
Identifiers: LCCN 2016002350 (print) | LCCN 2016012208 (ebook) |
ISBN 9780190215132 (hardcover : alk. paper) | ISBN 9780190215149 (pbk. : alk. paper) |
ISBN 9780190215156 (updf) | ISBN 9780190215163 (epub)
Subjects: LCSH: Social movements—Argentina. | Environmental policy—Argentina. |
Plant genetic engineering.
Classification: LCC HN263.5 .L37 2016 (print) |
LCC HN263.5 (ebook) | DDC 306.0982—dc23
LC record available at http://lccn.loc.gov/2016002350

9 8 7 6 5 4 3 2 1

Paperback printed by WebCom, Inc., Canada
Hardback printed by Bridgeport National Bindery, Inc., United States of America

CONTENTS

"What should we do? Should we park here?" asked Diego shyly from the wheel of his 1990s pickup truck. We did not answer, still feeling out of place. It was a foggy morning in March 2004, and I was sitting snugly between Pablo and Diego, friends and fellow sociologists from the University of Buenos Aires. We were driving stealthily alongside a highway near San Pedro, in the province of Buenos Aires. A wide, open meadow to our right led to Feriagro, an annual fair organized and promoted by a national media conglomerate. The entrance featured the logos of agribusiness companies, media outlets, and governmental offices sponsoring the fair where dozens of large white tents and colorful flags occupied an area of 1,000 hectares (the equivalent of nearly 1,900 American football fields). I was a bit nervous, as if dreading an impending embarrassment.

We had gathered in Buenos Aires two hours earlier, assembling a group of two dozen activists, rural sociologists, community organizers, and alternative journalists. All of us participated in the Land and Food Forum (Foro de la Tierra y la Alimentación), a loose network of academics, activists, and NGOs concerned about the social and environmental consequences of the vast expansion of genetically modified (GM) soybeans in Argentina. We were in San Pedro to partake in what we called "a counter-Feriagro," that is, a form of protest mimicking the countersummits of the antiglobalization movement at an infinitesimal scale. Our goal was "to discuss and think about alternatives, to regain the joy of a country and an agriculture that belongs to us all," as written in the leaflets we distributed.

Hesitantly, we parked near the main entrance to the fair where we erected a gazebo, installed two large wood panels to paint a mural on, and put up placards ("Glyphosate and 2,4D KILL," "There Is No Food Sovereignty with Transgenics"). We spent the day handing out flyers and painting two murals. The next day, we participated in a public presentation at the local library titled "San Pedro: From Orchard to Green Desert," in which an agronomist talked about how the area had gone from growing fruits to planting soybeans. We were glad to see many locals join us to hear a rock band that we had invited to close the event with a concert in downtown San Pedro later that night.

We had a great time even though the protest was largely inconsequential, barely reported in the media, and most likely did not change the minds of Feriagro attendants. I have briefly recounted this event as a way of making four points regarding my personal relationship with GM crops and social movements.

First, my participation in the modest counter-Feriagro suggests how and why I became interested in the social and environmental consequences of GM crops. Around 1998, as an advanced undergraduate student of sociology at the University of Buenos Aires, I joined a group in the School of Social Sciences doing research on rural sociology and social movements. In Argentina, and elsewhere in Latin America, the boundaries between social research and activism are porous, and the group I joined was not an exception. After 2001, like many Argentines around that time, group members, myself included, became even more involved in activism (in the context of the intensified social mobilization I discuss in chapter 1). In March 2003, I traveled to Formosa with two friends and colleagues, doubling as activists from the Land and Food Forum and sociologists from the University of Buenos Aires. As a result of this visit, we wrote a chapter in an edited volume and created a short documentary that we later showcased in Formosa.

"Soybeans and Power," however, is not a translation of activism into writing. While I entertain ethical and political questions, this book actually emerges from my *dissatisfaction* with what I came to see as Manichean views on the globalization of food and collective action. As I kept going to Formosa, for instance, I became increasingly aware of the dangers of projecting my own hopes onto the actions of others. My fieldwork, slowly but surely, convinced me that clear-cut narratives of global agrarian capitalism did not accurately depict the views of peasants, or rather tended to give credence to some voices at the cost of muffling others. In short, I believe that we should have a critical perspective not only toward the social processes we analyze but also toward the theories we use to make sense of them.

Third, I also candidly present my participation in anti-transgenic protests as a way of unveiling my own position. Issues of reflexivity and ponderings on the relationship between the researcher, her or his background, the field site, and fieldwork involve complex and lengthy discussions. I simply want to honestly disclose the conditions that led me to investigate the environmental and social issues surrounding the expansion of GM crops. Throughout this book

I am present in my own narrative not out of egocentrism, but because it is hard to disentangle my presence and the data I present. This is not a call for a radical constructivism or postmodern hermeneutics, but simply expresses my alignment with a straightforward realist constructivism in the sense articulated by Pierre Bourdieu: "Against the illusion which consists of seeking neutrality by eliminating the observer, it must be admitted that, paradoxically, the only 'spontaneous' process is a constructed one, but *a realist construction*" (Bourdieu 1999: 618, original emphasis).

Fourth and last, in this book I delve into the quotidian activities of social movements, coming dangerously close to airing dirty laundry. So a few words on the goals inspiring this research beyond my scholarly interests are in order. Romanticizing social movements may help in the way of garnering sympathy toward some causes, but this comes with the risk, I believe, of providing little in the spirit of constructive criticism or potentially useful cautionary tales for social movements. In other words, I think that a critical perspective should not stop at the door of a social movement organization, so to speak, or turn a blind eye (or a deaf ear) to the inequalities and subordination transpiring within and between movements and allies. Naturally, this critical perspective on social movements should always follow the mandate of "do no harm." I have made an effort to walk the thin line of being critical without spouting sterile criticism.

In any case, readers will ultimately decide how well I served the purposes I set forth when embarking on this endeavor.

ACKNOWLEDGMENTS

This book would not have been possible without all the people in Formosa who generously volunteered their scarce and valuable time to have conversations about experiences and events that oftentimes were not pleasurable to talk about. I am thus indebted to the members and leaders of MoCaFor for opening their organization, their homes, and their lives, to allow me to complete this project. *Muchas gracias cumpas!*

It is hard to find the words to thank my advisor and friend, Javier Auyero. He has always been there to generously support me—academically and otherwise. He goes above and beyond the call of duty, comments on my writings at shocking speed, and is overall an outstanding colleague. Let me just say (for those who are not fortunate enough to know him personally) that his superb abilities as scholar are only matched by his marvelous warmth and generosity as a person. *Gracias totales O'Sheer!*

This book is a thoroughly revised version of my doctoral dissertation, and I would like to express my gratitude to the exceptional members of my dissertation committee: to Michael Schwartz, because every meeting with him guaranteed insightful ideas and unparalleled enthusiasm; to Ian Roxborough, for constantly pushing me to make my arguments more precise and clear; and to Marc Edelman, for offering generous support and always providing a different and sophisticated viewpoint. I am also grateful to Eileen Otis, who encouraged me during the initial years of the PhD program.

I am very thankful to Katherine Jensen, Noël Norcross, and Pamela Neumann for their editorial assistance and extremely useful comments, and particularly to Katherine Sobering, a dear friend, insightful colleague, and editor extraordinaire. Brandon Adams, Diego Mourelos, and Inés Petz provided very useful assistance with the illustrations. A number of friends and colleagues read different portions of the manuscript (in its various iterations) and provided generous and constructive criticism: Claudio Benzecry, Oscar Chamosa, James Coverdill, Andrew Deener, Elizabeth Fitting, Melissa Forbis,

Susanna Hecht, Matthew Mahler, Emily Sahakian, Xiahong Xu, and the anonymous reviewers of the manuscript. At the University of Georgia, my colleagues Patricia Richards and David Smilde and PhD students Rebecca Hanson and Jeff Gardner contributed to improve key sections of the manuscript and to create a stimulating working environment.

In Argentina, Norma Giarracca and the members of the Grupo de Estudios Rurales of the Instituto de Investigaciones Gino Germani at the University of Buenos Aires (among others, Karina Bidaseca, Carla Gras and Daniela Mariotti) deserve recognition for enriching the early stages of my journey to become a sociologist. I would especially like to mention Pablo Barbetta, Diego Domínguez, and Pablo Sabatino for the many hours we spent writing, discussing, doing fieldwork, participating in demonstrations, or just enjoying time together. In Formosa, I am indebted with Cándida and Héctor Fernández and their family, Anny and Jorge Alcaraz, Luis Castellán, Sergio Sapkus, and Isabel Arguello and her family. Thank you so much for welcoming me during all these years.

In the United States, I was lucky to have friends who enriched my expatriate life and who were there through thick and thin: Bahar Aykan, José Aznarez, Natalia Chanfreau, Consuelo Figueroa, Angelo Guanazzi, Alberto Harambour, Barbara Orelli, Victoria Prieto, Alexis Stern, and Emilio Teubal. My friends and colleagues Diana Baldermann, Can Ersoy, and Lauren Joseph offered generous support during the long and winding road of my PhD.

I presented portions of this manuscript and benefitted from the comments of the participants at the Yale Comparative Research Workshop, the Taula workshop at the Center for Latin American and Caribbean Studies of the University of Connecticut, the Geography Colloquium at Department of Geography of the University of Georgia, the Forum of the International Sociological Association in Buenos Aires, the annual conference of the American Sociological Association in Denver, and a mini-conference of the section on Political Economy of the World-System (American Sociological Association) in New York.

I thank several institutions which supported this project in different ways and at diverse stages: the Tinker Foundation, the Social Science Research Council, the National Science Foundation, and, at the University of Georgia, the Sociology Department, the Latin American and Caribbean Studies Institute, the Willson Center for Humanities and the Arts, the Franklin College, and the Center for Teaching and Learning. Grant #P015A140046 from the US Department of Education supported this publication (however, the contents of this book do not necessarily represent the policy of the

US Department of Education, and endorsement by the federal government should not assumed).

At Oxford University Press, I was very fortunate to count on the diligent work of James Cook and Amy Klopfenstein, who did a superb work in bringing the manuscript to print.

My parents, Víctor Lapegna and Rita Calogero, my sister Alejandra Lapegna, my brother-in-law Claudio Meschini, and my nieces Malena Meschini and Lara Meschini always offered unconditional love and support.

It is not easy to express the many ways in which I am grateful to my partner in crime, friend, and lover, Roberta Salmi. *Tanti grazie* Rob, for bringing unexpected experiences to my life and for teaching me how to see things differently. Like everybody says but Ray LaMontagne sings like no other, "you are the best thing that ever happened to me."

While this book was in the making, two close friends and colleagues passed away: Gastón Joaquín Beltrán and Norma Giarracca. They will be sorely missed, both as exceptional people and insightful sociologists. This book is dedicated to their memory.

LIST OF ACRONYMS

ACINA	Asamblea Campesina Indígena del Norte Argentino (Peasant and Indigenous Assembly of the Argentine North)
CNIA	Comisión Nacional de Investigación sobre Agroquímicos (National Commission of Research on Agrochemicals)
FoNAF	Foro Nacional de Agricultura Familiar (National Forum of Family Agriculture)
FTV	Federacion de Tierra y Vivienda (Land and Housing Federation)
GM	Genetically modified
INTA	Instituto Nacional de Tecnología Agropecuaria (National Institute of Agricultural Technology)
MAF	Movimiento Agrario de Formosa (Agrarian Movement of Formosa)
MNCI	Movimiento Nacional Campesino Indígena (National Indigenous-Peasant Movement)
MoCaFor	Movimiento Campesino de Formosa (Peasant Movement of Formosa)
PAIPPA	Programa de Asistencia Integral al Pequeño Productor Agropecuario (Program of Integral Assistance to Small Farmers)
PJ	Partido Justicialista (political party, also known as Peronist Party)
PSA	Programa Social Agropecuario (Social Agricultural Program)
SAGPyA	Secretaría de Agricultura, Ganadería, Pesca y Alimentación de la Nación (National Secretary of Agriculture, Stockbreeding, Fishery, and Food)

SSDRAF   Sub-Secretaría de Desarrollo Rural y Agricultura Familiar (Sub-Secretary of Rural Development and Family Agriculture)

ULiCaF   Unión de Ligas Campesinas de Formosa (Union of Formosan Peasant Leagues)

LIST OF ILLUSTRATIONS

Figures

Map

SOYBEANS AND POWER

INTRODUCTION

GM CROPS, GLOBAL ETHNOGRAPHY, AND THE DYNAMICS OF DEMOBILIZATION

In February 2003, Nélida woke up on her small farm early as usual and went outside to feed her chickens.[1] Nélida lives in Monte Azul, a rural community in the province of Formosa, in northern Argentina. That morning she noticed that her manioc, corn, and vegetables were all completely withered. The day before, farmworkers had been spraying agrochemicals on a large nearby field of genetically modified (GM) soybeans. Carried by the wind, the agrochemicals had spread to the smaller neighboring farms, affecting Nélida and at least two dozen other peasant families.[2] This agrochemical drift destroyed the cotton that the peasants were about to harvest and withered the vegetables they sold at a local farmers market and used to feed their families. The damage was not isolated to the crops, but also affected the health of the surrounding community. Locals, and especially children, developed headaches, muscular pains, nausea, vomiting, breathing problems, skin rashes, and unusual pimples.

In the ensuing months, peasants reacted to this environmental damage by organizing some of the most disruptive and visible protests in the recent history of Formosa. In Monte Azul the affected families, many of them members of the grassroots organization MoCaFor (the Peasant Movement of Formosa, Movimiento Campesino de Formosa), organized several roadblocks and filed suits against agribusinessmen, demanding reparation for damages to their farms. The protests soon spread to other parts of the province. In Moreno, another stronghold of MoCaFor, peasants and local inhabitants seized a crop duster (the airplane used to spray agrochemicals) and occupied the local airport for a week. They did not leave until they were reassured that the fumigations would cease.

Fast-forward six years, to February 2009, when Nélida awoke to find an unsettling landscape: most of her chickens were dead or walking around the yard erratically. Throughout Monte Azul, nearly 100 chickens were dead and people (especially children) were again suffering from skin irritations and respiratory ailments, caused by another agrochemical drift. In Moreno, while aerial fumigations ceased after the 2003 protests, people continued suffering from agrochemical exposure and related health problems. Yet in 2009, unlike the response in 2003, no protests took place in either of these communities. Two points in time, two comparable problems of agrochemical exposure, and yet the same people reacted very differently: with intensive, disruptive protests in 2003, and with no collective action in 2009. Why, when facing environmental damage, do people from the same communities first react by organizing contentious protests and later fail to engage in collective action?

In this book, I scrutinize these events to tackle two issues: first, to analyze the social and environmental consequences of GM herbicide-resistant crops; and second, to understand the politics of demobilization in contemporary Argentina. Paying attention to subjective, organizational, and political dynamics, I analyze how peasants move from contention to accommodation, reconstructing the impacts of social movement alliances and evaluating the effects of authorities' responses (which change from dismissal to recognition). In short, this book is about the sweeping expansion of GM crops in Argentina, cases of agrochemical exposure, and processes of popular mobilization and demobilization as they open windows to agrarian, environmental, and political debates.

Why should we be concerned about GM crops and the fate of peasants and small farmers? What can we learn from the skyrocketing expansion of GM crops in Argentina and from an analysis of processes of demobilization? First, GM herbicide-resistant crops perpetuate an agricultural production centered on monoculture and agrochemical use. As such, they represent a hazard for populations exposed to agrochemicals and contribute to the economic concentration of agricultural production. This book shows that the widespread use of GM herbicide-resistant crops may create serious problems of agrochemical exposure and inhibit forms of production carried out by small farmers and peasants. Argentina, in short, provides critical lessons on the deleterious consequences of a massive experiment in transgenic monoculture and its negative socioenvironmental impacts.

The findings presented in this book apply to soybeans that were genetically modified to resist a specific herbicide and not necessarily to *all* transgenic crops (although I also briefly discuss the adoption of GM herbicide-resistant cotton). Although there is much discussion around the potential impacts of GM crops in general, whether positive or negative, analyzing Argentina and zooming in on specific rural communities allow us to inspect some of *the actual effects* of transgenic agriculture.

Second, by studying processes of demobilization, we can have a more comprehensive understanding of contentious politics, integrating concepts that explain the *emergence* of collective action with those that explain the *waning* of contention. I argue that the study of the ebb and flow of contention in the context of GM crop expansion offers lessons on how subordinate actors (in this case, peasants and the rural poor) think, feel, and act about socioenvironmental changes, and on how they resist *but also negotiate and accommodate* negative socioenvironmental impacts.

GM Crops as Global Project

The 1987 footage shows four men wearing suits and white lab coats, standing inside a greenhouse filled with plants. The intermittent clicking and flashes of photographers registering the event punctuate their conversation. "We have before the USDA right now a request to test this for the first time at a farm in Illinois this year," says one of the men to another who is listening attentively, arms crossed in front of the coat embroidered with his name and position: "Vice President George Bush." The vice president was touring a Monsanto Company research facility, and the executives and scientists were eager to test a genetically engineered soybean designed to resist the herbicide produced by the company. "And I will say quite frankly, we have no complaint about the way the USDA is handling it," continues the Monsanto executive. "They're going through an orderly process; they're making sure as they deal with these new things they do it properly . . ." After an awkward pause, the executive clarified: "If we're [still] waitin' until September and we don't have our authorization, we may say something different!" When chuckles subside, the Vice President Bush offers a word of comfort: "Call me. We're in the 'de-reg' business."[3]

Those "new things" that the executive referred to were seeds genetically engineered to resist Monsanto's herbicide, Roundup, and while Monsanto was initiating the biotech business, the government was promoting the de-reg business. By 1993, George Bush had gone on to become president of the United States and as part of his regulatory relief initiative the federal government authorized the release of biotechnology products into the environment. "The United States is already the world leader in biotechnology. And, we want to keep it that way. [The biotechnology industry] should reach at least 50 billion dollars by the year 2000, as long as we resist the spread of unnecessary regulation," said Bush's vice president, Dan Quayle, when he announced the new policy. In 1994, the first GM food was offered in the US market.[4] In 1996, GM herbicide-resistant soybean seeds were sold in the United States, unleashing the commercialization of other GM seeds and launching a profound transformation of agriculture around the world.

Genetically modified seeds were created in the 1990s, but are also a descendant of the "green revolution" in agriculture. Between the 1940s and the 1970s, philanthropic organizations (e.g., the Rockefeller and Ford Foundations) partnered with public institutions to support research and development initiatives to create hybrid seeds, crossing different varieties of plants and producing new varieties of maize, cotton, and wheat in Mexico, India, China, Pakistan, and the Philippines (Ross 2003). This process of technological diffusion known as the agricultural green revolution had at its core a "technological package" of hybrid seeds, agrochemicals (fertilizers, pesticides, and herbicides), and machinery (to sow, fumigate, and harvest the crops) designed to increase crop yields. The hybrid seeds of the green revolution and genetically engineered varieties, however, result from contrasting social processes and are different seeds. Hybrids are obtained from crossing different strands of plants while genetically engineered varieties result from recombining the DNA of plants with DNA of viruses and bacteria. Socially, whereas the green revolution was fueled by public–private partnerships, the "gene revolution" is overwhelmingly funded and controlled by corporations (Patel 2012, Pingali and Raney 2005, Kloppenburg 2005).

At least four salient features of transgenics allow us to identify them as *global crops*. First, transgenics are transforming agricultural production in diverse parts of the world. Second, they are created, patented, and commercialized by global corporations. Third, they have been adopted on the heels of the neoliberal globalization that spanned the globe in the 1990s. Finally, transnational social movements and NGOs have been resisting and opposing GM crops, mirroring their global diffusion (McMichael 2009, Heller 2013, Newell 2008, Otero 2012, Pechlaner 2012, Schurman and Munro 2010, Scoones 2008).

In the United States, GM crops have expanded rapidly since 1996. In 2011 they represented nearly 90% of soybeans cultivated in the United States, in addition to more than 80% of maize, and more than 75% of cotton (Lang 2013). In contrast, the production of GM crops in Europe is still restricted as a result of concerns raised by food scandals (most noticeably, "mad cow" disease), the adamant mobilization of environmental and farmers' organizations, and backlash to the aggressive marketing strategy implemented by Monsanto when trying to introduce GM seeds on the continent (Heller 2013, Schurman and Munro 2010). In so-called developing countries, the approval of GM seeds followed the track of the green revolution and found elective affinities with countries adopting neoliberalization policies. Argentina approved GM soybeans in 1996, China and India approved GM cotton in 1997 and 2002, and South Africa approved GM corn in 2001. By 2011, eleven countries accounted for more than 98% of the 170 million hectares planted with GM crops: the United States, Brazil, Argentina, Canada, India, China, Paraguay, South Africa, Pakistan, Uruguay, and Bolivia, in decreasing area (James 2012). Despite this global expansion, 83% of the world area planted with GM crops was concentrated in just four countries (the United States, Brazil, Argentina, and Canada).

In South America, the diffusion of GM crops intersected with processes of neoliberal globalization, which facilitated the increasing operation and control of agribusiness corporations over agriculture. In December 2003, Syngenta Company, one of the six biggest global biotech corporations, published a curious advertisement in an Argentine national newspaper. Next to the slogan "Soybeans Have No Frontiers," the ad showed a map of South America and a green patch covering most of Uruguay, northern Argentina, eastern Bolivia, southern Brazil, and all of Paraguay, with the words "United Republic of Soybeans" at its center (see Figure I.1). The ad prompted the reaction of anti-GM activists, since at that time transgenic soybeans were only legal in Argentina and Uruguay (Bravo 2010, Manzur et al. 2011). Transgenic seeds were smuggled from Argentina and illegally planted in Paraguay and southern Brazil in the late 1990s. Farmer associations and agribusiness lobbyists used the de facto situation of thousands of hectares planted with GM crops to pressure states and national governments, ultimately gaining approval for growing and commercializing GM crops.[5]

Ultimately, the United Republic of Soybeans ad proved to be premonitory: Paraguay officially authorized the production of GM soybeans in 2004, and Brazil and Bolivia in 2005. By 2011, GM crops in South America (mostly soybeans but also corn and cotton) had been sown across more than 66 million

FIGURE I.I United Republic of Soybeans

hectares, representing close to 40% of the global GM crop area (a landmass comparable to the states of California and Oregon combined). Argentina and Brazil are clearly the biggest GM crops growers in Latin America, with almost 24 and more than 36 million hectares of GM crops sown in 2011, respectively (James 2012). Argentine and Brazilian agribusiness have played a key role in the growth of transgenic production in Paraguay, Uruguay, and Bolivia (Bravo 2010, Galeano 2012).

During this period of global expansion, GM seeds developed two inter-twined lives. In one life they are a product, a seed genetically engineered to express a trait that simplifies agricultural production. Contrary to popular belief, GM seeds do not necessarily result in higher yields and fall short of solving the problem of agrochemical use.[6] The most widely sold GM seeds (soybeans, maize, canola, and cotton) are engineered to tolerate herbicides or eliminate insects, thus making production more standard and simpler to manage. Soybeans and canola were genetically engineered to resist Roundup (a glyphosate-based herbicide produced by Monsanto Company) and corn and cotton to produce a toxin that kills pests. In their life as seeds, GM crops are sown, grown, and harvested. But GM crops also have another life, expressed in the imagination, discourses, ideas, and projects of businessmen, policymakers, activists, scientists, scholars, and consumers. In this second life, GM crops elicit polarized views of aggressive promotion and entrenched opposition. As crops intertwined with projects and discourses, transgenics have incited both praise and condemnation throughout the world, receiving similar doses of enthusiastic adoption, critical appraisal, and adamant rejection.

The promotion of GM crops grew through a cross pollination of discursive themes that are highly problematic from a sociological perspective but are nonetheless deeply rooted among policymakers and the general public. I argue that technophile, productivist, Malthusian, and moral narratives are weaved into a highly influential "techno-productivist" discursive formation.[7] First, a technophile discourse taps into the ingrained idea of technology as a neutral tool; in the case of agriculture, a disembedded biotechnology is assumed to have the same results independently of the social context (Kinchy 2012, Levidow 1998, McAfee 2003).[8] Second, this idea is reinforced when combined with a productivist frame, that is, the unexamined assumption that agricultural production has to progressively increase yields.[9] Third, a neo-Malthusian narrative reinforces these technophile and productivist views, arguing that there is a pressing need to increase agricultural production in order to keep up with population growth (Ross 2003). Insufficient access to food is construed as a supply problem that can be solved by a "technological fix" (Goodman and Redcliff 1991: 142), thus excluding "the complex political, social and economic dimensions of the question of access to food in favour of the simplified notion of 'feeding the world' as a global project" (Brooks 2005: 367). The corollary of this techno-productivist discursive formation is a legitimizing moral imperative, presenting GM crops as a "pro-poor" technology that fulfills missions of corporate social responsibility (Glover 2007, 2010a, 2010b). This techno-productivist discursive formation is not entirely new but rather an extension of the ideas supporting the so-called green revolution (Patel 2012), and these discourses continue to be mobilized, for instance, to promote GM cotton in Asia and the introduction of GM corn in

Africa (Cohen and Paarlberg 2004, Cooper, Lipper, and Zilberman 2005, Paarlberg 2009).

A number of scholars have shown that the techno-productivist discourse relies on a series of highly debatable assumptions. First, as mentioned above, GM crops do not necessarily have higher yields than conventional crops.[10] Second, there is already more than enough food production to feed the world's population.[11] Third, GM crops have been commercially grown since 1996, yet the most popular and easily available seeds are soybeans, corn, cotton, and canola—crops produced as inputs for the feed, food, and fiber industries rather than staples of poor farmers. Fourth, the increasing concentration of the agricultural market in the hands of a few biotech and agrochemical companies makes the pro-poor argument of GM crops dubious, to say the least.[12] In spite of these objections, the storyline of GM crops as an altruistic and imperative endeavor still resonates among policymakers and the public, while opposition to transgenic seeds is sometimes framed as an expression of middle-class, well-fed northern activists.

In contrast to these approaches, other scholars have examined GM crops in the context of global capitalism and its articulation with the state, drawing from world-system theory and Gramscian analysis (McMichael 2009, Otero 2008a). In this perspective GM crops are commodities, goods created with the goal of making a profit. As such they are the expression of a global food regime, that is, relations of production and consumption of feed, fiber, and food spanning the world and led by corporations and usually supported by the state. From this viewpoint, GM crops are both an outcome and instrument of a neoliberal food regime. That is, they emerged from and reinforce the credo of free markets and unfettered trade fostered by international financial institutions, global corporations, and pro-business governments. The vignettes of the 1990s opening this section condense the salient characteristics of this neoliberal food regime: led by agribusiness, supported by deregulators, and seeking to extend US world hegemony.[13]

In this book I engage in a debate with techno-productivist viewpoints promoting GM crops, while seeking to extend the critical perspectives of food regime scholars. I do not aspire to find a safe middle ground between these positions, but rather to challenge the blind spots and assumptions of the former, while adding nuance to the latter. I elaborate this point below, but to anticipate my argument, my goal is to give serious consideration to mediations, contingency, cultural processes, situated meanings, spatial dynamics, and the articulation of multiple scales. For instance, while keeping in mind the key role of global capitalism underlined by food regime scholars, the ethnographic research presented in this book also highlights the articulation between global and national processes and, in turn, the dilemmas faced by peasant social movements as they seek to maintain national allies while acting at a provincial and localized scale. Along different lines, I also seek to challenge the techno-productivist assumption of an alleged unilinear progress heralded by science and (bio)technology. In the remainder of this introduction I elaborate these arguments, providing the theoretical framework that I empirically flesh out in the ensuing chapters using ethnographic evidence.

GM Crops, Space, and Scales

The challenge of inspecting GM crops from an ethnographic perspective is taking into account their world-spanning forces, regional dimensions, uneven national manifestations, and localized expressions. A first step in this direction is to refine our categories of "the global" and "the local," and offer a more nuanced account of the connections and disjunctures at different scales (global, regional, national, and local). An ethnographic perspective on global processes offers tools for improving the abstract conceptions of extant globalization theories, going beyond the global/local binary analyzing how global forces are experienced in concrete settings (Gowan and Riain 2000: xiv, Otis 2012) while also inspecting the articulation of diverse scales (Herod 2009). More specifically, an ethnographic approach to GM crops in Argentina allows us to simultaneously focus on the role of global corporations and the national state, while paying attention to processes of subnational differentiation (the varied impacts of GM crops in different regions) and the obstacles faced by peasant movements when navigating different political scales, from the provincial to the national.

This approach allows us to avoid the misconception of thinking of the local as the place the global impacts, and to rather see both as interconnected dimensions. The idea that the global can be developed by macrostructural views and then filled in by ethnographic portraits of the local fails to understand, as sociologist Michael Burawoy argued, that the "the global-local antinomy is itself misleading, for if something is global there can be nothing outside that is local" (2001: 156–157). "Global" and "local" can serve as shorthand expressions as long as we conceptually keep in mind that they articulate multiple scales and, as such, they are neither self-evident nor is one contained in the other. Taking this precaution circumvents the persistent identification of the global with the universal and the local with the particular, a conflation that confuses the level of analysis with the geographical scale (Massey 1994). As anthropologist Anna Tsing aptly put it, the schematic distinction between global forces and local places "draws us into globalist fantasies by obscuring the ways that the cultural processes of all 'place' making and all 'force' making are *both* local and global, that is, both socially and culturally particular and productive of widely spreading interactions" (2000: 352).

In this book, I considered the global forces driving GM crops as they manifest in regional, national, and local projects and analyze the connections enacted by social movement leaders, public officials, agribusinesses, and rural inhabitants. Zooming in on these connections illuminates the ways in which both the support and the opposition to GM crops combines global, national, regional, and localized discourses and actors. GM crops are part of a project promoted by global corporations but that gains ground, in Argentina and elsewhere, through the support of national and local actors. Similar to the environmental conflicts in Hungary analyzed by Zsuzsa Gille (2000) where people combined ideas of environmental racism in a post socialist context, my ethnographic data suggest that in resisting the negative consequences of GM crops peasants draw from global discourses while remaining bounded by their localized historical experiences. The connections fostered by GM crops also produce innovative exclusions. Like the trends studied by anthropologist James Ferguson in Africa, the study of GM crops in Argentina indicate the creation of "situated understandings of emerging global patterns" that "attend more adequately not only to exciting new interconnections, but also to the material inequalities and spatial and scalar disjunctures that such interconnections both depend on and, in some ways, help to produce" (2006: 49).

By studying the connections and disjunctures of global patterns, we can analyze the ways in which the benefits and impacts of GM crops are unequally distributed across different global regions and social classes, as food regime scholars argue. Yet we can take this insight a step further. The food regime perspective has been criticized for being too focused on European and North American trajectories and for its limitations in incorporating national and subnational processes (Moran et al. 1996). The critical literature on food and globalization also combines the strengths and weaknesses of Marxist theory, that is, "what it gains in historical sensibility it lacks in geographical sensibility," when "history is the independent variable, [and] geography the dependent" (Smith 2008: 2–3, 224).[14] Acknowledging these criticisms to the food regime literature, I pay attention to how the impacts of transgenic agriculture follow *uneven geographies within countries*.[15]

It is common to find the terms "Global North" and "Global South" when reading about the relationship between globalization and agriculture. Terms like the Global North and the Global South are useful heuristic devices, yet they may also suggest a dichotomous understanding of the world that may miss internal variation within countries and potentially give short shrift to the dynamics of space and place and the articulation of multiple scales (Herod 2009, Smith 2008: 228–230). A substantive body of literature discusses the inherent shortcomings of imagining nations as discrete units, what John Agnew (1994) calls "territorial traps." Heeding this insight, in chapter 1, I outline the process of agrarian neoliberalization in Argentina and the uneven geographies of the soybean rush, emphasizing its variegated effects across regions (i.e., the different impact of GM soybeans in the plains of the Pampa and northern Argentina). In chapter 2, I reconstruct the trajectory of grassroots peasant movements in Formosa, sketching the regional dynamics of radical mobilization in northeast Argentina in the late 1960s and 1970s. This close attention to the emplacement of peasantry in Formosa allows us to better understand their different reactions to the expansion of GM soybeans and to cases of agrochemical exposure. In chapters 3, 4, and 5, I complement this attention to uneven geographies and regional trajectories by showing how peasants' contention and demobilization is informed by the articulation of multiple scales, from the national, to the provincial, to the localized. More concretely, the processes of accommodation discussed in chapters 4 and 5 are informed by the ways in which peasants navigate national and provincial political scales; in other terms, by the vexed situation of supporting national administrations that are also allied to the authoritarian provincial government that peasants have to endure.

Attention to these political issues is useful in capturing the complex relationship between space and place resulting from the agrarian dynamics of the GM soybean rush. In their life as seeds and plants, transgenic crops transform concrete territories, changing the rural areas where they literally take root. In the process of being sown, grown, and harvested, GM crops change concrete *spaces*, generating effects in the agricultural and natural environments where they are introduced. This process of space-making, however, does not happen in a social vacuum but rather occurs in social geographies: the production of GM crops materializes in *places* with histories, institutions, and organizations entangled with individual and collective experiences (Massey 2005, Tuan 2001). That is why the up-close, long-term, and in situ tools of ethnography are especially well-equipped to capture the environmental *and* social effects of GM crops. By inspecting the effects of GM crop production in locations with specific histories, we have the opportunity to see how the technological package of GM crops unfolds in an environment in the broad sense of the term, that is, in a geographical space that is the substrate of social relationships. In the cases examined in this volume, GM soybeans transform the physical space of land, and as the use of herbicides affects the water and air of concrete territories, they also affect a place embedded in social relationships, places where peasant families have lived for generations but find it increasingly hard to continue doing so.

In summary, I reconstruct the articulation of global, national, and regional scales as they are experienced in specific localities, a perspective that reveals a "grounded globalization" that sees global processes as resulting from economic forces but also as a political accomplishment (Burawoy 2001). I pay attention to these articulations by reconstructing the links between global corporations (selling GM seeds and herbicides), regional actors like farmers from the Pampas (who adopt and diffuse GM seeds and herbicides), national administrations (regulating and deregulating GM seeds, herbicides, and appropriating part of the agrarian rent crated by soybean exports), regional agrarian histories (the specific relation of the Formosan peasantry, historically involved in cotton production), and localized experiences (the lives and everyday experiences of peasants, closely intertwined with place-making practices). Following anthropologist Sherry Ortner, I argue that the vantage point of a grounded globalization can circumvent the pitfalls of an "ethnographically thin" account of GM crops by paying close attention to the ambiguities and ambivalences of resistance, the "ongoing politics *among* subalterns," and their cultural contexts (2006b: 48, original emphasis). This book addresses these issues by analyzing how peasants resist *but also accommodate* transgenic agriculture.

Social Movements and Demobilization

Throughout the world, protests and social movement campaigns emerged as the inverted image of the intense promotion of GM crops. Scholars have investigated the mobilization of farmers, rural social movements, and NGOs against GM crops in Europe (Heller 2013, Schurman and Munro 2010), Canada (Andrée 2011, Eaton 2009, Müller 2006, Prudham 2007, Kinchy 2012), the United States (Buttel 2003, Carolan 2010, Pechlaner 2012, Schurman and Munro 2010), Mexico and Central America (Fitting 2011, Kinchy 2012, Klepek 2012, Pearson 2012, Poitras 2008, Wainwright and Mercer 2009, Motta 2014), Brazil (Jepson, Brannstrom, and De Souza 2008, Peschard 2012, Scoones 2008, Motta 2014), India (Roy 2013, Scoones 2008, Shiva 2000), and South Africa

(Scoones 2008). Researchers have also inspected controversies about GM food in the United States (Guthman 2003, Klintman 2002, Roff 2007), where at least 60 initiatives in over 20 states have pushed for GM labeling.[16]

Whereas this burgeoning research has provided insights on the mobilization against GM crops, we do not know much about the ways in which people accommodate or reconcile their negative influences or about how small farmers and peasants maneuver in territories transformed by the expansion of agribusiness through GM crops. In other words, we know more about protests *against* GM crops than about how their expansion and impacts are *negotiated*. This knowledge gap should not come as a surprise if we consider the concepts at our disposal when it comes to processes of demobilization.

Scholars of social movements have overwhelmingly focused on explaining *mobilization* and the *emergence* of social movements (Walder 2009). In comparison, processes and mechanisms of *demobilization* and social movement *decline* are much less understood. Piven and Cloward (1979) extended the classic thesis of Weber-Michels on the "iron law of oligarchy" (Michels 1962), arguing that demobilization was a function of institutionalization. Other scholars, however, have questioned this proposition (Clemens and Minkoff 2004, Voss 1996). Seminal studies argued that elite support and a lack of resources could lead to the taming of a social movement (McAdam 1982: 55–56) and similarly that movements supported by elites can be "channeled" (Jenkins and Eckert 1986) or "co-opted" when recognized as legitimate actors by authorities (Gamson 1975).[17] Sidney Tarrow's seminal concept of "protest cycles" (2005) demonstrated how political opportunities, information flows, the diffusion of collective action, and innovative tactics drove upward trends in contention, but paid less attention to the downward phase of cycles (Jung 2010). Scholars have also proposed the concepts of "abeyance structures" (Sawyers and Meyer 1999, Taylor 1989) and "organizational mortality" (Edwards and Marullo 1995) for those instances when movements vanish from the public sphere or dissolve completely. How can we understand social movements when they are neither institutionalized nor disbanded? What ideas and practices give meaning to political alliances, resources, and organizations that create opportunities *and obstacles* for contention?

This book addresses these questions to understand *why and how* social movements *cease* to mobilize or why people choose tactics other than transgressive collective action to address grievances. As sociologists McAdam, Tarrow, and Tilly argue, social movement scholarship has focused on the link between organization and action by "selecting on the dependent variable," that is, by observing how organization leads to collective action, a line of inquiry that "elide[s] the more numerous examples in which groups constrain action" (2008: 325). Similarly, most research has concentrated on how ideas and symbols inform framing activities resulting in collective action. But we know much less about negative cases, those instances "when framings fail to stimulate collective action" (Benford 1997: 412). In other words, the mechanisms causing demobilization beg for further elaboration, since our theoretical toolkit about *processes of demobilization* pales in comparison to the availability of concepts explaining mobilization itself.[18] This book contributes to efforts to observe how social movements mobilize *and demobilize*, combine contention *and negotiation*, seek to profit from opportunities and avoid threats, all while intertwining interests and emotions, developing relationships *within and between* movements, and interacting with authorities and adversaries.

I argue that, by and large, scholars have explained demobilization in negative terms, identifying what is lacking or merely seeing demobilization as the reversing of mobilization, thus paying scant attention to the *active production* of demobilization.[19] Whereas most social movement scholarship investigated the role of formal organizations in demobilization, here I focus on the cultural aspects that connect organizational pressures, political actions, and subjective experiences. Culture is, of course, a complex and debated term (Sewell Jr. 2005: 152–174, Williams 1983: 87). Meaning-making processes have been incorporated in the canon of social movements studies mostly as framing, or the alignment between individuals' interests and beliefs and social movement organizations' goals that result in collective action (McAdam, Tarrow, and Tilly 2001, Snow et al. 1986). This understanding of culture-as-frames inspired the critiques of scholars arguing that culture can facilitate *but also create obstacles* for contention (Polletta 2008), that discourses are multivocal, open-ended, and ambiguous (Steinberg 1998), and that meaning-making not only defines frames but also opportunities, resources, and organizations (Goodwin and Jasper 2004a, Kurzman 1996, 2008).

I use culture here to refer to forms of talk and interaction that both enable and constrain contention, providing scripts about what can or cannot be said and done, and as the context in which identifications are expressed, rejected, and redefined. In doing so, I take heed of an influential definition in which cultural symbols and meanings are understood as "toolkits" to solve problems and define strategies for action (Swidler 1986: 273). Throughout the book, I scrutinize language as it delineates the opportunities and obstacles for collective action, building on research that sees language and meaning as a key site to study political participation, contention, and the lack thereof (Baiocchi 2003, Comerford 1999, Eliasoph 1998, Gamson 1992, Lichterman

1998, Mische 2008, Tarrow 2013). I analyze how discourses define "a group's place within a social order, its relation to other groups, and thus its identity, thereby defining the limits of legitimate agency" (Steinberg 1999a: 16). I thus build on the "cultural turn" in social movements studies (Goodwin and Jasper 2004b) yet without disregarding the intertwinement of culture and situated political economies (e.g., Fantasia 1988, Steinberg 1999a, Thompson 1993).

Considering that the line of research on culture and social movements has overwhelmingly concentrated on the United States and Europe, more research investigating the enabling and constraining role of culture in diverse social settings is needed. Since Latin American polities have been historically shaped by patronage politics and clientelism (Fox 1994, Hellman 1994, Helmke and Levitsky 2006, Shefner 2008, Hilgers 2012a, Taylor 2004), an analysis of mobilization and demobilization in this region can strengthen social movement theories by inspecting the ways in which its insights on the role of culture can be extended to new social contexts. Whereas political phenomena like democratization, ethnic conflicts, and revolutions have been analyzed in tandem with social movements (McAdam, Tarrow, and Tilly 2001), here I expand our understanding of the links between social movements and other political phenomena by examining the connections *between contentious politics and patronage politics*.

The distribution of resources and the political opportunities afforded to popular movements in Argentina (and, more broadly, in Latin America and elsewhere) are embedded in the logic of patronage politics and clientelism (Auyero, Lapegna, and Page Poma 2009, Hilgers 2012a). At its most basic, clientelist relationships involve the exchange of resources or public employment (or its promise) for political support (usually as votes or participation in rallies) (Schmidt et al. 1977). These relationships, in turn, involve ideas of reciprocity and mutual obligations among unequal parties. An inspection of popular politics in Argentina can shed light on how political opportunities, organizations, and resources are interpreted through meaning-making process that, in turn, are imbued in the logic of clientelism. My goal is thus to incorporate meaning-making practices to understand mobilization *and demobilization*, claiming not only that culture matters, but also shedding light on *how* it matters. As Wendy Wolford put it: "How do cultural norms and practices shape the interaction between representation and that or those who are being represented? How do culturally specific understandings inform the making of categories through which people know their social universe and mobilize against injustice?" (2010: 24). In focusing on the connection between social movements and patronage politics to explain demobilization, we can better understand how a political culture is practiced in everyday interactions (Eliasoph and Lichterman 2003) while functioning as a *constraining* factor for contentious collective action (Polletta 2008).

Furthermore, inspecting patronage arrangements from the point of view of social movements contributes to discussions on the role of agency and strategy in clientelism and demobilization. When analyzed from the outside in, clientelist arrangements are usually depicted as a material quid pro quo in which resources are exchanged. In recent years, however, scholars have refined this traditional view of clientelism by emphasizing its *symbolic* aspects; that is, the quotidian interactions embedded in relations of reciprocity, and the affective and personalized dimension of exchanges (e.g., Auyero 2000, Gay 1994, Roniger and Günes-Ayata 1994, Lazar 2008). In this book, I pay close attention to different strategies deployed by social movements acting in clientelist contexts. I show that political support may also translate into eschewing contention, and that subordinate actors may choose different strategies to address their grievances—staging protests at certain moments, obtaining and distributing resources at others. In doing so, I join the conversation initiated by scholars of Latin American politics who study the strategic use of political networks among grassroots activists (Alvarez Rivadulla 2012, Canel 2010, Hilgers 2009, Lazar 2008, Quirós 2006). Adopting this perspective also bridges the literature on clientelism with social movement studies, given the latter's interest in strategic action (Fligstein and McAdam 2011, Jasper 2004, Maney et al. 2012). My argument, in a nutshell, is that people mobilize their agency in creating their demobilization.

GM Crops, Collective Action, and Global Ethnography

GM crops are a hotly debated public issue with little room for subtleties or nuanced arguments: analysts are usually in favor or against transgenics. From a techno-productivist perspective, GM crops are showcased as the silver bullet to end hunger, a marvelous technologic development that deserves nothing but praise, an instrument to lift the world's rural poor out of their misery. Within this camp—well entrenched in the business world, but also among policymakers, scientists, and academics—any hint of criticism toward transgenics is dismissed as Luddite, a stance ignoring how science works and what farmers need. Criticism of GM crops is even presented as a crime against humanity, committed by activists who put obstacles in the way of solving world hunger and helping farmers.

In the opposite corner, critics cast accusations at GM crops for tinkering with Nature (with a capital N), glossing over half a century of hybrid seeds and agrochemical use, and lending an ear to concerned consumers but not giving much importance to what farmers actually say and think. More often than not, anti-GM activists are quick to dismiss anything resulting from genetic engineering, and tend to idealize peasants and small farmers as inherently ecologically friendly or to project onto them their own environmental hopes. As a result, as anthropologist Glenn Davis Stone argues, both positions share a common ground in their "overriding commitment to an ethical black-and-white ... intended to delegitimate an examination of the grays" (2005: 208). Debates about GM crops are, in short, fraught with polarized positions.

In this book I do not attempt to find a *via media*, but rather to show the blind spots of these positions by analyzing the concrete consequences of GM herbicide-resistant crops in rural areas of Argentina (focusing mostly on the effects of GM soybeans and, in a lesser degree, GM cotton). On the one hand, as discussed above, I find that the pro-GM techno-productivist arguments are faulty on several points. By scrutinizing the uneven development of GM crops in Argentina, my goal is to underscore the deep entanglement of agricultural biotechnology and its social and political context. In doing so, my claim is that promoting transgenic crops as a strategy for development without considering this broader context misses the importance of power inequalities. Furthermore, promoting GM crops as a way to solve hunger glosses over the fact that the difficulties faced by the rural poor are, in large part, matters of livelihood and lack of access to key assets—land, water, credit, and *appropriate* technologies, to name just the most salient problems. I flesh out this argument in chapters 2 and 3, showing how peasants and small farmers in northern Argentina were developing environmentally friendly and socially oriented food production and commercialization initiatives that were cut short by GM soybean production in their communities.

On the other hand, while I draw from critical approaches to GM crops, I also seek to address some of their limitations. In chapter 1, I build on the framework developed by food regime scholars, while the ethnographies presented in chapters 3 to 5 address gaps in this perspective. The framework developed by food regime scholars combines a world-system perspective (attentive to the role of agriculture in propelling global capitalism) and Gramscian analysis (interested in the relationships between the state and civil society and the creation of hegemony). I found this framework extremely useful when putting Argentina in a broader context; yet the structural bias of this perspective did not fit well when making sense of my ethnographic data and the messiness of quotidian interactions. To put it in a metaphor: the world map of food regime scholars helped me to place Argentina in the region and on the globe, but I needed another cartography to guide my navigation during fieldwork. In other words, I do not object the accuracy of the broad picture outlined by food regime scholars. I seek, however, to also incorporate into their broad canvas the situated actions of social movement representatives, members, and sympathizers; their mutual interactions; their own understandings of GM crops and agrochemical drifts; and overall, the frictions and contradictions emerging from these processes. My goal is to take into account the ideas, interests, and actions of subordinate actors without considering their emotions as secondary or disregarding their worldview as inevitably shaped by the particular history of northern Argentina. Indeed, the variation I encountered *within* subordinated groups pushed me to rethink the influence that food regime scholars had in the way I initially conceived this study, leading me to reconsider many of the categories that I carried with me when entering the field for the first time.

These contrasts between the global project entailed in the expansion of GM crops and its situated, contextual manifestations beg a series of questions. Can an ethnographic approach capture the dynamics of GM crops as a global project? Are face-to-face interactions, interviews, and observations apt to address global processes? I believe that an ethnographic perspective on global process and social action is not only possible but also necessary, for at least two reasons. First, an ethnographic perspective may provide the tools to eschew globalist discourses, that is, monolithic and teleological renderings of global processes. Second, observing the concrete manifestations of global forces offers windows into the ways in which people experience them, thus revealing the role of agency and variation.

While it is important to account for the expansion of GM crops and its intersection with the forces of global capitalism, we need not see these processes in evolutionary terms. As historian Frederick Cooper rightly points out, "If one wants to use globalization as the progressive integration of different parts of the world into a singular whole, then the argument falls victim to linearity and teleology" (2005: 111). By imagining GM crops as embedded in the development of agrarian capitalism or in the progress of science applied to agriculture, we can inadvertently submit to the fallacy of globalism and understand global forces as unstoppable trends or predetermined destinies. GM crops are part of a broader global food regime in which powerful actors vie to incorporate increasing parts of the world into its circuits. Yet this process is not monolithic, but rather uneven and contested. From the perspective I develop here, the global project involved in the expansion of GM crops is neither universal nor predetermined, but rather "enacted in the materiality of practical encounters" (Tsing 2005: 1). The process of GM crop expansion is not simply imposed as an external force on the world's peripheries nor does it generate the same effects across different spaces. The expansion of GM crops is a global project but, as we will see, this world expansion also meets national, regional, and local projects resulting in diverse effects. In investigating GM crops from this perspective, I heed the insights of anthropologist George Marcus by developing "a research design of juxtapositions in which the global is collapsed into and made an integral part of parallel, related local situations rather than something monolithic or external to them" (1995: 102).[20]

Second, an ethnographic approach forces us to keep people's experiences and actions in sight, incorporating the role of culture, agency, and variation as part of our explanations. Inspecting the expansion of GM crops from this perspective illuminates processes of adoption but also of adaptation and accommodation to transgenic agriculture. By examining GM crops and their consequences as rural populations experience them, the project of transgenic agriculture becomes part of a social environment in which strategies of reproduction take central stage. Similar to the ways in which Elizabeth Fitting (2011) analyzes the impact of GM corn in Mexico by putting it in the context of a decline in peasant agriculture and the allure of migration to the United States, I analyze the effects of GM soybeans in the context of social policies and welfare programs targeting the rural poor and the neoliberalization of Argentine agriculture. This focus, in turn, provides access to the varied ways in which peasants and small farmers understand GM crops on their own terms, a topic that is still understudied (Ho, Zhao, and Xue 2009).

This attention to contingency and agency is particularly well captured by an ethnographic approach, which can make a key contribution to the study of social movements and contentious collective action. An ethnographic focus offers the benefit of observing both the micro-dynamics of mobilization *and* demobilization, and the role of agency in both processes. Research on social movements has mainly concentrated on discontinuous, public, and collective claim making (Tilly 2006a: 49). These events leave a "paper trail" than can be traced, thus classic social movement studies (McAdam 1982, Schwartz 1976, Tilly 1978) have used newspaper data and archives to assemble event catalogues in large datasets, a technique that became widely used (Earl et al. 2004). This strategy is logical when identifying relationships between significant variables while covering a large timespan (several decades or even centuries) or relatively vast geographical areas (one or more nations). However, certain correlations and their internal mechanisms may be hard to explain using this technique alone. Demobilization processes involve relationships that, by definition, do not evolve into open confrontations with authorities (and thus hardly leave public records). As such, these are processes that can be best identified by an up-close and in situ observation of practices and in-depth interviews. Furthermore, participant observation among social movements makes it possible to register the practices and discourses of both leaders *and* constituencies, thus avoiding the pitfalls of an "elite bias" (Benford 1997: 421–422) when scrutinizing meaning-making processes.

Ethnography is thus well equipped to delve into what Alberto Melucci (1985) calls the "submerged networks" of social movements, capturing the cultural practices of both mobilized and demobilized constituencies (Burdick 1995, Edelman 2001: 309). In delving into these submerged networks, I am interested in the micro-level dynamics of demobilization and the *role of agency* in these processes. My claim is that the lack of mobilization in a context where social movement organizations are still active is not simply an *absence* but rather a result of relationships between and within groups. I thus explain demobilization processes by taking agency seriously, observing variation within movements and changes over time, and closely scrutinizing the language used to make sense of contention. Specifically, I focus on the pressures created by clientelism in rural and deprived communities, the links between a local social movement organization and their allies (i.e., a national social movement and the national government), and the relations of cooperation and friction within a social movement.

The evidence presented in this book is culled from my long-term involvement with peasant activists in the province of Formosa, located in northern Argentina. While I visited several rural communities and conducted interviews in Buenos Aires, I did most fieldwork in four sites: the rural community that I call Monte Azul, the nearby town of Sarambí, the semirural town of Moreno, and the capital of Formosa. I modified the names of specific localities and people to ensure anonymity, although I use the real names of the province and public figures. As I further explain in the appendix (where I elaborate on other methodological details), I first met the peasants of Monte Azul in 2003, shortly after the case of agrochemical exposure analyzed in chapter 3. I collaborated in the creation of an amateur documentary film about what happened, and we came back in 2004 to present it at a public event. I returned to Formosa every year between 2007 and 2011 for a total of 12 months, revisited the province in 2013, and met with Formosan informants in Buenos Aires in 2012, 2013, and 2014. Throughout these multiple visits I conducted a total of 45 interviews, collected an array of documents, and took extensive notes on the interactions that I witnessed during fieldwork. I took part in activities held in MoCaFor offices in Surumbí and Moreno, lived in the houses and on the farms of peasant families in Monte Azul, and participated in rallies and meetings held by MoCaFor leaders and members in Formosa and Buenos Aires, all the while taking extensive notes on actions and dialogues. I also reviewed three provincial newspapers and several documents produced by MoCaFor and by public agencies. Whereas the events analyzed in chapter 3 are reconstructed from interviews and archival sources, the situations and processes analyzed on chapters 4 and 5 come mostly from notes taken during my participant observation.

My initial goal was to conduct research on the social and environmental impacts of the expansion of GM crops, and the collective resistance to their negative consequences building on an analysis of the 2003 events. In early 2009, while I was in the United States, I received an email from members of MoCaFor telling me there had been another agrochemical drift in Monte Azul similar to the one in 2003. I traveled to Formosa some months later and found out that no protest had taken place following this environmental problem. For reasons that will become clearer as you keep reading this book, I ultimately decided to focus my research on processes of mobilization and demobilization, contrasting different reactions to agrochemical drifts over time.

Throughout the process of writing this book, I strived to keep the narrative as faithful as possible to what I registered during fieldwork. This had, I believe, the advantage of avoiding archetypes and simplifications. The pages you are about to read can be seen as a story in the sense that events and situations are presented from a particular perspective, mostly as they emerge from the viewpoints of social movement participants. Yet it is not a story with villains and heroes. In writing this book, I kept two tempting narrative plots at bay: one, exuding miserabilism, would have led me to describe Formosan peasants as victims. The other plot, that can be labeled populist, would have steered me into presenting Formosan peasants as a unified group fighting resolutely against GM crops and voicing their rights in unison. Whenever these siren calls were about to seize my imagination or the storyline, my fieldwork, fieldnotes, and interviews provided the discomfort and disconcert I needed. The more time I spent in Formosa participating in meetings, interviewing peasants, and listening to their quotidian conversations, the less plausible narrative plots of defenseless victims and stoic heroes seemed.

This story thus takes the tensions, frictions, and contradictions I heard and observed in my fieldwork as opportunities (Hale 2008), seeking to go beyond black-and-white accounts and explore the productivity of gray areas. It is a story about seeds that simplify agrarian production, creating wealth for nations and (some) farmers while contributing to the poisoning of the environment and the marginalization of peasants. It is a story about resistance and contention against GM crops and agrochemical drifts, but also about peasants accommodating transgenic agriculture and about the contradictions, ambiguities, and "internal politics of the dominated" (Ortner 2006b: 49). It is about local authorities dismissing claims, disregarding rights, and disrespecting people, but also about well-intentioned public officials trying to support popular organizations while creating obstacles for their contentious mobilization.

Road Map

The ensuing chapters present the context of Argentina and a narrative arc of the emergence, contention, and demobilization of the Movimiento Campesino de Formosa, MoCaFor (Peasant Movement of Formosa). Chapter 1 introduces the dark side of the GM soybean boom in Argentina by answering a set of questions. Why did GM soybeans expand in Argentina so broadly and quickly? What are the socioenvironmental consequences of this "soy rush"? And how do farmers, the government, and rural social movements think about and react to this process? I first reconstruct the agrarian neoliberalization in Argentina in the 1990s, the approval of GM soybean seeds in 1996, and the sweeping expansion of transgenic soybeans. I then focus on the dark side of the boom, describing the negative socioenvironmental consequences of Argentina's soy rush: deforestation of native woods, violent land evictions suffered by peasant and indigenous families, and a myriad of agrochemical exposures in rural areas and small towns. I next turn to the political context of these processes by discussing the changing relationships between the government, popular social movements, and agribusiness associations since 2003.

Chapter 2 zooms in on the province of Formosa, reconstructing the history of peasant organizations, the local impacts of neoliberalization, and the pervasiveness of patronage politics. I review the economy and politics of the province as seen *from the points of view of peasants and their organizations*, introducing the rural communities where I did fieldwork. While the ensuing chapters delve into events of contentious mobilization and processes of demobilization throughout a decade (circa 2003–2013), this chapter serves as a broader historical canvas that allows us to situate that decade within a longer history of peasant struggles in northern Argentina.

Chapter 3 centers on the contentious events described at the beginning of this introduction. What can we learn from these protests? What do they tell us about GM crops and popular contention? GM soybean production in Formosa exposes the disjuncture between the official script of GM crops and their concrete realities. When I saw how GM crops were produced *on the ground*, I could not help but conclude that the discourses and propaganda of agribusiness were at odds with the realities of agricultural production. What the cases of Monte Azul and Moreno (and agricultural production in Argentina at large) show is that the *potential* environmental advantages of herbicide-resistant GM crops are countered by their *actual* environmental impacts—at least when it comes to transgenic soybeans in northern Argentina. I inspect these protests as an opportunity to bridge structural and cultural perspectives on collective action, showing that they were as much about material demands and interests as about recognition, emotions, and identity.

Chapter 4 scrutinizes the relationships between local social movements, authorities, and local populations to shed light on processes of demobilization. I explain these processes by pivoting between *organizational* dynamics (social movements), *institutional* actions (government), and *subjective* understandings (people's views). I introduce the concept of dual pressure, which refers to the relationships between leaders, constituents, and allies. Then, I analyze the institutional recognition implied in the agrarian social policies of the national government and its impact on rural social movements. I argue that, taken together, dual pressure and institutional recognition shape the organizational dynamics of MoCaFor, helping to keep the social movement running while posing obstacles for contention.

Chapter 5 dissects the events surrounding the agrochemical drift of 2009, arguing that the response of authorities can be seen as a mechanism of "performative governance" whereby the relationships between peasants and authorities are shaped by practices of impression management (Goffman 1959) and discourses that "do things with words" (Austin 1962), which combine to create obstacles for contention. This chapter closes with an examination of the *subjective* understandings of contention, GM crops, and agrochemical drifts, showing the accommodations and adaptations developed by peasants, and the strategies devised by peasant households to make ends meet in the midst of an encroaching transgenic agriculture.

The conclusion returns to the puzzle of mobilization/demobilization posed in the initial pages of this introduction and answers it by discussing the links between institutional politics and social movements, and the relationships within and between social movements. It closes by critically examining the techno-productivist discourse on GM crops and arguing that a closer inspection of social movements and the incorporation of multiple scales can improve the literature on agriculture and globalization.

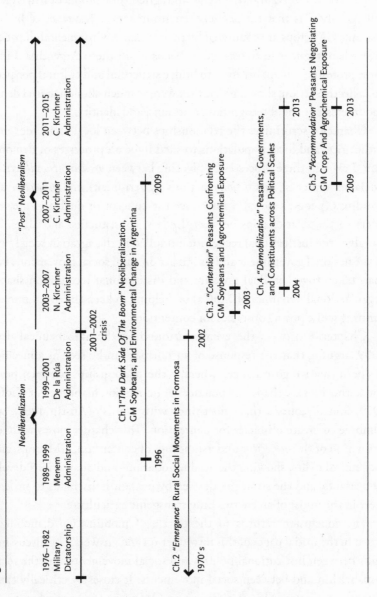

Argentina: National Administrations

Neoliberalization

"Post" Neoliberalism

| 1976–1982 Military Dictatorship | 1989–1999 Menem Administration | 1999–2001 De la Rúa Administration | 2003–2007 N. Kirchner Administration | 2007–2011 C. Kirchner Administration | 2011–2015 C. Kirchner Administration |

2001–2002 crisis

Ch.1 "The Dark Side Of The Boom" Neoliberalization, GM Soybeans, and Environmental Change in Argentina

1996 ——— 2009

Ch.2 "Emergence" Rural Social Movements in Formosa

1970's ——— 2002

Ch.3 "Contention" Peasants Confronting GM Soybeans and Agrochemical Exposure

2003

Ch.4 "Demobilization" Peasants, Governments, and Constituents across Political Scales

2004 ——— 2013

Ch.5 "Accommodation" Peasants Negotiating GM Crops And Agrochemical Exposure

2009 ——— 2013

THE DARK SIDE OF THE BOOM

NEOLIBERALIZATION, GM SOYBEANS, AND ENVIRONMENTAL CHANGE IN ARGENTINA

Imagine yourself in Buenos Aires, a large metropolitan area of more than 13 million people. Because the city sits on the flat plains known as the Pampas, you would only be able to see this large urban sprawl from an airplane, or from one of the skyscrapers that dominate the city's skyline. Driving northwest crossing the Pampas, in a few hours the green fields stretch as far as your eye can see and soybean plants reach the shoulders of the road, almost touching your car. Maybe you would notice the colorful signs attached to the wire fences, reading "Dekalb," "Nidera," or the name of another seed or agrochemical company.

Four hours or so after your departure from Buenos Aires, you would arrive in the city of Rosario, in the province of Santa Fe, located on the banks of the long and wide Paraná River (see Map 1.1). Rosario is a major hub for Argentina's soybean exports: the city port receives crops from hinterland provinces (e.g., Córdoba and Santiago del Estero) and from provinces along the river (Santa Fe, Chaco, Formosa, and Entre Ríos). From there, soybeans are shipped down the river, or processed and exported to the rest of the world (mostly to Europe, China, India, and Southeast Asia). If you drive through Rosario, the proliferation of high-rise buildings and the construction boom in several neighborhoods may draw your attention. If you venture to the outskirts of the city, however, you would find a different landscape, dominated by shantytowns and precariously built houses. On the radio you might catch Hermes Binner, a former Rosario mayor and a former governor of the province, explaining the growth of marginal neighborhoods in the city, mixed with doses of concern and social phobias: "There are people who have migrated and are

MAP 1.1 Center and North of Argentina

Argentines struggling to eat every day ... They come from other provinces, they come here permanently. Well, Paraguayans and Bolivians come too, right? But basically they are from the Argentine provinces. Here, we have whole barrios of Chaqueños [people from Chaco province]; we have four huge neighborhoods of all Tobas [an ethnic group from the Gran Chaco region, self-identified as Qom]. They've been run off their land by the soybeans."[1]

Continuing north, driving parallel to the Paraná River for eight hours or so, you would arrive at Resistencia, the capital of Chaco province, in the Chaco region. The weather would be warmer than in Rosario, and the palm trees lining the road would let you know that you have entered a subtropical area.

The Argentine countryside has been undergoing a profound process of environmental change since the 1990s, mostly driven by the sweeping expansion of GM soybeans that have increased agricultural production and exports. But there is also a dark side of the soy boom, an underbelly that can be grasped through the experiences of people living in the countryside, particularly peasant-indigenous families. The concerns of the former Santa Fe governor quoted above hint at the social hierarchies, uneven geographies, and regional inequalities stirred up by the soy boom. In the next chapter we will keep traveling north, to Formosa, to further scrutinize these issues. But before examining changes in space and place, we first need to go back in time.

Neoliberalization and the Argentine Soybean Rush

On March 25, 1996, Felipe Solá, the Argentine Secretary of Agriculture, signed a resolution that would radically change the agriculture and the environment of the country in the years to come. The resolution was concise: "The production and commercialization of the glyphosate-resistant soybean seed, its products and derived sub-products, is authorized."[2] The Secretary's decision employed the same rationale that was used that same year in the United States to approve GM seeds, namely, the "principle of substantial equivalence." This principle claims that overall GM soybeans are similar to their non-GM equivalent, and thus represent no risk to the public health or the environment (Levidow, Murphy, and Carr 2007). Fifteen years later, by 2011, GM soybeans covered close to 19 million hectares of Argentina's farmland (more than 46 million acres, an area larger than the states of New York, New Jersey, Connecticut, Massachusetts, Delaware, and Rhode Island combined).[3] In 2012, almost 200 million liters of glyphosate were sprayed across Argentina (a hard to fathom volume of almost 53 million gallons, equivalent to 80 Olympic-size swimming pools).[4]

The approval of GM soybeans unleashed the expansion of transgenic agriculture in Argentina. But lest we endorse a technological determinism, we need to situate the adoption and expansion of GM soybeans in its social context. The Argentine "soy boom" and its geographical diffusion is best explained by the interplay between the policies of neoliberalization (providing a favorable institutional frame), the unique features of genetically engineered soybeans, and the practices of social actors that adopted, promoted, and disseminated both agricultural biotechnology and neoliberal principles.

The 1990s are frequently referred to in Argentina as the "neoliberal decade." In 1989 the country was crippled by inflation, the national government had been delegitimized, and riots erupting in several major cities. Seeking to overcome the crisis, President Alfonsín step down from his position six months before his term ended, handing over the government to President-elect Carlos Menem. After spending several months trying to find a way out of the quagmire, the new government adopted the policies recommended by global financial institutions such as the International Monetary Fund and the World Bank. The national government privatized public companies, reduced public employment, and eliminated import tariffs and export taxes, resuming a socioeconomic project partially implemented during the 1976–1983 military dictatorship.

In 1991 the government pegged the Argentine peso to the US dollar, a policy that greatly facilitated the import of foreign goods and promoted the export of primary goods. These policy orientations were applied on the agricultural sector through the dismantling of regulatory measures (controlling the prices and the commercialization of grains, meat, cotton, sugar, etc.), the elimination of barriers to the importation of agricultural supplies (seeds, agrochemicals, machinery), and the promotion of export commodities (Teubal, Domínguez, and Sabatino 2005).

By the mid-1990s, neoliberal policies paved the way for the adoption of GM crops. A business-friendly context facilitated the marketing of the technological package sold by transnational corporations (TNC): genetically engineered seeds, agrochemicals (herbicides, fungicides, fertilizers), and heavy machinery (to sow and harvest soybeans and apply agrochemicals). Furthermore, the reintegration of Argentina into global markets took place in a context of high commodity prices; soybean production thus became an attractive venture to meet a rising global demand (fueled, in great part, by the imports of feed and vegetable oil in China, India, and Southeast Asia).

These national and global processes interacted with specific features of genetically engineered soybeans that facilitated their expansion. Soybeans seeds were genetically engineered by Monsanto Company to make the plants resistant to the agrochemical Roundup, a glyphosate-based herbicide sold by the same company. Herbicide-tolerant soybeans do not necessarily result in higher yields, but do have three characteristics that greatly facilitate the productive process. First, GM soybeans can be sowed without harrowing the land, using "no-till" practices. In traditional agriculture, farmers plough the land to eliminate weeds *before* planting a crop. GM soybeans, in contrast, are planted *directly* into the soil without harrowing the land because weeds are eliminated using Roundup soon after sowing the seeds. Second, producing GM soybeans is a highly standardized process. Unlike the growing of a traditional crop that requires close monitoring (to determine whether grow-ers should use agrochemicals to control pests or stimulate growth), GM soy-beans follow a preestablished, step-by-step process that is relatively easy to follow. "You can produce soybeans by email," joked Norberto, a Formosan agrarian engineer, during a conversation we had in the agricultural experi-mental station where he works. Third, GM soybeans allow for shorter ag-ricultural cycles. That is, they can be sowed and harvested twice in a given year unlike other crops that need more time to come to fruition. No tilling practices and a standardized productive process mean fewer laborers to hire, which, combined with a shorter harvest cycle, usually result in higher profit margins.

Technical and economic dimensions, however, only partially explain the shocking speed and vast geographical expansion of GM soybeans in Argentina; the traits of genetically engineered seeds combined with the idiosyncrasy of local agribusiness. Argentine farmers are used to reproducing their seeds, a practice protected under national laws. Unlike the hybrid seeds of the green revolution, which usually have a much lower yield if farmers re-produce and replant them, GM soybeans can be reused as seeds and planted again. Argentine farmers engaged widely in this practice, selling and ex-changing unregistered GM soybean seeds—a practice known as "white bag," *bolsa blanca*, probably because the bag of seeds shows no logos or trademarks. This practice allows farmers to circumvent the payment of royalties to the owners of seeds' patents (reducing the costs of acquisition), and contributed to the availability of GM soybean seeds.[5] The proliferation of unregistered GM seeds affected corporations' intellectual property rights, but also con-tributed to capturing the Argentine market for transgenic agriculture.

Neoliberal polices developed a series of elective affinities with agricultural biotechnology. Lower costs of production, increased profit margins, favor-able external demand, seed availability, and rising global prices combined to quickly expand the planting of GM soybeans in the Argentine plains (Bisang 2003). By the mid-2000s the area cultivated with GM soybeans soared, cov-ering nearly 50% of the country's arable land, more than 18 million hectares (almost 44.5 million acres). By 2013, GM soybeans were sowed in more than 20 million hectares (more than 77,000 square miles). Production figures pres-ent similarly skyrocketing trends. In 1997–1998, shortly after the approval of GM varieties, Argentina produced close to 19 million tons of soybeans. By 2006–2007, production rose to 47.5 million tons and by 2012–2013, it reached 49 million tons (MAGyP 2013, see Figures 1.1 and 1.2). In 2010, the exports of the soybean agro-industrial complex (soybeans, oil, and flour)

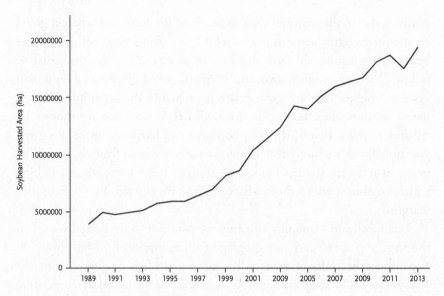

FIGURE I.I Soybean area in Argentina

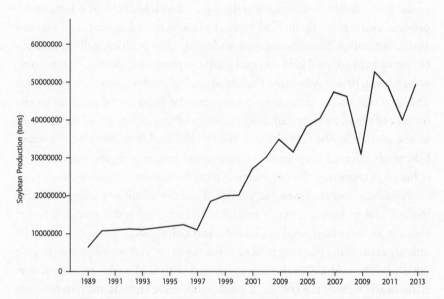

FIGURE I.2 Soybean production in Argentina

made up to one-fourth of the total exports, worth more than 17.3 billion dollars (MAGyP 2011). By mid-2000s, virtually all soybeans produced in Argentina were genetically modified. A USDA report aptly summarized this process, stating: "No other Latin American country embraced Genetically Modified Crops as wholeheartedly as Argentina" (Yankelevich 2006: 3).

But soybeans do not grow by themselves; which actors led this process? When people ask me about my research and I mention GM crops, they quickly connect the topic with Monsanto Corporation. Likewise, scholars analyzing these processes from a neoliberal food regime perspective put TNCs and the state as the leading actors driving the expansion of agricultural biotechnology in Latin America (Otero 2008a). TNCs indeed dominate several important parts of the soybean business in Argentina. They sell inputs (such as seeds, agrochemicals, and machinery), process soybeans (into oil and animal feed), and export the output. They do so in an increasingly concentrated market: in 1990, eight companies controlled 67% of the soy flour market; by 2002, six companies dominated 92% of it. Similarly, in the soy oil market, the eight biggest companies increased their market share from 72% to 92% between 1990 and 2002. The economic concentration that occurred during the years of neoliberalization is also reflected in the reduced number of firms controlling agricultural exports. In the mid-2000s, seven TNCs (Cargill, Bunge, Nidera, Vicentin, Dreyfus, Pecom-Agra, and AGD) controlled 60% of this market (Teubal, Domínguez, and Sabatino 2005: 46–47). This dominant position of TNCs, however, should not obscure the fact that the *actual production* of GM soybeans is mostly carried out by Argentine agribusiness. Global agribusiness corporations are a powerful and necessary actor in the expansion of GM crops in Argentina, but the picture is not complete without considering national and local actors.

Beyond Transnational Corporations: The Role of Argentine Agribusiness

"The weather forecast, and the global demand for food and energy offer a great opportunity for entering the business that identifies us as Argentines. With a historical average rate of return of 20%, this is an attractive investment." I read this statement from an email I received in May 2012 while working at my desk in Athens, Georgia, in the southern United States. The message was sent by an agricultural investment fund, and included a brochure luring investors by comparing the rates of return of soybeans to other investments. The banner on top of the brochure showed pictures of large extensions of crop fields, and a big tractor crossing one of them. There were no people in sight. The message invited people to informative talks in Buenos Aires the following week. Piqued by curiosity, I sent a brief email inquiring if there were any meetings scheduled for June (during my next visit to Buenos Aires). Minutes later, I received a reply from Felipe (pseudonym) describing the investment opportunity and attaching a sample of the contract to join the group. The message explained that the minimum investment was $15,000 US dollars, with a rate of return of between 15 and 25%. They estimated that for this growing season the firm would rent 35,000 hectares. Felipe explained the steps to become an investor: sign the contract and the document joining the investment fund (*fideicomiso*), and deposit the money in a designated account within 72 hours. "Then you send us the receipt and your investment is effective," Felipe wrote in an informal and amicable tone (using the *vos* instead of the formal *usted*).

I was fascinated by the implications of this fleeting exchange of emails, which exemplify the speed, tone, and style of some of the social actors behind the Argentine soybean rush. In half an hour, I had all the information I needed to invest in soybean production in Argentina. Anyone, in any part of the world, could become a soybean investor almost overnight. Still mesmerized, I searched for more information about the company. The four heads of the firm are between 38 and 40 years old; their meetings were held in the offices of the firm, the Sheraton Hotel, and a place called Urban Station, located in the so-called neighborhood of Palermo SoHo—an area of Buenos Aires that is the tourist area par excellence. I had trouble wrapping my head around the sharp contrasts between the global sites that the firm used for their meetings and the places where I did my fieldwork in Argentina, where the actual production of soybeans takes place. I could not help thinking that the areas of Buenos Aires connected to this venture had more in common with SoHo, New York than with Monte Azul, Formosa.

Agricultural investment funds like the one I contacted in May 2012 are one of the agents leading the process of soybean expansion, together with others: mega-agricultural firms, agribusiness contractors, and a minority of medium-scale farmers. During the years of neoliberalization, these actors took hold of Argentine agriculture. The aggregated data of National Agricultural Census shows that in the 1990s, one fifth of existing farms went out of business.[6] In the early 1990s, family farmers tried to adapt to the new scenario by taking on debts to expand their scale of production. The downward trend of commodities in the mid-1990s, however, forced many of them to sell their land after going bankrupt. The upward trend of international prices of soybeans in 2001–2004 arrived too late for most family farmers, but stimulated the creation and expansion of agribusiness companies (see Figure 1.3). Agricultural investment funds or "sowing pools" (as they are called in Argentina) mushroomed in the 2000s. These arrangements consist of joint ventures of associated investors (agrarian and nonagrarian), who contribute

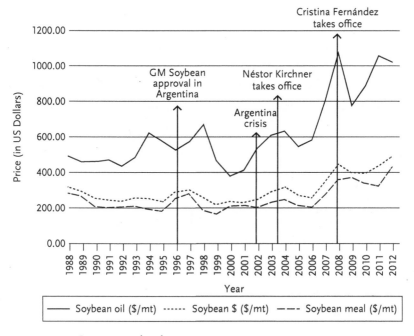

FIGURE 1.3 International soybean prices

capital in order to rent land for two or three harvests and hire an agronomist to manage the fields. The soybean growers responsible for the agrochemical drifts described in chapter 3 are an example of this type of scheme. These arrangements are just one of the diverse forms of short-term investments that have flourished in the Pampas region over the last decade (Bisang, Anlló, and Campi 2008).

Mega-agricultural firms are another type of agribusiness companies and ventures that have come to dominate Argentine agriculture. These firms reach economies of scale by *renting* hundreds of thousand of hectares instead of *buying* lands, which would immobilize their capital (de Martinelli 2008, Posada and Martínez de Ibarreta 1998). One of the most emblematic examples of these firms is Los Grobo, a company that cultivates more than 150,000 hectares in Argentina but owns a very small percentage of it. Instead the company leases most land under temporary contracts in exchange for a percentage of the harvest. Medium-sized agribusiness companies that offer agricultural services also expanded in the last two decades. These contractors (*contratistas*) are in charge of spraying, dust cropping, sowing, and harvesting crops. Many of them are former family farmers who became small rentiers, now leasing their land to large agribusiness and then offering their services to other agribusiness companies or farmers nearby (Gras 2009). The expansion of these different agrarian and financial actors helps explain the accelerated and aggressive diffusion of GM soybeans. In the mid-1990s, these arrangements were also combined with a sort of business activism on the part of companies (for instance, Monsanto), which hired local community leaders, organized meetings with local farmers, and distributed publications and videos to actively promote the adoption of GM soybeans (Gras and Hernández 2009: 20, see also Gras and Hernandez 2013).

From the Pampas to the North: The Uneven Geographies of GM Soybeans

The expansion of GM soybeans in Argentina is a geographically uneven process. The growth of agribusiness has different implications for different regions, and taking the country as an undifferentiated whole misses key spatial dynamics of the soy boom. Between 1996 and the early 2000s, GM soybean production rapidly expanded in the Pampas; that is, the area comprised of the provinces of Buenos Aires, Santa Fe, Córdoba, and La Pampa (see Map 1.1), which is historically characterized by its commercial and export-oriented agriculture. The so-called *Pampa gringa*, populated in the late nineteenth and early twentieth centuries by European immigrants (Gallo 1983), followed a historical trajectory and economic development similar to other regions of recent settlement, like the American Midwest or the Australian plains (Font 1990, Sábato 1988).[7]

The Argentine North, in contrast, was populated by the descendants of indigenous populations and developed through agrarian production oriented toward the internal market rather than to the global trade. The image of wheat-growing farms and the proverbial *gaucho* hardly reflect the experience of northern Argentina. In the twenty-first century, soybean agribusiness expanded to a space historically shaped by the production of sugar, tobacco, yerba, and cotton, and the exploitation of native forests. During the nineteenth and early twentieth centuries, British companies decimated native forests by enlisting rural workers as woodcutters (Dargoltz 2003). The state-sponsored agro-industrialization developed throughout the twentieth century promoted sugar production in the provinces of Tucumán and Salta; cotton in Chaco and Formosa; tobacco in Misiones, Salta, and Jujuy; and yerba mate and tea in Misiones. Peasants provided these industries with raw materials by working in the fields and in the processing plants, while agro-industries captured the lion's share of the profit by commercializing the products in the internal market.[8]

The neoliberalization of agriculture initiated in the 1990s radically altered the agro-industries of the Argentine North and the social fabric built around them. As national economic policies reoriented agriculture toward global markets and eliminated the state regulation of regional productions, small farmers and peasants that were a subordinated but integral part of regional development became increasingly marginalized. These dynamics, in turn, nurtured regional inequalities that were not only economic but also social and cultural. Throughout the twentieth century, a process of *mestizaje* of indigenous and rural workers (Gordillo 2014: 33–36) represented an expression of a long-term process of erasing indigenous heritage and "whitening" Argentina (Chamosa 2008, Gordillo and Hirsch 2003, Quijada 2000). By and large, public policies and research "invisibilized" peasant populations, subsuming the regional economies of the Argentine North into the Pampas while conceptualizing peasants in negative terms—as an actor lacking capitalization or having only a marginal participation in the creation of value (Barbetta, Domínguez, and Sabatino 2012). This dominance of the Pampas in both material and symbolic terms meant that Argentine peasants never gained the recognition that they had in other Latin American countries like Mexico, Bolivia, Peru, or Paraguay.

The expansion of GM soybeans reinforced the unequal development that has characterized Argentina historically. Circa 2003, with mounting international prices for soybeans and land prices in the Pampas increasing up to 50% (INTA 2004), transgenic agriculture began to expand to the north (Leguizamón 2014, Pengue 2005, Goldfarb and van der Haar 2016). Agribusiness companies and large farmers sought to reach economies of scale; that is, increase their operations by taking advantage of their machinery, know-how, and access to inputs while profiting from cheaper lands and the subtropical climate of northern provinces. Agribusiness companies producing soybeans in the provinces of the Pampas could extend their cycle of production by renting land in provinces farther north, like Santiago del Estero, Chaco, or Formosa. They usually did this for a three-year period and then left the plot cleared for the owner (i.e., ready to use again). This expansion allowed companies to produce "winter-spring" soybeans: while soybeans sowed in the Pampas are still growing, they can harvest the soybeans in the warmer lands of Formosa or Chaco and extend the creation of profits from a six- to nine-month period.

Norberto Schmidt is a tall, slender, and loquacious man in his late sixties, who talks about rural life and agricultural production with an unmatched enthusiasm. In June 2009 I met him in his office at a national institute of rural development in a small Formosan town, where he has worked as an extension agent for more than three decades. His experience offers an account of how the process of GM soybean expansion takes place in northern Argentina. During our interview, Norberto recounted conversations he had with agribusiness representatives asking about the availability and quality of lands.

> I ask everyone arriving here what they will be growing and they all say, "Soybeans." [I told them] "Mind you, the soil of Formosa is not good for soy. A 1,000 hectares land is for cattle and woodland." [They asked me] "Can the trees be cut down?" [I replied] "Well, there are regulations, and it's better to leave the trees because it is wealth, there are animals, there are fence posts." "No, we just want to cut down." So they come here to "Pampeanize" Formosa [to reshape the province following agricultural practices prevalent in the Pampas]. And the model from the *Pampas* . . . should never have been implemented here. Because the soil is rapidly depleted . . . But they started coming. And they do so with the knowledge from the South [the Pampas region]. They do not come with the knowledge from the local producers and technicians. They just ignore it all. They arrive with the arrogance of productivism: cut down, clear, and sow soy. The thing is soybeans can be grown by email [in jest], since it's a very easy crop.

His amusing manners grew more serious when he described the rampant deforestation in the area.

> There was a property of seven thousand hectares of woodland here; they could use it for fifty years of sawmill productivity. What they did instead was to fence and burn [*acordonaron y le prendieron fuego*]. The children had to leave school because of the smoke. A livestock auction was delayed because of the smoke, too. And here our nature reserve was suddenly full of pumas escaping from the fire. Without the woods, the rain takes all the soil.

Norberto's concern provides a first glimpse of what I call the dark side of the boom; namely, the environmental and social consequences of GM crop expansion. Besides deforestation, these negative outcomes also include the violent expansion of the agricultural frontier and the environmental suffering caused by agrochemical exposure, as we will see next.[9]

The Dark Side of the Boom

The extraordinary transformation of Argentine agriculture fed by the soy boom of the last two decades has been touted by a series of analysts. Some studies stress its economic benefits, framing them as a natural process of integration into global agriculture (Trigo and Cap 2003). Others see the expansion of GM crops as resulting from the dynamism and innovative practices of agribusinesses (Hernández 2007). Critical perspectives, in contrast, draw attention to the negative social and environmental consequences of GM expansion in Argentina. Are these impacts an unintended consequence of agricultural biotechnology? Are these externalities the necessary price to pay for economic growth? The answers may vary diametrically depending on whose perspective is considered. What does the soy boom look like from the standpoint of peasant-indigenous families and rural inhabitants?

Violent Outcomes: Land Conflicts and the Killing of Indigenous-Peasant Activists

On November 16, 2011, two armed men showed up at the humble house where Cristian Ferreyra lived with his wife and two children in a rural community in the northern province of Santiago del Estero. The two men, security guards hired by an agribusinessman, shot Ferreyra and beat his wife and a family friend. Some hours later Ferreyra bled to death. Nearly a year later, on October 10, 2012, a goon showed up on the farm of Miguel Galván in a rural community 40 miles from where Ferreyra was shot. Galván was stabbed in the neck and died shortly after. Just a few days earlier, he had gone to the local police to report the harassment by individuals hired by an agribusinessman from the nearby province of Salta.

Ferreyra and Galván were members of MOCASE, the Movimiento Campesino de Santiago del Estero (Peasant Movement of Santiago del Estero), an organization created in the early 1990s to defend peasants' land rights that has become the largest peasant movement in Argentina. In the late 1990s, MOCASE was instrumental in creating a national alliance of peasant organizations in Argentina called the MNCI (Movimiento Nacional Campesino Indígena, the National Indigenous-Peasant Movement). MOCASE is also an active member of CLOC (Coordinadora Latinoamericana de Organizaciones del Campo, the Latin American Coordination of Agrarian Organizations) and the transnational peasant movement Via Campesina.[10]

The murder of Ferreyra and Galván are not isolated incidents, but rather the deadly result of mounting tensions between agribusinessmen and organized peasant families and indigenous peoples. In recent years, several more activists have died in the context of land conflicts in northern Argentina (Domínguez and De Estrada 2013). In October 2009 Javier Chocobar, a member of an indigenous organization, was murdered in the province of Tucumán. In March 2010, Sandra "Ely" Juárez, another peasant activist in Santiago del Estero, died of a heart attack while resisting an eviction. In November 2010 during a roadblock, police shot and killed Roberto López, a member of an indigenous organization in the province of Formosa, who was claiming rights to lands that had been taken from the Qom people.

In the case of Ferreyra, human rights activists claim that eight months before the killing, the businessman accused of instigating the attack enclosed a large tract of land (more than 8,600 acres), leaving peasant families without access to the local school. The provincial Ministry of Education paid no attention to the protests about this situation. The local judge never responded to the complaints about the presence of armed groups harassing peasant activists and local families. Likewise, Galván had denounced the enclosing of land that the peasant-indigenous families wanted to reclaim after living in the area for generations. Between 2008 and 2010, MOCASE held a series of meetings with the governor of Santiago del Estero, who finally signed an agreement pledging to solve the more than 250 land conflicts in the province—a situation that resembles the institutional recognition and performative governance I analyze in chapters 4 and 5. In spite of this agreement, thugs hired by agribusinessmen continued to harass peasant-indigenous families until their threats materialized.

The situation in Santiago del Estero exemplifies the deadly consequences of the soybean rush and the complicity of agribusiness, provincial administrations, and the judiciary power, a situation that several human rights organizations have documented in other provinces of Argentina such as Chaco, Córdoba, and Mendoza (REDAF 2010, UPC and UNESCO 2009). A report of the United Nations concluded: "As a result of the expansion of agricultural activities, indigenous peoples [in Argentina] have lost large tracts of their traditional lands . . . These activities are also harmful to the health of indigenous people because crops are sprayed with toxic agrochemicals" (United Nations, Human Rights Council 2012: 9–10).

Peasant and indigenous movements and human rights organizations in Argentina have mobilized to demand legal protections at the national level. In 2006, the national Congress sanctioned a law to protect the rights of indigenous communities to their lands. The law was only partially implemented to the point that it was extended in 2009 because it failed to meet its stated goals (for instance, the cadastral registration of indigenous lands).[11] Paradoxically, Galván was killed after his local organization mobilized to enforce this law. Since 2010, peasant organizations have demanded a similar law to stop evictions affecting peasant families.[12] On the heels of the killings of Ferreyra and Galván, peasant movements organized demonstrations in Buenos Aires and lobbied the national Congress in support of the law (now dubbed "Cristian Ferreyra law") and its urgent enforcement.[13] Although some legislators support these peasant organizations, the bill is still under debate.[14] Land conflicts in Argentina continue and peasant activists live under frequent threats.[15] These conflicts are about land and the "control of the territory," as peasant leaders put it, but they are also about the access to and use of native resources. Whereas rural families use forests as sources of firewood, honey, and pastures, soybean growers understand the woods in different terms.

Ecological Fallouts: Deforestation, Super Weeds, and Degraded Soils

Three ecological problems stand out as a result of the soybean rush: deforestation, the appearance of "super-weeds," and soil degradation. With the diffusion of GM soybean production from the Pampas to other regions of the country, problems of deforestation increased dramatically (Gasparri, Grau, and Angonese 2013). In certain eco-regions, like the Mesopotamian Forest in the northeast and the jungle of Yungas in the northwest, the agricultural frontier has advanced at the cost of natural forests (Pengue 2005). According to government reports, between 1998 and 2008 almost 1.7 million acres of native forest were lost (Leguizamón 2014). The environmentalist organization Greenpeace denounced the annual deforestation of nearly 250,000 hectares and exposed companies and governors for their involvement (Greenpeace 2006). In light of this dramatic effect of agricultural expansion, in 2007 the national Congress passed a bill known as the "Bonasso law," which requires that the provinces promote mechanisms of "territorial organization" by designating three types of areas: red (prohibiting deforestation), yellow (authorizing deforestation under certain conditions), and green (allowing deforestation).[16]

"In conclusion: we have to destroy and deforest, in order to live," Roberto Leburay told me in 2007 at his house in downtown Formosa. He was 45 years old, the owner of a ranch that spanned 18,000 hectares (an area two times larger than the island of Manhattan). He spoke frankly, giving me the impression

of a person who enjoys an intense exchange of ideas. During our interview—
interrupted by the directions he gave on his cellphone for cashing checks, filling
out forms, and buying feed for his cows—he candidly expressed his views:

> A bill like the Bonasso law says that we can't touch the forest, and
> you have to go to Buenos Aires to get permission . . . I think what
> they're doing is condemning those of us who live here, in the *monte*
> [the bush], to die in poverty so that over there [in Buenos Aires] they
> can live much better on the resources of the state . . . This is my vision
> of agricultural development: if the forests are untouchable, the land
> will be neglected [*se ensucia*], it won't produce. What it's going to bring
> is much more poverty to the provinces [*el interior*] . . . I think all of the
> environmentalist movements, more than environmentalists, they are
> conservationist and anti-production: [they say] don't touch the forests;
> when in doubt, don't touch the forests. I don't agree with that . . . This
> law, is trying to do just that. From Buenos Aires, they tell us here in
> Formosa, if I am going to deforest my land . . . it seems to me that this
> law doesn't match the reality of the countryside [*el campo*].

Leburay's opinions shed light on why the law has been so slowly implemented in Formosa and elsewhere. Agribusiness representatives see the regulation of deforestation as contrary to their economic activities, but they also
frame these initiatives as "anti-growth" while tapping into an ingrained dis-
like of Buenos Aires in northern Argentine provinces.

As agricultural production expanded by cutting down trees to plant GM
soybeans, growers faced two more ecological backlashes: the appearance
of super-weeds and the depletion of soils. A whole set of weeds that resist
glyphosate (the active ingredient in Roundup) have sprouted in Argentina's
countryside, causing soybean growers to apply even more toxic agrochemicals (Faccini 2000, Papa 2002, Puricelli and Tuesca 2005, Vitta, Tuesca,
and Puricelli 2004).[17] This massive and uncontrolled use of herbicides has
contaminated water sources (Jergentz et al. 2005). A study succinctly summarizes the situation: "The substitution of traditional crops by GR [glyphosate-
resistant] soy within the last couple of decades represents a large-scale,
unplanned, ecological experiment, whose consequences for natural ecosystems, and aquatic environments in particular, are poorly understood" (Perez
et al. 2007: 2311). In addition, soils have been degraded by a lack of agricultural rotation. This occurs because GM soybeans are produced over two or
more consecutive harvests instead of rotating different crops or alternating

between agriculture and cattle breeding (Binimelis, Pengue, and Monterroso 2009, Cerdeira et al. 2010, Pengue 2005). The increased use of agrochemicals has created not only ecological and agronomic problems; it has also triggered processes of environmental suffering throughout Argentina.

Agrochemical Exposure and Environmental Suffering

It was a cloudy winter morning in June 2012 when I arrived at the courthouse in the city of Córdoba, a province in the center of Argentina. A few hours later, two farmers and the pilot of a crop duster were going to trial for the use of agrochemicals in Ituzaingó Anexo, a neighborhood on the outskirts of the city of Córdoba. The Madres de Ituzaingó, a group of mothers from this neighborhood, had organized the case against the soybean growers. Their leader, Sofía Gatica, has become a symbol of the struggle against agrochemicals in Argentina. She was drawn into activism after her daughter died of kidney failure. Gatica and other women in her neighborhood sued the farmers and the crop dusters for the indiscriminate use of agrochemical and the increase in the number of cancer cases in their community.[18]

A large tent had been pitched next to the court building, where members of peasant organizations and environmentalist groups sold honey, jam, handicrafts, T-shirts, and DVDs of documentaries. Peasant and environmentalist groups were meeting to support the trial, participate in a demonstration against Monsanto, and hold an assembly to discuss possible strategies for joint action (see Figure 1.4). In the afternoon, all the people in attendance gathered under the tent in a wide circle. One by one, people presented their pleas and struggles against agro-toxics (they favor this term over agrochemicals). As I listened, I soon detected diverse accents in individuals' speech: those coming from Buenos Aires, like myself, are easily identified by the strong pronunciation of the "ll" and the "y," the same letters that others pronounced in a subtler way, suggesting that they arrived from the Western part of the country (*Cuyo*). I recognized participants from Santa Fe province because, like my relatives there, they inhaled the "s"; and locals from Córdoba stood out by extending the vowels in each word they pronounced.

I was not surprised by the diversity of people in attendance who were affected by agrochemicals, but I thought that the diverse accents were a telling indication of the regional expansion and the wide reach of agrochemical exposure. Agrochemical use in Argentina has risen steeply in recent years, in close connection to the expansion of GM soybeans. At the end of the 1990s, 42% of the agrochemicals used in the country were destined for the production of GM

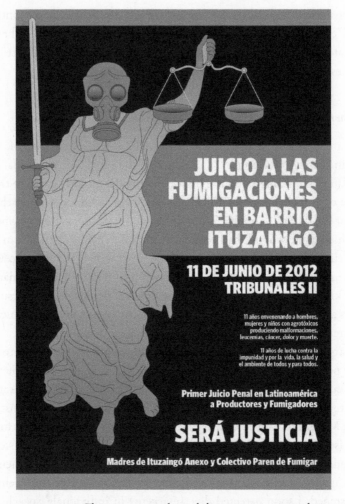

FIGURE I.4 Flyer to support the mobilization against agrochemical use in Córdoba

soybeans (Casabé et al. 2007, Clua, Conti, and Beltrano 2012, Druille et al. 2013). In 1997–1998, 28 million liters of glyphosate were sold in Argentina and in 1998–1999 this quantity doubled to 56 million liters (Pengue 2004b). By 2003–2004, conservative estimates indicate that glyphosate use reached 100 million liters (Pengue 2004a), increasing to 200 million liters by 2012.[19] In Argentina, the herbicides containing glyphosate are surprisingly accessible, costing one-third of a comparable herbicide in the United States (Benbrook 2005). On average, soybean growers in Argentina apply glyphosate 2.3 per year whereas farmers in the United States do so 1.3 times per year (Benbrook 2003).

Since the early 2000s, journalists and NGOs have reported cases in which agrochemicals drifted from the fields onto people's houses and farms, affecting their health and contaminating water streams (GRR 2009, Joensen, Semino, and Paul 2005).[20] In 2006 environmental activists launched a campaign and organized meetings in several provinces to raise awareness about agrochemical exposure (Arancibia 2013).[21] A study published in 2010 documented 32 cases of agrochemical drifts throughout Argentina (Domínguez and Sabatino 2010).

The issue of agrochemical exposure sporadically gained public attention, and affected populations obtained some pyrrhic victories. In 2009 Andrés Carrasco, a molecular biologist from the University of Buenos Aires, publicized his research on the deleterious impact of glyphosate on embryos (Paganelli et al. 2010). Activists cited the study to bolster their claims, and the research prompted a group of representatives to present a bill in the National Congress to ban aerial crop dusting and limit the terrestrial applications of agrochemicals.[22] The vitriolic reaction of companies only further publicized the issue.[23] In 2010 and 2011 in the provinces of Santa Fe and Chaco, provincial courts supported the demands of exposed neighbors and ordered the suspension of agrochemical applications near populated areas.[24] In spite of the creation of buffer zones in some provinces, studies continued to find a series of ailments caused by agrochemical exposure. Moreover, some provincial governments backtracked on their initial attempts to regulate agrochemical use.[25] In 2010 concerned scientists, doctors, activists, students, and neighbors from several provinces organized the First National Meeting of Physicians in the Crop-Sprayed Towns in the city of Córdoba.[26]

Considering all these initiatives and some modest but significant victories, why is agrochemical exposure and the concomitant environmental suffering still so prevalent throughout Argentina? Given the scope and gravity of the problem, why is it hard to organize a national campaign or broad mobilizations to address the issue? An ethnographic foray to the Second Meeting of Crop-Sprayed Towns sheds light on these questions.

Neighbors from towns exposed to agrochemicals, together with activists, students, and social movement representatives, gathered in a large classroom of the University of Córdoba in June 2012. They met during the trial over agrochemical use waged by the Madres de Ituzaingó. The goal of the meeting was to discuss strategies for organizing a national campaign against agrochemical use. The debate exposed not only the variegated regional composition of the participants, but also their different problems and motivations, their disagreements over agendas and strategies, and the tensions between and within organizations.

Soon after the assembly began, I noticed that many people provided testimony about the environmental suffering in their communities. An impatient coordinator soon intervened, asking for presenters to focus on concrete initiatives for the national campaign. When some of the participants showed their enthusiasm about the creation of buffer zones, another organizer reacted:

> The buffer could be 200, 500, or 800 meters, but that keeps us on the productivist discussion, without debating the productive model. We have to say that we're against the productive model, [it] doesn't matter how many meters. Otherwise, we're not getting at the bottom of the matter. They [the advocates of GM agriculture] unify their discourse saying that agrochemicals are harmless, that everything depends on how they're used. That's why they're going to say that the guys on trial just behaved badly.

The critique prompted the reaction of a neighbor from Santa Fe: "Having 800 meters [of buffer zone] won't spark an agrarian revolution, but now we don't even have 100 meters!"

Debates about organization, politics, and factional disputes also emerged. A woman opened her speech by introducing herself as member of CTA, a national union. She was cut short by one of the meeting coordinators: "But, which CTA do you belong to? Because there are two CTAs, the organization is split."

Her reaction was adamant and triggered a murmuring on the whole room: "I'm from the one and only CTA, the other one doesn't exist!" The organizer sought to compromise and bring order to the assembly: "Well, the fact that the two CTAs are here is already a triumph."

The discussion veered toward issues of representation and organizational structure. Some people argued that they needed to consult their constituents before making a decision, while others claimed that decisions should be taken then and there: "That's why we're here, because we represent our organizations!"

When someone proposed to create a national committee (a *mesa coordinadora nacional*), one of the local organizers disagreed: "In the 1970s we created a lot of organizations, structures . . . and that didn't work. No, we have to make the road while we walk [*tenemos que hacer camino al andar*]."

A woman from an NGO agreed: "If you create a commission, soon after, you will see the members running for a seat on the municipal council or the legislature." Her speech launched a debate on the relationship with politicians. "Politicians are looking for us to support them, this is a good moment, and we need to take advantage of it," said a man from Santa Fe.

Others had quite different views: "I stopped going to the national conferences of women organizations because the last ones were controlled by political organizations," said a woman from Córdoba.

The representative from Santa Fe disagreed: "In our speeches we shouldn't dismiss those participating in political parties, because 80% of them are lay people."

Disagreements petered out toward the end of the meeting and participants agreed on three points: asking for justice for the Ituzaingó neighborhood, "promoting a critique of transgenics and agro-toxics," and "emphasizing the lack of popular sovereignty to protect public health and the environment."

In the ensuing chapters of this book, I revisit many of the points discussed during this assembly by zooming in on the case of Formosa, scrutinizing issues of factionalism, the relationship between social movements and politics, and the tension between short- and long-term goals. Formosa exemplifies dynamics of agrarian change, social movements, and mobilization writ large. But to better grasp the issues debated in Córdoba in 2012 and the Formosan context, we also need to look at transformations that were taking place at the national level. Of specific importance are the economic and political changes ushered in by the national administrations of Néstor Kirchner (2003–2007), and of his wife and successor, Cristina Fernández de Kirchner, who became president in 2007 and was reelected for the 2011–2015 period.

Postneoliberalism? Changes and Continuities in Kirchner's Argentina

At the end of 2001, Argentina was submerged in a deep crisis. In mid-December, a series of lootings spread throughout the country (Auyero 2007). Then-president de la Rúa declared a state of siege on the night of December 19, only to prompt further protests in response. That night, thousands of people marched to the Plaza de Mayo, the central square in Buenos Aires next to the Pink House (the Presidential building), chanting "*Que se vayan todos / Que no quede / ni uno solo*" ("All of them must go," in reference to politicians and representatives). The next day, thousands of protesters flooded the streets of downtown Buenos Aires. The police shot tear gas, rubber bullets, and deadly ammunition, killing at least 39 demonstrators. On December 21, the president resigned.

The events of December 2001 were arguably the endpoint of social processes harkening back to the previous decade. During the 1990s, popular sectors exhibited a twofold response of contentious reaction and strategies of accommodation as they confronted the effects of neoliberalization. Riots, roadblocks, and massive demonstrations were staged in opposition to the negative consequences of neoliberalization policies (Auyero 2003, Cerrutti and Grimson 2004, Farinetti 2002, Giarracca 2001, Silva 2009, Svampa and Pereyra 2003). These conflicts amounted to a cycle of contention, that is, "a phase of heightened conflict across the social system, with rapid diffusion of collective action from more mobilized to less mobilized sectors, a rapid pace of innovation in the forms of contention employed . . . and sequences of intensified information flow and interaction between challengers and authorities" (Tarrow 2005: 199). At the same time, popular sectors adapted to the circumstances by resorting to patronage networks that distributed welfare resources and provided access to public services and employment (Auyero 2000, Brusco, Nazareno, and Stokes 2004, Giraudy 2007, Levitsky 2003, Lodola 2005, Weitz-Shapiro 2014).

In the aftermath of the 2001 crisis, both collective action and welfare programs expanded. The *piqueteros*, unemployed workers movements that burgeoned in the 1990s, maintained a high level of mobilization, while factories were occupied by laid-off workers and turned into cooperatives, and neighbors created popular assemblies in several cities (Dinerstein 2003, Sitrin 2006, Villalon 2007). The institutional crisis of December 2001 resulted in a string of three different presidents until Eduardo Duhalde, the leader of the Peronist party, became interim president in January 2002. His provisional government launched a vast welfare initiative, the Unemployed Head of Households Plan (Plan Jefes y Jefas de Hogar Desocupados), reaching more than two million households by 2003 (CELS 2003). Duhalde's government was scheduled to last until the end of 2003, but he called early elections after the police killed two activists during a demonstration in June 2002.[27]

Néstor Kirchner, one of the Peronist candidates of the Partido Justicialista (PJ), was elected president of Argentina in 2003, normalizing the country after the economic and institutional crisis triggered in 2001. Kirchner's administration transformed both the macroeconomic policies and the political landscape of Argentina by breaking away from the neoliberal policies of the 1990s (Levitsky and Murillo 2008) and forging international alliances with left-wing leaders in Latin America. The national administrations of Néstor Kirchner (2003–2007), and of his wife and successor, Cristina Fernández de Kirchner, deployed a series of policies aimed at redistributing income in favor of workers and popular sectors. In building their political powerbase, they enlisted the support of several social movements.

During the initial years of his administration, Néstor Kirchner courted popular social movements and incorporated a series of their leaders into the government.[28] Two organizations exemplify these dynamics: the FTV, Federación de Tierra y Vivienda (Land and Housing Federation), and the MNCI, Movimiento Nacional Campesino Indígena (National Peasant-Indigenous Movement).[29] As mentioned above and in the next chapters, these two organizations play a key role in understanding the dynamics of mobilization and demobilization linked to the expansion of GM soybeans in Argentina.

. The FTV is an alliance of grassroots organizations working at the community level. It emerged during the 1990s and grew exponentially in the early 2000s by enrolling unemployed workers in the province of Buenos Aires (Svampa and Pereyra 2003).[30] The FTV was also instrumental in supporting Néstor Kirchner during his presidential campaign, and, since 2003, it received the largest number of unemployment subsidies from the national government (Silva 2009: 80).[31] Additionally, the administrations of Néstor and Cristina Kirchner granted the FTV control of the offices in charge of public housing and regularization of lands at the national level. This offered the FTV and its leader, Luis D'Elía,[32] a series of advantages. First, it provided a national organizational structure for the grassroots group. Second, it provided opportunities for the FTV to give input on the policies targeting their constituents and opened job positions for member-activists. The FTV also developed a good and lasting relationship with the national Ministry of Social Development, directed by Alicia Kirchner (Néstor Kirchner's sister). This alliance allowed FTV to appoint employees to direct programs of the Ministry of Social Development in several provinces and gain access to greater resources.

The Kirchner administrations also built an alliance with the MNCI, a network of peasant and indigenous organizations that operate at the provincial and local level. In 2005, the national government offered the MNCI the management of the PSA (Programa Social Agropecuario, Social Agricultural Program), a program coordinating rural welfare under the national Secretary of Agriculture. After an internal debate, MNCI leaders accepted the offer and a leader of a peasant organization became the head of PSA. Upon taking control, peasant leaders in their new role as national public officials decided to redesign the program. Instead of distributing money among small groups of *individuals*, PSA funds were distributed directly to *organizations*. The goal of this change was to strengthen grassroots, peasant, and indigenous organizations vis-à-vis provincial governments that were often opposed to local social movements. MNCI's control of over PSA came to an end in 2007 when the national minister of economy was replaced. This change had a chain effect: the secretary of agriculture was also replaced, and the leader of MNCI was forced to relinquish the control of PSA. This coincides with a moment in 2008 when the links between the national government and peasant organizations were redrawn, as we will see below.

As social movement organizations became more involved in welfare policies and some leaders were appointed to public offices, popular movements in Argentina underwent a striking demobilization (Delamata 2004, Svampa and Pereyra 2004, Villalon 2007, Wolff 2007). The administrations of Néstor and Cristina Kirchner gradually moved their alliances with social movements to the back burner, as they concentrated on gaining the support of two key institutional actors in Argentine politics: the Peronist party and provincial governors. In doing so, their administrations increasingly relied on patronage politics to obtain political support. From the 1990s and onward, the Peronist party became synonymous with clientelist practices (Auyero 2000, Levitsky 2003). Argentine presidents often seek the support of governors to ensure votes in the national Congress (Jones and Hwang 2005), and the Kirchners were no exception. In forging these alliances the Kirchners approached governors who had held office for decades, who relied heavily on political machines to maintain power, and who firmly controlled provincial legislatures and the judiciary (Gibson 2012). Provincial governors, for the most part, also discourage protests and autonomous social movements (Moscovich 2012: 47). As two scholars with extensive knowledge on the Argentine political system summarize: "Because most legislators owe their nomination to a provincial boss rather than the national party leadership, discipline within the PJ's [Peronist party] legislative bloc hinges to a considerable degree on the president's ability to maintain the support of governors. Thus even powerful Peronist presidents . . . have governed in coalition with—and with the negotiated consent of party bosses" (Levitsky and Murillo 2008: 20). As we will see in detail in the next chapter, as in the case of Formosa, most governors and party bosses in Argentine provinces have built veritable "authoritarian sub-national regimes" (Gibson 2012, Giraudy 2015). Moreover, in northern provinces, provincial party bosses and their families often double as business partners of soybean growers, agribusiness people, and large landowners. Why did the Kirchner administrations increasingly rely on the Peronist party, political bosses, and provincial governors? A conflict dominating the political scenario in 2008 provides some answers and sheds light on the importance of soybean production in the economic and political life of Argentina.

The Government Against El Campo: Diehard Neoliberalism and Agribusiness Mobilization

Following the devaluation of the Argentine peso after the 2001 crisis, the national government established taxes on agricultural exports to appropriate part of the extraordinary rents produced from the difference between national prices (in pesos) and export revenues (in dollars).[33] Beginning in 2003, the administrations of Néstor and then Cristina Kirchner tapped into this revenue, mostly yielded by GM soybeans (the exports of the soybean agro-industrial complex account for nearly one-fourth of the total Argentine exports). The Kirchner administrations used these export taxes to fund redistribution policies and welfare programs, creating what some call an "export-oriented populism" (Richardson 2009).[34]

In March 2008, the national Ministry of Economy raised export taxes on soybeans, triggering the opposition of medium to large landowners and farmers' associations. Supported by media conglomerates and their main national newspapers, *Clarín* and *La Nación*, farmers blocked roads throughout Argentina and mobilized between March and July. Massive demonstrations in the cities of Rosario and Buenos Aires emboldened landowners, who took the offensive and deployed a free-trade discourse to demand the complete elimination of *all* export taxes (Aronskind and Vommaro 2010, Giarracca and Teubal 2010).[35]

Cristina Kirchner reacted by sending a bill to congress, Resolution 125, which modified the export tax on soybeans by tying the taxable percentage to the ups and downs of international prices. The bill was approved in the lower house (Diputados), but the parties of the opposition and agribusiness lobby fiercely opposed the bill in the Senate. During a dramatic nationally televised congressional debate, votes were tied but the bill was finally overturned when Vice President Julio Cobos (in his capacity of head of the Senate) verbally cast his negative vote. Cobos's decision was significant not only because it determined the failure of the bill, but also because he belongs to the UCR (Unión Cívica Radical), a centrist party that historically opposed Peronism. Cristina Kirchner had invited Cobos to be part of her running ticket in the 2007 national election to build transversal alliances that would bring together leaders from different political parties who shared similar ideas. Cobos's betrayal put an end to that initiative, and from then on Cristina Kirchner increasingly relied on fellow Peronists.

The defeat of Resolution 125 had broad political implications. During the protests, soybean growers and the mass media exhibited a keen capacity to deploy their hegemonic position, installing the idea that "what is good for agribusiness is good for the country" and successfully presenting themselves as *el campo*, or the countryside (with little or no mention of peasants and indigenous peoples).[36] The events exemplified what Peter Newell calls "(bio) hegemony" in reference to "the alignment of material, institutional, and discursive power in a way which sustains a coalition of forces which benefit from the prevailing model of agricultural development" in Argentina (Newell 2009: 38). While the conflict revealed the dispute between the national government and agribusiness regarding the appropriation of the wealth created by soybean production, the environmental and social consequences of transgenic agriculture were strikingly absent in the discussion. In terms of contentious politics in Argentina, the events had an ironic twist: the streets, roads, and squares where popular social movements voiced their claims in previous years were now occupied by the mobilized middle and upper classes.

As a counterreaction to the contentious collective actions of soybean growers, popular social movements marched in support of the national government (among them, the MNCI and the FTV). In April 2008, groups organized a massive demonstration in Buenos Aires to express their support for the president. In June, peasant and indigenous organizations created a *mesa coordinadora* in response to the conflict, demanding their "effective participation ... in the design of agrarian policies" (besides the suspension of land evictions and new land legislation).[37] Following the confrontation with large agribusiness, the national government launched a series of initiatives directly aimed at garnering the support of small farmers and peasants. One of these initiatives was the transformation of the Social Agricultural Program (PSA), a program that was renewed annually, into a permanent office. The PSA was upgraded and turned into the Sub-Secretaría de Desarrollo Rural y Agricultura Familiar (SSDRAF, Sub-Secretary of Rural Development and Family Farming).[38] Likewise, in 2009 President Kirchner addressed the demands of the "sprayed towns," ordering the creation of the Comisión Nacional de Investigación sobre Agroquímicos, CNIA (National Commission of Research on Agrochemicals). The decree creating the commission explicitly cited the legal case brought forth by the Madres de Ituzaingó as a rationale.[39] I scrutinize the implications of these initiatives in chapters 4 and 5.

In the ensuing chapters I further examine the relationships between popular social movements, the state, and patronage politics in the context of agricultural change and environmental transformations. While this chapter on Argentina focused on the 1990s and 2000s, the next chapter extends farther back in time and zooms in on a specific place. In doing so, I show the ways in which economic, agrarian, environmental, and political changes involve multiple scales and become enmeshed in individual and collective histories. Let us, then, continue the trip that opened this chapter by traveling further north to the province of Formosa.

2

EMERGENCE

PEASANTS, POLITICS, AND PATRONS: RURAL SOCIAL MOVEMENTS IN FORMOSA (1970s–2000s)

Know that the problems of social science, when adequately formulated, must include both troubles and issues, both biography and history, and the range of their intricate relations.

—C. WRIGHT MILLS *(1959: 226)*

Arriving in the city of Formosa from the south, the visitor is greeted by a monumental white cross standing 100 feet tall in the middle of a square. Continuing straight for 2.5 miles, you would reach the city's main square, Plaza San Martín, at the center of the downtown area. If you traveled for another half a mile, you would reach the esplanade alongside the Paraguay River. The area has been recently revamped and the passerby is constantly reminded about the changes by large billboards "signed" by the longtime governor of Formosa, Gildo Insfrán. The esplanade is a stone's throw from the Republic of Paraguay and the Paraguayan town of Alberdi is clearly visible just across the river.

Several murals and monuments dot the esplanade, one of which has caught my attention ever since my first visit to Formosa. The monument is occupied by the figures of a mustached man wearing a rolled-up shirt and a woman wearing a long skirt and a handkerchief on her head, while holding a baby (see Figure 2.1). Behind the couple, three columns are emblazoned with telling symbols. In the center, the province's coat of arms shows two hands shaking under a blooming cotton plant. The left column sports a thick white cross while the column to the right presents a sword. Two European-looking farmers, under cotton, situated in between the Catholic Church and the Army. The monument encapsulates the dominant version of Formosan history, not only by showing but also by concealing. Official discourses highlight "a provincial identity based

FIGURE 2.1 Monument to the immigrants

on the idea of a relatively recent frontier society, produced through military campaigns against the 'wild Indians' of the Chaco and forged by peasants who migrated from Paraguay and the Argentinean northeast (in the east of the province), *criollo* cattle-herders who moved in from Salta (in the west), and European immigrants" (Gordillo 2008: 337–338). This established narrative—and the monument on Formosa's esplanade—downplays the genocide against the Wichí, Qom, Pilagá, and other indigenous groups and the state's appropriation of the territories they used to inhabit.

The national state initiated its control of the northeastern region of Argentina after the war of 1865–1870, in which the allied armies of Brazil, Uruguay, and Argentina defeated the Paraguayan armed forces and claimed swathes of territory. In 1872, President Sarmiento signed a decree creating the National Territory of Chaco (encompassing the current provinces of Formosa and Chaco), and in 1884, the Army launched a military campaign that decimated the indigenous populations (Gordillo 2014: 53–72). At the end of the nineteenth century, the national authorities distributed land titles among a small group of families with strong ties to public officials. Almost 1 million hectares (2.3 million acres) were adjudicated to just 14 owners, each receiving around 66 thousand hectares (more than 163 thousand acres, 7.5 times the size of Manhattan island) (Slutzky 1973: 7).

The occupation of the territory continued during the first decades of the 1900s through the exploitation of forests and the breeding of cattle on large ranches (Brodersohn and Slutzky 1975). By then, the die was cast for land distribution. Since its inception and still today, a polarized agrarian social structure dominates the province of Formosa: small properties of up to 100 hectares (almost 250 acres) have historically represented around 70% of the farms, but they only have had control of 3 to 4% of the land. In contrast, large properties of 1,000 hectares or more (nearly 2,500 acres) constitute between 10 and 15% of the farms, but make up around 80% of the total arable land.[1]

This chapter delves into the history of the Formosan peasantry as seen through the experience of peasant activists, thus heeding the advice of C. Wright Mills on the importance of linking biography and history to create worthwhile social science. Cases of agrochemical exposure can be best understood when seen as the product of experiences anchored in the routines and interactions that shape specific places (Auyero and Swistun 2009: 144). By conveying the particular relationship that peasants created with their territory, we will be better equipped to understand the actions, feelings, and ideas that inform their processes of mobilization and demobilization analyzed in the ensuing chapters.

Cotton, Migration, and State Intervention (1930s–1960s)

"Here, for most small farmers, if you don't grow cotton you're not a farmer," an agronomist with decades of experience working in Formosa told me in 2007. Cotton has historically been the cash crop from which Formosan small farmers make a living. A crop that is preyed by a variety of insects (e.g., bollworms, aphids, and beetles), conventional cotton production involves the use of a number of pesticides and other agrochemicals (e.g., growth regulators and defoliants before harvest). In the 1940s, DDT was widely used to control insects (Tripp 2009: 38) and until the mid-1990s, "the organophosphate group, one of the most hazardous in terms of worker's risks, represented the majority of the insecticide market in cotton cultivation in many developing countries" (Kooistra, Termorshuizen, and Pyburn 2006: 13). While talking with an agronomist in Formosa about cases of contamination, he recalled how small farmers growing cotton "yearn for" parathion, an extremely toxic organophosphate agrochemical that EPA has classified as a possible human carcinogen.[2]

—Parathion is the classic for cotton ... You talk with producers here and they long for parathion. They love parathion.
PABLO: Why do they miss it?
—Because they say that it controlled bollworms really well. If you were going to applying it, when you came back, the insects were on the ground [dead] ...When people see the insect attack the leaf, they become desperate ... and they go looking for [agrochemical] products.

In the 1930s, the national state promoted cotton production by distributing seeds, facilitating access to credit, and creating the National Board of Cotton (Junta Nacional del Algodón), which regulated its production and commercialization (Girbal-Blacha 2004).

Small farmers growing cotton populated the east and center of the province creating villages that, even today, are called "colonies" (*colonias*). Analysts characterized the settlement of small family farmers as "interstitial," since they occupied "the reduced free spaces enclosed by large cattle properties" (Brodersohn and Slutzky 1975: 103).

"All of us worked. All of the children worked the land with our parents. That's how we know how to work the land, and it's all we know to do well. Work the land. Some say they don't want to be peasants [*campesinos*], but we're proud to be *campesinos*. Those of us who were born in the countryside, we want to stay in the countryside. No matter how poor we might be," Nélida told me in 2007 as we sipped mate sitting on front of her farmhouse in Monte Azul (see Figure 2.2). Her parents were born in Paraguay and they migrated to Formosa, fleeing the devastating aftermath of the Chaco War (1932–1935) between the Bolivian and Paraguayan armies. They met, got married in Formosa, and in 1958 they settled in Monte Azul. Nélida was eight years old. She grew up working in the cotton fields with her parents and her 11 siblings. "We all [her siblings] finished primary school. Hardly anyone finished secondary school, only Horacio [her youngest brother and also a MoCaFor leader]. I went to secondary school in Sarambí but only for two years. I couldn't go anymore because we were poor, and we couldn't leave my younger brothers with my mother, so I had to come to help."

Monte Azul, a colony or rural community of nearly 800 inhabitants, is located 70 miles from Formosa's capital. An unpaved vicinal road connects

FIGURE 2.2 Nélida's farm

the elementary school, the church, and the small healthcare center, and then continues to connect with the paved national highway leading to Sarambí (a town of around 35,000) located 14 miles away (see Figure 2.3). Most families settled in Monte Azul during the 1930s, when a state-owned company was installed in the area to produce wood and coal. Locals and migrants were hired as loggers, and families occupied vacant lands and grew cotton as a cash crop, as well as manioc, corn, pumpkin, and other vegetables for self-consumption.

Between 1945 and the 1960s state intervention in cotton production intensified, both in the province of Formosa and Argentina as a whole. During the governments of Juan D. Perón (1946–1952 and 1952–1955), cotton production was stimulated by the creation of factories that bought and industrialized the fiber produced in the region, while cotton cooperatives were created in Formosa and in the neighboring provinces of Chaco and Corrientes. Throughout this period, cotton production became the main source of income for small farmers. In 1955, shortly before Perón was ousted by a coup d'état, Formosa was upgraded from the status of national territory to become a province. The provincial coat of arms, showing two shaking hands under a cotton plant, suggests the importance of this crop in Formosa (see Figure 2.4).

FIGURE 2.3 Entrance to Monte Azul

From 1955 to 1973, the military controlled Argentine political life. Although it discouraged political activism and outlawed Peronism, it nonetheless maintained a regulated cotton market.

Nélida grew up during the golden age of cotton production. In 1969, when she was 19 years old, she got married and moved with her husband to the farm where she lives to this day. She has good memories of her first decades living there, especially in contrast to the present, something I heard her say on several occasions: "In the early years, when we got married, and my husband worked the land, it was very profitable, everything we planted. Cotton had a good price. My husband got credit from the bank to plant on all of our land, paid all the bills, we never owed a cent to anyone. We had money to spare to enjoy ourselves, to buy what we wanted, to build our house little by little . . . But now it's impossible. There's a big difference."

Nélida and her family were part of the large group of peasants that produced cotton and grew other crops for self-consumption. Until the end of the 1960s, peasant families lived side-by-side with large ranches where landowners bred cattle. By the end of the 1960s, cattle production in Formosa became increasingly complementary with this activity in the Pampas region: calves bred in Formosa were exported to the Pampas for their final fattening. The

FIGURE 2.4 Formosan coat of arms

acquisition of agricultural land in Formosa thus became increasingly appealing for cattle breeders interested in using this land to grow fodder and calves. In addition, between 1966 and 1972, the provincial administrations appointed by the military gave large areas of fiscal lands to middle- and large-scale cattle ranchers (Brodersohn and Slutzky 1975: 104).

Around the same time, peasants also began to demand more land. Toward the end of the 1950s, the introduction of synthetic fibers in the world market led to a decline in the price of cotton. Small farmers responded to the drop in prices by increasing the cultivated area in an attempt to maintain their income by producing more (Brodersohn and Slutzky 1975). In short, by the end of the 1960s, the social actors behind cotton and cattle production—two economic activities that until then had run relatively independent from each other—began to have increasingly conflicting interests (Roze 1992: 92–93). In the 1970s, these mounting tensions escalated into open conflicts that ended tragically.

The Peasant Leagues and Military Governments: Radical Mobilization and Repression (1970s)

Elisa was born in a rural village in the north of Formosa to a family of small farmers. In 1968 when she was 15 years old, she began to participate in the Rural Movement of the Catholic Church, an organization inspired by the principles and the practices of Liberation Theology (Ferrara 1973). In 1971 the bishop of Formosa, Monsignor Scozzina, encouraged the organization of assemblies that ultimately resulted in the creation of ULiCaF, Unión de Ligas Campesinas de Formosa (Union of Formosan Peasant Leagues). The ULiCaF was the Formosan variant of the Peasant Leagues that were created during the 1970s in Paraguay, Brazil, and throughout the Argentine northeast (in the provinces of Misiones, Chaco, Corrientes, and Santa Fe).[3] ULiCaF sought to address the unequal distribution of land and improve the terms of negotiation between cotton growers and the cotton industry.

In 2007, I sat with Elisa on her patio in the city of Formosa and I asked her what she remembered about those years. "The struggle was very important, because all of the peasantry [el campesinado] were involved. And it was beautiful because it was totally a grassroots effort. The leaders were campesinos, and there were lots of youth," she told me. It was during this time that she met Nahuel through her participation in the movement. He was a Catholic priest deeply involved in the Leagues, but in 1974 Nahuel left the priesthood and they got married. Elisa was 21 years old.

A close reading of the statutes of ULiCaF shows peasants' concern with the interference of political parties in their organization, and at their public demonstrations, they eschewed the participation of politicians (Ferrara 1973: 235, 243, 287), a relevant distinction in comparison to the 1980s, as I discuss in the next section. Peasant Leagues were characterized by vibrant grassroots mobilization and ULiCaF in particular allowed the participation of nonassociated peasants in a bottom-up decision making system. ULiCaF had a keen concern about bureaucracy: leaders refused to participate in government commissions, refrained from becoming a legal entity (personería jurídica), and had reservations about receiving resources from the government (Ferrara 1973: 302–304).[4] In 1971 the military government offered an extensive tract of land to ULiCaF, but the organization rejected the offer because of the bad quality of the plot and the conditions that came with it.[5] Three and a half decades later, Elisa regrets the decision: "A commission traveled to examine the land. And they didn't accept it. Later, when time had gone by, we said 'Damn, if only we had accepted.'"

ULiCaF mobilized intensively between 1971 and 1975, staging massive demonstrations in the Formosan capital and occupying lands. Local committees in several areas of the province engaged in direct occupations of plots of fiscal lands that had been previously transferred to private owners in the 1960s.[6] "When it's bottom up, it's stronger. I felt that way in the Leagues. I felt like we participated, that we thought, we debated: if we're going to take these lands, why are we going to take them, why should we, what are our advantages, what was against us, what was the possibility of winning, what happens if we lose? It wasn't just 'let's do a roadblock and that's it.' Now it's easier. As I see it, it's not the same. Before it was more thought out," Elisa told me.

In 1973, Perón returned to Argentina after being in exile and the country held the first free elections since he was overthrown in 1955. He was elected president in a landslide and the Peronist candidate for governor of Formosa obtained more than 70% of the votes. The new authorities soon became immersed in a fierce dispute, pitting the governor (supported by ULiCaF and the left-wing faction of Peronism) against the vice governor (supported by unions and the right-wing faction of Peronism). The national Congress approved a federal intervention in the province in November 1973, in large part due to the anxieties spurred by the land occupations organized by ULiCaF (Servetto 2002: 31–32).

In March 1976, the military organized a coup d'état against the national government and launched a systematic repression of popular organizations and left-wing groups.[7] The dictatorship of 1976–1983 in Argentina involved the repression of radical movements in the context of the Cold War, but it was also a project of national elites to redraw society along lines favoring their interests vis-à-vis popular sectors (Azpiazu, Basualdo, and Khavisse 1986, Jozami, Paz, and Villarreal 1985).

In Formosa, colonel Juan Carlos Colombo was appointed governor with strong support from the provincial Rural Society (Sociedad Rural), an organization of large landowners (two of its members were appointed minister of the economy and minister of agriculture in the province). During the Colombo administration from 1976 to 1981, several publicly owned companies were privatized, including cotton gins, a textile factory, and a meat processing plant (the latter was acquired by the Rural Society).[8] In addition, the provincial Cotton Board (Junta Provincial del Algodón) was transformed and its regulatory functions were curtailed. As a result, "in three years the structure of the cotton industry took a decisive turn, coming under private sector control with a total absence of the State in the regulation of market policies and prices" (Rofman et al. 1987: 241).

During the military dictatorship ULiCaF members were harshly repressed, imprisoned, and tortured like activists of other popular movements throughout Argentina.[9] "It was awful not knowing anything . . . there was like a silence," Elisa reflected, decades later. "You could never relax, because you never knew when they might get you. People disappeared all the time." At the end of the dictatorship the Formosan economy was more polarized than ever, and the negotiating power of small cotton farmers was greatly reduced. In terms of land distribution, fiscal land was transferred to medium and large proprietors, and a special commission was created with the specific purpose of evicting peasants occupying lands without legal titles (Rofman et al. 1987: 242–243).

The Agrarian Movement of Formosa: Democratization and the Peronist Political Machine (1980s–1990s)

In 1983, Argentina initiated a transition toward democracy that began with free elections nationwide. In Formosa, the candidate of the Peronist party, Floro Bogado, was elected governor and held office from 1983 to 1987. After the traumatic experience of the dictatorship, former activists of the Peasant Leagues were at a loss but trying to regroup. "There was a hunger to know what the hell had happened. Because the media was talking about 'the *guerrilleros*,' 'the communists,' 'the subversives,'" Elisa said. She saw an opportunity to reconnect over the baptism of one of her daughters and invited her former *compañeros* to the party. "My concern was how we were going to find each other again. For me, the organization was my life. We did the baptism, and it was the first encounter [since the dictatorship]. It wasn't a meeting, but it was a chance to find each other." Following their initial meetings, a group of former leaders of ULiCaF decided to recreate the organization under a different name: Movimiento Agrario de Formosa, MAF (Agrarian Movement of Formosa). Discussions about the name were an early indication that the character of the movement was beginning to change. As Elisa said: "No one wanted to call it Leagues. I wanted it to be called Leagues, but no . . . [Others said] that it didn't matter, that our struggle is what matters." The attempts to reorganize the movement soon showed that the bottom-up and grassroots spirit of the 1970s was not an easy feat to achieve in a different political context.

Rafael was another former activist trying to recreate a peasant organization. I talked to him in June 2009 at his farm, when Julio drove me there on his motorcycle. Julio is a local leader of MoCaFor in Monte Azul and also Nélida's son. Rafael and Julio had never met, but Rafael knew Pedro, Julio's father and Nélida's husband, who had also participated in MAF. We stayed in the area for a few days and visited Rafael three times. During our conversations I felt that Rafael was not only talking to myself as a sociologist, but was also passing along the history of peasant struggles to Julio (who began to participate in MoCaFor in the 2000s).[10]

Rafael offered a candid and insider account of how the MAF became a springboard for political careers and an appendage of the provincial political machine. In 1983, Rafael was in a meeting called by the soon-to-be governor, Floro Bogado. Rafael remembered that Bogado had convinced local leaders to remain quiet. Bogado had told them, "I'm going to win, but don't agitate, don't mobilize the base, we're returning from the dictatorship. So whatever you need, deal with me. But the base, keep them quiet. No effervescence, no land occupations. There were land occupations here, but we don't need that [now], because we are coming out of a really complicated period." In 1992 a cadre of MAF leaders organized a roadblock, demanding economic support for farmers. But they were also seeking, as Rafael put it, "to clean the MAF, and overthrow the mobsters associated to the political power [*tumbar la mafia que estaba con el poder político*]." The leaders of the roadblock seized the momentum and in the next general assembly of MAF, they garnered the majority of votes and gained control of the movement.

In the early 1990s, the new leadership of the MAF took over the organization with the idea of regaining autonomy and rekindling the organization. But this spirit did not last long. "They became arrogant, the new leaders." Rafael said with resignation. "They had all the power. They were on TV, in the papers ... They were there 4, 5 years, and didn't renew their posts, they didn't hold assemblies ... that was a mistake." By then, Vicente Joga, the president of the Peronist party in Formosa, had finished his first term as governor (1987–1991) and was reelected for a second term (1991–1995). Policies of neoliberalization were in full swing, combining "roll back" deregulation in the cotton industry and "roll out" interventions through rural welfare.[11] "Then the MAF enters in the PSA [Programa Social Agropecuario, a national welfare program for the rural poor launched in 1993]. The PSA was managed by MAF [in Formosa] and controlled a lot of resources. Our strategy was to get resources and contract our technicians," Rafael recalled. "And later, they went too far and problems arose with the leadership. They weren't careful, they were there 4, 5 years, through inertia. They did what all the others did, they stayed in the central office and didn't do the grassroots work. And there was bad money management. They didn't want to do the accounting because they couldn't justify it."

In 1995, Gildo Insfrán was elected governor and soon after, MAF leaders negotiated a pact with him, becoming fully integrated into the provincial political machine. Insfrán had been vice governor between 1987 and 1995, and once elected governor, he reformed the provincial Constitution to remove term limits and allow the indefinite reelection of the governor. He has been governor since, and was reelected for the 2011–2015 term. At the end of this term, he will reach 20 years of uninterrupted control over the Formosan government. Elisa and Rafael have not talked in years, but they offered me similar interpretations of the changes in MAF, linking the changes in the structure of the organization to its relationship with the Peronist political machine. "It's hard for me to talk about MAF," Elisa admitted in 2007:

We tried to be democratic; we called on the people to participate. But there was no response from the base, from the people in the *colonias*. There were leaders from every zone [in the MAF]. But it was no longer like the Leagues. With the Leagues, every *colonia* had their delegate, who respected what their *colonia* told them. They represented the *colonia's* views in the central meeting, in the assembly, and brought information back to their *colonia*. But with MAF, it wasn't like that. There was already control by the popular ... democratic, let's say Peronist, government. They bought off the delegates! I mean, I say "bought," but they gave them a job, a salary. Maybe a job in the *colonia*. And to the strongest, they gave land.

Rafael interpreted the failure of MAF in similar terms:

The MAF failed because it had a big structure, the leadership arrives up there, it disconnected from the base, they negotiated ... there were lots of things I didn't share with MAF because it sold itself to the political power ... The leaders received tractors. "And with this, we do politics [*hacemos política*]," they thought. Some received salaries, others [received] candidacies, [and] became representatives [*diputados*], councilmen, mayors. And things got quiet [*se adormeció*].

In 2009, I visited the offices of MAF to gain a fuller understanding of the claims about their involvement with the provincial government. The following excerpts from my fieldnotes provide an idea of the pervasiveness of patronage politics in Formosa and give a glimpse of how provincial authorities and MAF leaders see MoCaFor.

I arrive at the office of MAF in the city of Formosa for an appointment with Miriam. She manages the organization's tasks in the capital of the province, because Carlos Arroyo, the provincial head of MAF, is the mayor of a town in the countryside (I learned that at least five MAF leaders are also mayors of small towns). I arrive at the offices and am welcomed by a man in his fifties, who tells me that Miriam is not there yet. As we chat, he explains that delegates come to that office "to do paperwork or bring concerns [*para hacer trámites o traer inquietudes*]."

While I wait for Miriam, I look at the pictures hanging on the wall. In one of them, Arroyo is smiling next to a minister of the province of Buenos Aires and Gildo Insfrán (the governor). Next to the picture, a bronze plaque reads: "From the government of the province of Formosa to the Agrarian Movement of Formosa recognizing its permanent struggle in defense of the countryside. Formosa 1993." Three other framed pictures hang next to the plaque. In one of them, Arroyo is talking into a microphone next to a table where Governor Insfrán and other men in suits and ties look on attentively; the caption reads: "Don Carlos Arroyo, Mayor of [town], November 2006, 6th floor of the Government Building" (the floor where official ceremonies take place). In another picture, the governor and Arroyo walk together down a street. The caption reads: "Don Gildo Insfrán and Don Carlos Arroyo, Formosa's boardwalk, March 1997." In the last picture, Arroyo, the governor and other men smile while eating at a table under a gazebo.

I receive a SMS from Miriam asking me to come to the headquarters of PAIPPA, the Program of Integral Assistance to Small Farmers (Programa de Asistencia Integral al Pequeño Productor Agropecuario), a provincial welfare program that many interviewees told me works as an extension of the patronage network of the Peronist Party.

Once at the PAIPPA building, a picture hanging on the wall draws my attention. It reads "Delivery of motorcycles to promoters" and a group of more than twenty people wearing the same shirt and cap pose behind a banner that reads "Thanks, Mr. Governor." I finally meet

Miriam and she tells me that she is "running all over the place" to obtain the subsidies that the government is distributing among cotton growers. She introduces me to several people, and I notice everyone in the office addresses each other as *compañero*, the way Peronists refer to their fellow party members.

We enter an office to meet Fabio Casone, the provincial secretary of rural development, and we sit with Miriam and three other people in front of his desk [the following year, Casone became provincial minister of production and the environment]. Casone gives me a long speech about Formosa, mentioning the governor in every other sentence, saying things like "Gildo is a man of dialogue," or "the message of Gildo is that we always have to have hope." According to Casone, the PAIPPA only covers basic needs, "but we have organizations like MAF that give us a hand." He contrasts MAF with MoCaFor, saying the latter "does not look for dialogue, only confrontation." Towards the end of the talk he adds, matter-of-factly, "It's in our genes, we don't like to fight."

I leave the building with Miriam and go back to the MAF office, where she has to take care of the paperwork for credits from the national ministry of human development. She praises Arroyo, saying that he knows how to maneuver politically (*tiene cintura política*) and that he became mayor because "we realized that we lacked a political branch" (*nos dimos cuenta que nos faltaba la pata política*) (fieldnotes, June 8, 2009).

Dirty Politics, Helpul *Políticos*

The most difficult task in social anthropological fieldwork is to determine the meaning of a few key words, upon an understanding of which the success of the whole investigation depends.

—E. E. EVANS-PRITCHARD *(1951: 80)*

The limits of my language mean the limits of my world.

—LUDWIG WITTGENSTEIN *(1949: 5.6)*

Within Peronism, you hear about social justice and a lot of stuff that happened under Peronism, but they don't practice even half of that. Still, we're all Peronists, without even knowing why.

—ISIDORO, *local MoCaFor leader.*

While doing fieldwork in Formosa and, later on, when transcribing interviews and coding fieldnotes, I noticed two tropes that constantly reemerged in peasants' voices: the disparaging ways in which they referred to politics and the use of the term "*ayudas*," or "help," in reference to welfare resources. Discerning the meaning of "politics" (*la política*) and "help" thus became an important part of my fieldwork and analysis—a "difficult task," as Evans-Pritchard noted, in which I was guided by the work of qualitative sociologists that sought to determine the meaning of terms that encapsulated a social world (Becker 1993).

Talking about politics and resources in these terms is certainly not unique to Formosa or Argentina. The idea of politics as a "dirty" activity, infused with petty bickering and controlled by self-serving politicians, is found in a variety of social settings (Baiocchi et al. 2014, Bilakovics 2012, Eliasoph 1998, Lazar 2008: 198–203). The use of "help" may be less widespread but, interestingly, it also emerges among Nicaraguan peasants involved in development projects, who "talk the languages of both vertical patronage and horizontal solidarity" (Fisher 2012).

Below I delve into the language that peasants use to talk about politics and resources to gain access to the "political common sense" that permeates MoCaFor participants; that is, the seldom articulated ideas that allow people like Isidoro observe that they are Peronists "without even knowing why." MoCaFor confronts the governor and the Peronist political machine, yet the movement shares the same political milieu (a point that I further elaborate in chapter 3 by exploring the language that peasants use to make sense of collective action and contentious identities, and in chapters 4 and 5 by analyzing how unspoken ideas of reciprocity and performative speech acts create obstacles to contention).

"Politicians have a clean conscience . . . because they never use it!" This joke, which I heard a few times while doing fieldwork, encapsulates the ways in which many peasants and poor Formosans think about *políticos*, namely, politicians and political brokers. In the initial stages of my fieldwork, I noticed two tropes about politics: peasants talked about it as a spurious activity, and, among social movement leaders, as an interference to their activities.

Peasants saw politics as something dirty, driven by personal, selfish interests, and tainted by corruption. I repeatedly heard stories of corrupt politicians, and people referred to politics as an impure realm. Nélida, for instance, frequently voiced her critiques of politics and politicians: "I don't see anything clean or healthy within politics . . . If you are in politics, if they tell you to steal, you have to steal; if they tell you 'go this way,' you have to do it, even if you don't want to . . . I don't want to be in politics because politicians have to lie," she told me in 2009. The pervasiveness of this understanding of politics was evident in that many of the people I talked to took for granted the meaning of "being political." During a conversation with Isidoro, a current local leader of MoCaFor, he mentioned that a person was "very political." I asked him what he meant. "Well, because he wants everything to be in line with the government [*quiere llevar todo para el lado del gobierno*]. One time, we went to a meeting. We arrived, in the morning we talked a little, then we ate lunch, and by the end of lunch the final document was already written."

These views toward *politicos* turned even more acrimonious when peasants talked about resources (or the lack thereof), conveying their resentment toward patronage networks; in other words, needing to be politically connected in order to receive public resources. Nélida told me countless anecdotes about how she was denied access to public subsidies for cotton production because she was not "politically connected." Peasants also linked their economic demise to politics, using phrases like, "Before . . . we had the support of the province. Now, everything is political." They also perceived the pressure for land as a result of politicians' actions. Facundo, a peasant from Monte Azul, told me in an interview at his farm in 2007:

> Before, we weeded everything with two people and two plows, because we had credit with the provincial bank and we had a surplus so we could pay it back and still have money left. But now, our leaders want you to go asking for the little bag of goods [*la bolsita de mercadería*, in reference to the food that political brokers give in exchange for political support during elections]. Those who come to rent [lands] are from the government, because they hire a government agronomist who finds land for them, and that's why they first speak with Gildo [the governor]. The governor lets them come here . . . Before, with two plows we could work our land, we had the support of the province. Now everything is political.

Horacio, a leader of MoCaFor, exemplified the obstacles posed by *politicos* when trying to obtain legal status (*personería jurídica*) to represent the farmers market in which many MoCaFor members participate (more on this below): "We were told that we needed the support of a politician, that we should bring his business card with a telephone number. Then they told us that the governor should authorize it. Finally, when Valencia [the local political boss] went to Buenos Aires, a member of the movement who is an evangelical talked to Valencia's niece, who is also an evangelical. That is how we got the *personería jurídica*" (fieldnotes June 27, 2007). These ideas were applied to the politicians of the perennial incumbent party, the Peronists, but also to the main opposition party, the Radical Party (UCR). Another joke peasants made repeatedly was, "This year I will sow *radicales* ... they sell fast!"

Not all the participants in MoCaFor, however, thought about politics in the same way. For several members and leaders, for instance, politics was a tool and the only way to effect a social change. Seeking to gain access to diverse views and problematize a monolithic representation of peasants' ideas about politics, I took advantage of a technique called "the barometer of values." The activity consists in proposing an ambiguous statement; then, the participants place themselves along an imaginary scale ranging from "total agreement" to "total disagreement." Each person explains their position and then they debate the statement.

In June 2009 I stood in front of a dozen members of MoCaFor in Sarambí, inside the warehouse that serves as their headquarters and meeting place. "So, we have this phrase: 'Politics only serves to make politicians rich,'" I said, trying to make myself heard over the screeching of tables and chairs and the murmurs of people moving along the imaginary scale of "agreement" and "disagreement." The majority (nearly 10 men) converged in the "total disagreement" zone, while three women gathered around the "agreement" area. The first intervention came from Isidoro, one of the local representatives of MoCaFor:

ISIDORO: I came over to this side [disagreement] because I don't agree that politics is only good for politicians ... To me, if you practice politics, I think it functions more like ... part of a job that you delegate, and it's not about getting richer. If politics is carried out well, as it should be, I think that everyone benefits, not just some, not politicians, or foreigners/outsiders, or businesses. ...

NÉLIDA: I placed myself here [agreement] because I am not as smart as them [gesturing to the men], but from what I've seen so far, it's what it says there, it's just about the politicians and the powerful getting richer. And people with money get more money. And the poor get poorer. It doesn't do anything else, but it doesn't have to be that way.

The ideas of Isidoro and Nélida reflected the agreement/disagreement distinction, yet both converged on seeing politics as a tool, an instrument.

During the discussion, the disagreement mostly revolved around what can be done with that tool: whereas some (mostly men) saw politics as an instrument that could be used in different ways, even to effect a positive change, others (mostly women) articulated their idea of politics as a tool used by self-serving politicians reproducing inequality.

As the debate became heated, Isidoro took the floor to cast a challenge: what would MoCaFor members do if they were president? The question triggered a discussion on elections as a vehicle for change.

ISIDORO: I want to give an example. What would happen if this year you get elected president [directed a no one in particular]. Would you do the same thing? Would you use politics like this?

NINA: Yes! [Everyone laughs].

ISIDORO: Because let's suppose that we vote for president and you put your team, would everyone do the same?

HORACIO: No, because my way of seeing politics is not that same as Gildo Insfrán [the governor]. [Several people talk at once, some call for silence].

NÉLIDA: But the same thing is going to happen, you're going to bring the same thieves.

NINA: I want to be a politician to do the same thing they do [the women laugh]. To make myself comfortable, to become wealthy, and let the rest take care of themselves [Laughter and various comments].

EMILIO: But if they elect him [Horacio] as a politician, I don't think he will do the same thing. So politics is not just about making yourself rich.

RODO: Are you sure? [Laughter].

Toward the end of the debate, two interventions by Eduardo and Horacio elaborated on the relational aspect of clientelism and the expectations of reciprocity embedded in it.

EDUARDO: You say that Gildo bribes [people], that he puts pressure on people [*que aprieta*] . . . I think it's the lack of awareness, of having consciousness . . . Because no one is going to see your vote. And today you are in power, but I can vote against you.

HORACIO: I don't know if it is the lack of ideology among the people, or if they strongly value being sincere. When they committed to receive the bag [with food and other items], they gave their vote, and they didn't say one thing here and do another there. [Politicians] promise you tons of things, and later they don't do anything. The people are not practicing the same politics that they do.

Another way in which peasants revealed the weight of patronage politics in Formosa was in the term they used to talk about public resources. Peasants usually referred to these resources as "help" (*ayuda*), suggesting that they receive them as a favor rather than a right. For instance, in 2009 I asked Telma, a representative of MoCaFor in Moreno, about what they were aiming at in the 2003 protests (discussed in the next chapter): "What we wanted the most is that they would give them some *help*, or something, to those families who were affected." When I asked Nélida how MoCaFor members managed to make ends meet, she answered that they obtained things from the PSA, the Social Agricultural Program of the national state. She contrasted the help they receive from the PSA with the relationship with the provincial government: "The Ministry of Agriculture in Formosa didn't even give us a gram of anything. It's all talk, nothing else. . . . They come and say they are going to do trainings [*capacitaciones*], but if they don't help you with something else, you can't do anything. And this is what we fight with them about, the trainings are good, but along with the training, they need to give us credit or subsidies so we can work."

Ignacio lives with his mother on a small plot of land where they built a house out of wood and adobe bricks. I asked him, "Who helps the community?" inadvertently using the emic language. "The one who *helped* us was Julio, to get the plan [unemployment subsidy]. Julio and Isidoro *helped* us a lot. Through them we got the plan, me and my mom." When I asked him what community project he was involved in (a condition to be a beneficiary of an unemployment subsidy), Ignacio replied: "We're cleaning up to build a plaza. But help is still needed to put up hammocks for the kids."

MoCaFor members and representatives also expressed ambivalence toward clientelism when criticizing the patrons who fail to deliver. I witnessed several instances when people, paradoxically, condemned clientelism while also complained about its malfunctioning:

Valencia [the local political boss] stole but he would do stuff. If you were going to ask for medicine, or if you needed money to travel to Formosa [the capital city] at least he gave it to you. If you ask Salinas [the then-current mayor] for something, he tells you to come back tomorrow. But you need it for today. That's why I get mad when they say that it's just the politician's fault. If we go and vote for them, if people get their little bag of goods and they go and vote for him, even though they know that after the elections they are not going to give them anything else (Eduardo talking with Julio, fieldnotes June 18, 2009).

Valencia is a son of a bitch, but the type of person that would solve problems for you. When someone would lose a family member, he took care of everything. He paid for trips to Buenos Aires, the old man gave you things. Those who are around now . . . don't give people anything (Isidoro, fieldnotes June 19, 2009).

Sensini [a local political broker] is a millionaire . . . If you're a leader, you have to leave a good legacy so that God will receive you with open arms, because the wooden suit doesn't have pockets [referring to a coffin]. The leaders make schools, Gildo steals but he does things, he builds things, you can see that he has already stolen plenty (Adela, interviewed in 2009).

In Formosa and elsewhere, social movements and civil society organizations usually conceive of politics as transcendent (coming from outside) and polluting (contaminating social relations with manipulations and insincerity) (Goldman 2001: 165). Among MoCaFor participants, negative views of politics combined with ambiguities toward *políticos* and, particularly, clientelism. In interviews and everyday talk, I noticed that people referred to clientelism and *políticos* disparagingly, all the while resorting to a lexicon imbued with the logic of patronage. MoCaFor representatives not only complained because political bosses were gatekeepers, but also because these patrons did not deliver like they used to. My interpretation of the ubiquitous use of "help" suggests that people tended to see public resources as a right but also as a favor delivered personally. This, in turn, shows not only the prevalence of clientelism among popular sectors in Formosa, but also the ambivalence toward politics and politicians when the latter were criticized not only for putting obstacles to social movement organizations but also for not delivering as expected.

With this analysis, I do not want to imply that Formosans have a spurious understanding of rights. Rather, I interpret their views through the lenses of research proposing that political claims can be expressed using different languages (Lazar and Nuijten 2013). Rather than considering the local meaning of politics in Formosa as "degraded," I make an elemental ethnographic effort of capturing politics "in their own terms." This analysis of how the logic of patronage and clientelism makes its way into the language of activists allowed me, in turn, to outline the boundaries of the local political imagination. Insofar as the limits of a language draw the limits of a given world, as Wittgenstein's epigraph above suggests, attention to local meanings of politics sheds light on the subjective roots of mobilization and demobilization that I scrutinize in the following chapters. This foray into peasants' understanding of politics, politicians, and resources also provides an overview of the context in which MoCaFor emerged in the late 1990s, to which I turn next.

MoCaFor: A Peasant Movement in the Midst of Neoliberalization and Clientelism (1990s–2000s)

"We are like a piece of meat stuck in your teeth [*somos como carne en el diente*] ... they don't like us. Many people depend on public employment, the school, the municipality, the police, and they all answer to the government that doesn't want us to exist," a MoCaFor member told me in 2008. His statement reflects a sentiment that, in the eyes of many Formosans, activists are "weird" or bothersome, hinting at the vexed process of becoming an oppositional voice in the province.

When MAF struck a pact with the governor in the mid-1990s, nearly a dozen members of MAF broke away, unsatisfied with the subordination to the provincial government. Around the same time, two Catholic nuns and Benito García created a grassroots peasant committee in the rural town of Moreno and a group of women organized a peasant group in the town of Sarambí and the nearby rural community of Monte Azul. By the end of the 1990s disgruntled MAF members, the local organization in Moreno, and the group in Sarambí/Monte Azul came together to form the Peasant Movement of Formosa, MoCaFor (*Movimiento Campesino de Formosa*).

MoCaFor triggered three distinctive and interrelated processes. First, participation in the movement contributed to a subjective transformation, especially among peasant women. The grassroots work of MoCaFor created a space where peasant women could speak up. "What I most value about this period with the MAF is the work with women," Elisa told me in 2007. "Because during the presidency of Menem, it was the women who put food on the table. There was no work and women were the ones who dealt with everything." In the 1990s, while the MAF was in the process of becoming a close ally to the provincial government, Elisa asked for funds from the leaders but to no avail. "We didn't have money. Everything went through the central commission [of the MAF], who told us, 'yes,' but didn't give us funds," Elisa recalls. When they obtained funds from a Dutch foundation, she created a team with a social worker and an agronomist, and they developed a grassroots project with peasant women in rural communities. The Team of Peasant Women (*Equipo de Mujeres Campesinas*) organized workshops with a broad conception of women's rights. As Elisa put it, "We talked about their rights in all aspects. Not just as a woman producer participating in the organization, [but] also in a more integrated way; it wasn't just feminism."

In most of my conversations with Nélida, she brought up the influence that the *Equipo de Mujeres Campesinas* had in her process of becoming an activist, learning to speak up, and being vocal about the problems of peasant families and rural communities. Nélida began to participate in the *Equipo de Mujeres Campesinas* and then in MoCaFor thanks to Elisa. They met through Pedro, Nélida's husband, who was a member of MAF before he passed away in 1999. Nélida's understanding of her participation sheds light on the obstacles peasants face when trying to voice claims—a germane factor to understanding processes of activist mobilization and demobilization. She tied her process of becoming an activist to the struggle for resources and the relationship of conflict and cooperation with authorities:

> They [the *Equipo de Mujeres Campesinas*] taught us not to be afraid of anyone, to bang on the doors of officials, to demand of the government that they do what they ought to do. And to claim our rights . . . I learned many things. In the case of PROINDER [a welfare program], we were already fighting in the province because we did the projects here and we didn't get anything [in return]. They [the resources] all went to other places. Later, we went to Buenos Aires and they told us that we could get projects in our area. And we came to fight with the government people, the people in the ministry in charge of all of this. They didn't take us into account. All the people who are in the government don't like the organization. They don't like that people realize things [that] only *they* should know. When they feel like it, they give you crumbs.

In one of the many conversations we had on her farm, Nélida elaborated on the obstacles she had to overcome to articulate her claims:

> You feel yourself valued when you go to a meeting and you can argue with a minister, and show him he's lying, that what he's saying is not true. And before we didn't have that capability to confront them, to argue with a minister, for instance. But not today, thanks to the

organizations, thanks to a lot of women who taught us during the conferences [women's conferences she attended to as MoCaFor representative]. Well, I learned there. Before that, I didn't want to speak; in Buenos Aires when a journalist came, I used to tell them "don't interview me, I don't want to do it because I don't speak well—everything will go wrong, and the only thing that will happen is that I will be laughed at." And the other women from other organizations used to tell us, "It's not true that you don't know how to talk; you should talk the way you know how."

Second, MoCaFor organized a series of contentious collective actions to defend the interests of their members and obtain resources, establishing itself as a dissenting voice in provincial politics. Furthermore, MoCaFor became an instrument not only for voice but also for action. In the late 1990s and early 2000s, MoCaFor organized a series of contentious collective actions to address the lack of access to land and the difficulties their members were having trying to make a living. In 1999 MoCaFor organized roadblocks in different areas of the province, and the movement held two assemblies attended by hundreds of people, where leaders delivered speeches that were highly critical of the provincial government (Sapkus 2002). In 2001 MoCaFor organized an occupation of a neighborhood built by the provincial government in Moreno, denouncing the fact that public houses were being given to political brokers and demanding a fair allocation of the houses.

Third, in a context of dwindling opportunities for cotton growers, the organization underpinned new development strategies for peasant families. MoCaFor was instrumental in providing members with economic alternatives in a context where cotton barely allowed peasants to break even. In one of my first conversations with Nélida, in 2003, she sketched the dire situation of cotton growers.

For the last three, four years, there was no way to harvest. The harvesters charged you 150 pesos per ton, and you had to sell at 150, 180 per ton, so it didn't cover the cost. So the people started letting everything rot in the ground so the cows would eat it. And this is what really hurts the poor. Because all year long you work but then you don't get back all the money you spent . . . [it's like] you're going backwards like a crab. But those who have money can recover their losses, they can start over. But for the poor, once it's gone, it's gone.

In 2001, addressing the crisis in cotton production, Monte Azul peasant families participating in MoCaFor created a farmers market (*feria franca*) in Sarambí and began to sell vegetables, meat, and dairy products (see Figure 2.5). The initiative provided a source of income but also of pride, and became a badge of independence for Monte Azul peasants. As Nélida said in 2003 in the square where the market was held every week:

> The farmer's market started because nothing was profitable. What we planted, for example, we had to give away the pumpkin to those who were going to buy it. But then we started to make a change: we talked to the *compañeros* in the association, and [said] "we're going to organize ourselves and have a *feria*" . . . In the supermarket, they charged 50 cents a kilo [of pumpkins]. And we sold it for 5 cents [at the farms]. So if here [in Sarambí], we sell at 30 cents, it benefits us and it benefits the people . . . We did this all ourselves, we didn't ask for help from the government, nothing, just the producers [the small farmers]. We feel very proud of this because it's ours. We got together, *we* did everything we had to do to get legal status, *we* inaugurated it over there [indicating the central square], *we* were the speakers [emphasizing the "we"] . . .

FIGURE 2.5 Farmers market

> So people in the government got angry, because they wanted to do
> it, they want to be involved. They wanted to inaugurate [the farmers
> market] and say that they did it, but it wasn't like that.

The weekly farmers market helped to connect MoCaFor peasants with the local community, while also encouraging peasants to change their productive practices. Most peasants grew cotton for most of their lives, an activity that demands the use of toxic agrochemicals, as explained above. Through their participation in the farmers market, in contrast, peasant families began to grow food instead of fibers, minimizing the use of agrochemicals or using homemade, natural pesticides.

MoCaFor also provided its members access to welfare funds. Access to these resources came from the national state and helped peasant families to make ends meet, while allowing the organization to maintain a certain level of autonomy from the provincial government and thus avoid repeating the history of MAF. As the national state was deregulating the economy in the 1990s, it also instituted a series of social policies that increased resources assigned to welfare during this period (Isuani 2010). By collectively organizing as MoCaFor, many peasant families gained access to the targeted social programs created by the national state to replace universal social programs for the rural poor. The national state implemented a series of programs and projects through the Secretary of Agriculture and the INTA (National Institute of Agricultural Technology), usually framing their efforts as providing "assistance" to "vulnerable groups."[12]

In addition to rural welfare funds, MoCaFor also gained access to subsidies for the unemployed through its participation in the FTV, the Federación de Tierra y Vivienda (Land and Housing Federation), a national social movement organization. MoCaFor was one of the founding organizations of FTV in the 1990s, and its main leader was the vice president of FTV for more than a decade. From 1999 on, FTV gained access to unemployment subsidies, many of which were passed on to MoCaFor. Since 2002, FTV managed a large amount of benefits from the Unemployed Head of Households Plan (PJyJHD, Plan Jefes y Jefas de Hogar Desocupados), a national welfare plan providing 150 pesos (then 50 dollars) a month. In 2003 the plan reached almost two million beneficiaries, and it was both praised as a much-needed safety net for the poor and criticized on the grounds that "far from its supposed consecration of a right, the plan limits itself to distributing precarious welfare benefits that do not meet the basic needs of the indigent population" (CELS 2003: 3).

This expansion of welfare had a series of implications for social movement organizations. Namely, their increasing entanglement with patronage politics and clientelist arrangements, as I analyze in the following chapters. But why did Formosan peasants have to rely on welfare to make ends meet in the first place? What was the economic context of the province in the early 2000s?

GM Soybeans and Agrochemical Drifts in Monte Azul and Moreno

As I discussed in chapter 1, in the early 2000s the production of GM soybeans began its geographical expansion from the Pampas, in the center of Argentina, to the provinces of the north. By 2002, large plots of GM soybeans were encroaching upon peasant families in Monte Azul and Moreno. GM soybeans were grown next to their small farms and the local elementary school (see Figure 2.6 and Figure 2.7). Two soybean growers rented plots in the area at that time: farmers from Santa Fe (the *santafesinos*, as locals called them) and agribusinessmen from Salta (the *salteños*). Although both were cultivating GM soybeans, locals talked very differently about them. They referred to *santafesinos* with respect, describing how they lent them machinery,

FIGURE 2.6 Local school, next to soybean plots

FIGURE 2.7 Local farm, next to soybean plots

gave peasants rides to Sarambí, pulled over when crossing paths with locals riding their horses, and generally behaved as good neighbors. In contrast, peasants repeatedly remarked on how *salteños* drove SUVs at high speed on local roads, sometimes running over chickens, and showed little interest in interacting with locals. These differences are relevant because, as we will see, a feeling of disrespect played an important role in the dynamics of mobilization and demobilization.

The *salteños* arrived to Formosa as part of a joint venture, CEFA, created in April 2002. As described in chapter 1, short-term ventures to grow soybeans have become a common practice in contemporary Argentina: entrepreneurs obtain capital, rent land for two or three years, hire machinery and agrarian engineers, and then redistribute the profits after the harvest is sold. CEFA rented almost 6,000 hectares in Formosa (more than 14,800 acres), which was divided in several plots, the largest of which covered an area of 700 hectares (almost 1,730 acres). The joint venture was attracted by the low prices of land in the province and the chance to produce soybeans during the winter–spring season, due to the subtropical weather (thus increasing the yearly profits of their agricultural business). In Monte Azul, CEFA rented around 350 hectares (more than 860 acres), divided in several plots ranging from 11 to 90 hectares (27 to 222 acres), all of them located close to farms of peasant families. In advance, CEFA paid 10 pesos per hectare (around 3 dollars at the time, per 2.5 acres). Locals landowners found the deal hard to refuse: they would be paid less money than they could get from a hectare of cotton, yet without having to farm the land by themselves. Ironically, some of the families renting their plots out to soy growers later experienced the negative effects of agrochemicals.

In Monte Azul, CEFA hired an agrarian engineer, Julio Cortello, to provide on-the-ground information about the best plots to rent and to take care of striking deals with locals. Cortello had a good knowledge of the area since he worked for the provincial Ministry of Production coordinating programs for small farmers. The company employed local youth for the preparation and fumigation of agrochemicals under the direction of Cortello. These employees worked between 10 and 18 hours a day, and although they were paid not much more than the minimum wage, they told me that they received "good money" (¡nos pagaban buena plata!).

In Moreno, a rural community north of Monte Azul, farmers and agribusinessmen from the Pampas region also rented plots of land. There, Formosan landowners and politicians also began to plant soybeans. The most prominent was Anselmo Cabral, a provincial representative (diputado), local political boss, and large landowner, whose father acquired lands during the military dictatorship by evicting peasant families with precarious land titles. Another main soy grower in the area was the nephew of the then-provincial minister of production. Soy growers in Moreno used the water tank and the tractor that belonged to the municipality to carry water to their private fields. They hired a company from Buenos Aires to perform the aerial fumigations, but the municipality gave them permission to use the local airstrip to land and refill the airplane with agrochemicals.

After soybean production started in Monte Azul and Moreno, peasants noticed that their tomatoes and lettuces began to wither, their cassava grew smaller roots, and their fruit trees did not flourish as they used to. They also were experiencing headaches, soreness in their throats and faces, muscular pains, and skin rashes. Locals initially did not know the cause of these problems in their crops and bodies, but after a series of agrochemical applications, they connected these issues with nearby herbicide use.

In 2008, I sat for a conversation with Isaías under a tree on his farm, close to Moreno, where he and his family suffered the effects of agrochemical drifts firsthand. Isaías is in his fifties, and has the furrowed face of someone who has worked the land his whole life under the blazing Formosan sun. He proudly told me that he was born and raised in the area; his parents had a farm nearby and he managed to buy his own plot of land. His farm is located in between two plots of GM soybeans; each time the plots were sprayed, his house and crops were also drenched in herbicides. "This is not an area to use an airplane, they're crazy!" Isaías told me, visibly agitated. His daughter was seven years old at the time; she fainted on several occasions and had sudden episodes of nausea after the fumigations. Isaías also noticed that his cotton plants were losing their cotton balls and new sprouts were not growing, and the leaves of his manioc withered. He went to the police station in Moreno to file a complaint. Some days later, a policeman and then a public official from the provincial ministry of production visited his farm. "They came to take a look, to see if it was true. And that was it. They told me they would come back . . . but I'm still waiting for them." Isaías did not harbor many expectations about sanctions or warnings reaching soybean growers: "The agrarian engineer working for the soybean growers is the nephew of the minister . . . The minister has always supported them."

In Moreno, agribusinessmen rented several plots of land situated between small farms of peasant families: nearly 2,000 hectares (almost 5,000 acres) divided in smaller plots of 80–100 hectares each (200–250 acres). Soybean growers used a fumigation plane to spray herbicides, a technique prone to produce agrochemical drifts. As Angus Wright explains: "One of the most difficult safety and economic problems of using aerial rather than ground spray techniques is the control of what is called 'drift,' the pesticides carried outside of the target field. Under normal circumstances in developed countries, 20 to 80 percent of sprays applied land outside the targeted field and may injure nontarget crops twenty miles downwind . . . , and under specially adverse conditions, investigators have shown that 95 percent can miss the field" (Wright 2005: 20).

Omar is burly middle-aged man with calloused hands who works on a 140 hectares (346 acres) plot of land that is owned by a local political boss. We conversed outside a local grocery store while he explained the way that weeds are managed in the fields, helping me to understand why soybean production uses not only glyphosate (the active ingredient in Roundup) but also the more toxic herbicide 2,4D. While we sipped mate, Omar said that the subtropical climate in Formosa promotes the growth of weeds that are uncommon in the temperate climate of the Pampas region. In Formosa, soybean growers use 2,4D because they would have to use large quantities of glyphosate to destroy the persistent weeds: a quart of 2,4D will do the work of 20 liters of glyphosate. To fumigate the fields, workers mix 60 liters of glyphosate, 25 liters of

2,4D, plus sulphosate and other chemicals to regulate the water's pH level. He had become accustomed to finding dead foxes and armadillos after each spraying. "I tell the agronomists and the owner to plow the land instead of using so many chemicals, but they don't pay attention to me . . . The agronomists want to sell their products," he told me with a shrug.

This intensive use of agrochemicals is an open secret, as agrarian engineers publicly discuss it with the media. In 2010, a consortium of farmers and agribusiness rented 3,500 hectares (more than 8,600 acres) near Moreno to grow soybeans during winter. In a nationally circulated newspaper, the consortium's agrarian engineer said that the treatment of "diseases" in soy plants grown in Formosa was "more demanding," so they applied two extra agrochemicals: strobilurin and triazole. Strobilurin-based pesticides are regarded as "a family of relatively safe pesticides in terms of acute, chronic, and long-term effects" yet they are "toxic to fish and aquatic invertebrates."[13] Triazole, in turn, is considered by the EPA to be a carcinogen, and a suspected endocrine disruptor.[14] It is also a potential water contaminant and raises serious concerns about its negative effects on fish and other aquatic organisms.[15]

In Monte Azul, I interviewed two locals hired by CEFA (the company from Salta province described above), who also told me that glyphosate was frequently mixed with a more toxic herbicide, 2,4D. The workers' main tasks were to "prepare" the seeds with fungicides, mix concentrated agrochemicals with water, and to stand on the borders of plots waving flags to guide the tractor driver doing the fumigations. Sprayings were done using a "mosquito," an agricultural machine similar to a tractor with faucets on the sides to spread agrochemicals (see Figure 2.8). Following the orders of Cortello, the company's agrarian engineer, employees cleaned the tanks used for fumigations in public water reservoirs in the area, where they also dumpled remaining agrochemicals. "Sometimes there were leftover bags of Roundup and one day there was a lot of leftover poison ["*veneno*," the term locals use for agrochemicals]. A thousand liters. So we dumped it in the entrance where the school is, the thousand liters. . . . And I don't know what it may have done, but the water was contaminated, for sure. It was an order from Cortello: [he told us] 'go there, and dump it,'" one of the CEFA workers told me.

Fumigations were making local inhabitants uneasy. They were conducted during lunch hours, forcing residents to seclude themselves within their houses in a province where temperatures easily reach 100 degrees Farenheit during the summer. Emilia tackled the situation individually when the fumigations greatly affected one of her sons, who suffered from respiratory problems. During one of the sprayings next to her farmhouse, she went to the soybean

FIGURE 2.8 Mosquito fumigating machine
Photo by Alvaro Ybarra Zavala, Getty Images

field: "I screamed at the tractor driver, asking him to stop the fumigation," she told me. When she got back home, her daughter was in shock: "Mom! How did you do that?! Don't you see he's just working?!" On the patio of her farm, Emilia still sounded apologetic when we talked, years later: "I looked like a crazy person, but I didn't know what else to do; I was seeing my son who couldn't breathe and I just did it, without thinking about it." Soon after these incidents, in February 2003, the individual complaints transformed into collective actions, a process that I analyze in the next chapter.

Conclusion

Sociologist C. Wright Mills (1959) famously coined the idea of "the sociological imagination," defining it as the capacity to identify the connections between history, society, and biography. In this chapter I explored the history of the province of Formosa, outlining its economic and political features as they intersect with the lives of peasant families and the trajectories of rural social movements. This exploration illuminates three issues that I scrutinize in the ensuing chapters by zooming in on rural communities within a shorter time frame.

First, my incursion into Formosan history delineated the relationships between the peasant economy, rural social movements, the state, and political machines. The relationships between authorities and activists that I analyze in the next two chapters are best understood when seen in the context of their longer history of conflict and cooperation. An exploration of the local history also shows how political and economic elites are intertwined, and hints at the challenges faced by peasant organizations in a province dominated by social inequality and patronage politics. The virulent discourses of provincial elites in reaction to the 2003 mobilizations, for example, are best understood when keeping in mind their relationship with the former military dictatorship. In addition, exploring Formosa's history situates the decisions made by peasants when facing pressing dilemmas. For instance, the historical weight of patronage politics and importance of cotton production in Formosa contextualize the processes of demobilization and peasant's strategies of adaptation that I discuss in chapter 5.

Second, an exploration of the ups and downs of rural social movements situates MoCaFor within a longer line of peasant mobilization. The lives of activists show how their experiences in the 1970s were passed on to a new generation. Reconstructing the ebb and flow of peasant organizations suggests that the demobilization process examined in the chapters 4 and 5 is not an end stage, but rather a phase of popular mobilization.

Third, reviewing the connections between history, society, and biography in Formosa familiarizes the reader with the places and territories conquered by agricultural biotechnology in the 2000s. As I argued in the introduction, GM crops in Argentina expand geographically, transforming territories with distinct histories and affecting changes in places that are intertwined with people's lives and social movement's trajectories. As transgenic agriculture advances over territories, it intersects with a sedimented past of oppositions and negotiations between farmers, agribusinesses, activists, peasants, and authorities, whose visions and actions are informed by history and shape their reception of agricultural biotechnology. Let us, then, continue the journey and immerse in the places where GM crops take root.

3

CONTENTION

PEASANTS CONFRONTING GM SOYBEANS AND AGROCHEMICAL EXPOSURE (2003)

In January 2003, during the hot and dry summer in Formosa, Julio Cortello was growing anxious. As the agrarian engineer working for GM soybean growers in Monte Azul, he wanted to prepare the soil and plant new soybeans as soon as possible to obtain three harvests, instead of two, during the 2002–2003 agricultural campaign. On February 1, a windy Saturday, he ordered the company workers to fill the tank of the fumigating machine with herbicides and spray the fields. The agrochemicals drifted from their intended target—something to be expected given the weather conditions—and destroyed the plants of the peasant families neighboring the soybean plots.

The affected peasants of Monte Azul reacted by organizing the most contentious events in the recent history of Formosa. With the support of MoCaFor, peasants blocked provincial roads, denounced the contamination in provincial and national media, and sued the soybean company. In Moreno peasants marched to the local airport, seized the airplane soy growers used to fumigate fields, and occupied the airport for a week while refusing to return the aircraft. The authorities' response was victim blaming, denial, and dismissal. Provincial public officials reported to the media that people's ailments were due to a "lack of hygiene" and poor education. Representatives of agribusiness associations downplayed the effects of contamination and dismissed the protests, depicting demonstrators as troublemakers.

This chapter reconstructs these events to illuminate, in microscopic fashion, two issues of this book: the social and environmental consequences of GM crops and agrochemical exposure, and the intertwinement of material and symbolic dimensions among social movements.

GM soybean production in Formosa reveals the disjuncture between the official script of GM production and its concrete realities. GM soybeans are usually touted as more environmentally friendly than conventional crops, and this claim has a grain of truth to it when taken at face value. Farmers using herbicide-resistant GM seeds do not need to plow the soil before sowing (a technique called "no tillage"), and thus soil erosion is avoided. Instead of getting rid of weeds by tilling the soil, farmers apply an herbicide (glyphosate) shortly before and after planting the seeds, and GM soybean plants are engineered to resist this herbicide. In addition, glyphosate (the active ingredient of the commercial herbicide Roundup Ready) is considered a less harmful agrochemical than many of those traditionally used.[1]

However, as the cases presented below exemplify, the realities of agricultural production in Argentina belie these arguable environmental advantages. Unlike traditional crops that require closer monitoring to control pests or stimulate growth, GM soybeans follow a simple, preestablished, step-by-step process. In northern Argentina, agribusinesses usually rent fields for two or three consecutive seasons and grow GM soybeans without rotating crops, a practice that may make economic sense. Yet besides being detrimental to soil nutrients, these agronomic practices encourage the use of more toxic agrochemicals, severely affecting people's health and the environment. When GM soybean plants are harvested, some soybeans inevitably fall to the ground. The plants growing from those soybeans need to be eliminated before planting new GM soybean seeds, but they cannot be eliminated using Roundup (like other weeds) because they resist glyphosate. This means that other more toxic herbicides (often 2,4D) must be used to clear the field before replanting.[2] Furthermore, as mentioned in chapter 1, the lack of crop rotation usually results in the appearance of herbicide-resistant weeds, which also contributes to the use of toxic herbicides. This process leads to the "transgenic treadmill" that I discuss in the conclusion.

When we pay close attention to how GM crops are produced *on the ground*, we see that the discourses and propaganda of agribusiness are often at odds with the realities of agricultural production. What the cases of Monte Azul and Moreno show (and agricultural production in Argentina at large) is that the *potential* environmental advantages of herbicide-resistant GM crops may be countered by their *actual* environmental impacts.

It may be argued that the negative social and environmental impacts of GM soybeans have little to do with the technology itself and are rather a result of its misuse. Farmers and companies do not apply herbicides properly; authorities are not able or willing to address environmental issues—or so the argument goes. One of the main points of this book, however, is to show that transgenic crops entwine with (often highly unequal) social milieus, transforming agricultural practices and environments. In other words, as GM crops are sowed and grown in concrete places, they inevitably become part and parcel of environmental, political, and economic processes, and thus cannot be considered neutral or aseptic technological tools (Kinchy 2012, Levidow 1998).

The protests analyzed in this chapter also open a window to observe issues of subordination and inequality that shape the social context in which GM crops are grown, at least in rural areas of northern Argentina. This, in turn, allows us to capture the intersections of emotions and interests, of identification processes and material claims, and of people's agency and their political and economic constraints. MoCaFor peasants mobilized against the damage to their farms caused by agrochemical drifts, but their grievances were also imbued with demands for recognition of their worthiness as peasants and small farmers (*pequeños productores*). Furthermore, these protests reveal ways in which inequality and subordination engage definitional struggles about the meanings of transgenic crops and agrochemicals, contentious collective action, and identities. To put it bluntly, protests against GM crops and agrochemical exposure are as much about material grievances and interests as they are about demands for recognition and processes of identification. The analysis below thus bridges structural and cultural perspectives on social movements while paying attention to different understandings of transgenics, contention, and identity *within movements*. In doing so, I also seek to sensitize food regime scholars who, overly influenced by a classic Marxist account of consciousness and collective action, may underestimate the importance of emotions and miss peasants' ambiguous stances toward contentious actions and identities.

I tackle these issues of contention and meaning following a narrative line inspired by my ethnographic research. I zoom in on the events pitting peasant families and social movements against soybean growers and authorities, and how they engaged in a battle that was not only about agrochemical exposure but also about the status of peasants in the public sphere. Then I take a step back and scrutinize the backstage of these protests, paying special attention to the different discourses of spokespersons and the rank-and-file within the movement, and bringing in the voices of "half-hearted" social movement participants and others in the community (Eliasoph 1998, Wolford 2007). I observe the variety of identifications and interpretations within the movement, analyzing women's views of their participation as an issue of motherhood, the ambivalence toward disruptive forms of protest, and the ambiguities and tensions of identifying demonstrators as troublemakers. In doing so, I pry open a social movement organization to interrogate the ontological status that we often assign to them. As Wendy Wolford (2009: 412) explains: "We typically assign a higher degree of coherence to social movements than is appropriate. Movements—or 'the movement'—are regularly invoked as coherent actors (the movement says this or the movement does that) when in fact decisions are made (and unmade or contested or negotiated) by a complicated web of activists on the ground" (see also Edelman 1999, Rubin 1998, Burdick 1995). Building on a dialogic approach to social movements (Holland, Fox, and Daro 2008, Steinberg 1999b), I scrutinize discourse to illuminate the situated and negotiated meanings of social movements and contention, an analysis complemented by the next two chapters on discourses and processes of *de*mobilization.

Peasants Against Poisons

In February 2003, CEFA's managers were eager to sow new soybeans in Monte Azul. To get rid of weeds the agrarian engineers considered plowing the land, but when rains prevented this, they decided to apply 2,4D to ensure three harvests for the 2002–2003 season. On February 1, CEFA employees received orders to fumigate from early evening until nightfall, in spite of the intensely hot weather and strong winds. The high temperatures made the agrochemicals vaporize quickly, and the wind carried them toward neighboring plots.

The next day, locals woke up to an environmental disaster on their small farms. They found their cotton and food staples (cassava, beans, pumpkin, lettuce, tomato, etc.) totally withered. Instead of the gradual withering seen on previous occasions, herbicides had had a powerful negative effect overnight. Plants looked "as if someone had put a flame next to them" or "as if someone had doused them with chlorine," locals told me. The cotton bolls peasants were expecting to harvest a month later, and from which they receive their main income, had fallen to the ground; the staples they rely on to feed their families and to sell in the farmers market were destroyed, their leaves completely withered.

Nélida's farm is located between Horacio's and Luisa's, two of her siblings, and she and Horacio represent MoCaFor in the area. As soon as Nélida saw the destruction of her plants, she went to Horacio's and Luisa's farms, where she encountered a similar poignant landscape. Joined by Luisa's husband, Facundo, Nélida and Horacio went to Monte Azul's police station to file a report. The policemen, however, refused to file the report or to go to their farms and see the damage; they dismissed them, telling them to file a report at the police station in Sarambí, a town 14 miles away. At Sarambí's police station, Horacio filed a formal statement in spite of the policeman's hostility. A policeman told them, "You won't get anywhere; there have been many reports but nothing has ever come of them." "You take our report and we'll see how far we can go," Nélida replied, undeterred.

Back in Monte Azul, Nélida and Horacio visited the farms of neighbors also affected by the agrochemicals and called a meeting to discuss what they should do. The next day, more than two dozen peasants met at Nélida's farm and agreed to hire a notary and bring an agrarian engineer to document the damages to their crops. Soon, they realized these were not easy tasks to accomplish. Nélida and Horacio contacted an agrarian engineer who confirmed that the plants appeared to be affected by the herbicides used in soy production, but he refused to write a report, let alone sign it, out of fear of losing his job.

Nélida and Horacio then got in touch with Mario Hispano, an agrarian engineer working for PSA, the Social Agricultural Program (Programa Social Agropecuario), a national welfare program for poor rural families. Hispano agreed to collaborate with the peasant families but only as a private consultant because he was wary of potential retaliation; in fact, he later learned that the provincial minister complained to the national coordinator of PSA about his report. Hispano and a notary visited Monte Azul on February 6, and his observations confirmed the peasants' suspicions: the deformed leaves showed the typical effects of 2,4D (curled and withered leaves, and unusual growth caused by hormonal changes). Hispano recommended that the peasants cease consumption of the crops affected, stop selling them in the farmers market, and destroy all the plants. Questioned by the peasants about their vomiting, headaches, skin rashes, and throat and face soreness, he answered that those symptoms were typical of people affected by herbicides. Hispano also told them that the rain probably transported remnants of pesticides to the reservoirs where they obtained water on a daily basis. A professor of ecology from the University of Formosa also visited Monte Azul and wrote a report confirming the environmental wreckage caused by agrochemicals and the conclusions advanced by Hispano.

Peasant leaders were bolstered by the two reports confirming the effects of herbicides on their plots. "The State has to assume its responsibilities to the affected people and recognize their rights," reads the petition presented to the Municipal Council of Sarambí. The petition demanded the council's intervention to stop fumigations as well as to report on the environmental damage. The request also included demands for healthcare, the provision of seeds for the following agricultural campaign, subsidies, and food for the affected families.

The note framed the demands as rights to be guaranteed by the state but also deployed terms frequently used in patronage politics: "It is requested . . . help with merchandise" (*Se solicita . . . ayuda con mercaderias*), for instance, reflects the use of the trope "help" discussed in the previous chapter. Some days later, Horacio (on behalf of the farmers market association) sent a certified letter to the provincial Ministry of Production demanding that they "stop fumigations immediately and [conduct] a study of environmental impact." Using far more contentious terms than the note to the municipal council, Horacio addressed the Minister saying: "I DEMAND that [soybean growers] be held responsible for the damages, without foregoing the penal responsibilities that may correspond" (emphasis in original).

The meetings among affected families and the environmental impact studies show the relational and dialogic work involved in transforming an "objective" situation into a collective problem.[3] The meetings among the affected peasants created the sense that the agrochemical exposure was not an individual problem but a collective issue. Furthermore, Hispano's recommendation to destroy the crops revealed that peasant families could not eat their produce or sell it in the farmers market, and the studies confirmed that the withering of their crops was attributable to the agrochemicals used by soybean growers. Similarly to the peasants studied by James Scott (1976), who questioned economic exploitation only when it affected resources needed for subsistence, Formosan small farmers were not troubled by GM crop production until it threatened their daily survival. In other words, this situation reveals that deprivation and environmental damage are defined as such through interaction and meaning-making processes; material grievances combine with emotions to generate collective action (Goodwin, Jasper, and Polletta 2001, Aminzade and McAdam 2002, Gould 2009, Emirbayer and Goldberg 2005, Jasper 2011).

Rage Against the Machine: Peasant Women Confront Soybean Growers

In the midst of these events, a group of Monte Azul women met at the local school to complete paperwork for a welfare program provided by the national government and brokered by local MoCaFor leaders. A discussion about the damage to their farms quickly consumed the meeting. Nélida, whose son was working for CEFA, provides a glimpse of how people, especially women, felt about what was happening:

> I was enraged when we learned that [the agrochemicals] were very poi-
> sonous, very dangerous, and that these people [the managers] didn't
> even tell the kids "use gloves and be careful." Only after everything
> happened, when the animals and plants had died and the kids got
> sick, did we talk to other people who told us [agrochemicals] were
> very poisonous . . . They had not even told the kids "wash your hands"
> [after working]. And they drank water from the same place where
> they cleaned the tanks. The kids didn't know about the danger either.
> And all that got me *so* enraged, when people told me that you may not
> notice it now but in the long term . . . that they may not be able to
> have kids, or their sons could be deformed . . . I was so pissed off . . .
> I couldn't talk to anybody, let alone them [the managers]. Because the
> plants and the soil may get sick and you can recover from that, but
> recover a son . . . you don't know. If I had known, I never would have
> let my son do that for a miserable ten pesos [for a day of work]. But
> I used to teach him to work, no matter for how much. Ten, five pesos;
> anything but stealing or getting into drugs. And for those ten pesos,
> he might be sick for the rest of his life.

Nélida's testimony encapsulates the views of many in the community, intertwining the pressures of material survival and the simmering emotions
of many women in the community who were enraged by the situation and
compelled to define it in terms of their identity as mothers.

While in the meeting, the women got word that the "mosquito" (the machine used to fumigate) was working in one of the soybean plots. They went
to the entrance of the soy plot to be fumigated next, determined to not allow
the mosquito in. Armed with rolling pins and pieces of wood, more than
a dozen women gathered at the entrance to the soybean plot. Juana, one of
Nélida's sisters, told me that in the meeting they decided that

> We had to do something. Because if [one round of herbicides] killed
> everything around, what was in store for us next? To be killed our-
> selves? . . . So, little by little, we gathered courage, and we did some-
> thing to defend what is ours. And then we, the mothers, made the

decision [to block the entrance of the soy plot]; several of us, Nélida and other *compañeras* . . . So we, the women, because we were mainly women there, we said, "send word to the husbands, the kids, the neighbors, tell them to come."

The *empresarios* (businessmen, as locals call CEFA's managers) arrived with the mosquito, but found the group of women obstructing the entrance to the plot. In a menacing tone, the *empresarios* told the women to let them in or else face the consequences of criminal charges. The women, however, were not discouraged and replied that they would not move. With the argument escalating, entrepreneurs threatened to run into the women with the tractor. "I would rather die here and now than be killed little by little," Nélida replied. "They didn't run into her, which gave us courage," Juana recalls. The *empresarios* left the field and went to Monte Azul's police station. In less than half an hour, they arrived at another of their soybean plots, accompanied by two police officers. There they found an even larger group obstructing the entrance, as men had joined the women. The peasants were adamant in their resolve to not let in the mosquito. Outnumbered by the peasants, the entrepreneurs took the mosquito with them and left the area (see Figure 3.1 for a timeline of peasants' action and elite's reactions).

By late February, MoCaFor leaders issued press releases declaring the movement "in a state of alert and mobilization." Determined to obtain legal protection, their lawyer filed an injunction in court, based on two provincial laws protecting environmental rights. News of the conflict reached radio stations and local TV networks, granting the issue high public visibility. In the midst of this heightened publicity, Marcelino Trillo, a legislator and leader of the main oppositional party, the UCR, visited Monte Azul accompanied by councilmen of Sarambí. He made public statements supporting the pleas of the peasant families and some days after, he presented a bill to enforce the provincial environmental laws. Juana's interpretation of these actions hint at how peasants were yearning for recognition of their pleas: "Some people, I think lawyers, came and . . . they gave us some advice, but without taking the initiative . . . like saying: do what you can do and defend yourselves that way. At least, they told us 'Do that'; it was better than nothing."

Following the political and media attention, peasants held meetings and decided to block the main paved road at the entrance of Monte Azul. They spent three intense days obstructing the road, showing passersby the cassavas and sweet potatoes visibly affected by agrochemicals. When recalling the roadblock during our interviews, peasants usually brought up the disparate

February 1, 2003
Soybean growers spray herbicides, which drift to peasants' farms

February 2, 2003
Peasants file a police report in Curuzú

February 6, 2003
An agrarian engineer visits Monte Azul to assess the damages in peasants' crops

Mid-February
Women block the entrance to a soybean plot

March 2-4, 2003
Roadblock in Monte Azul organized by MoCaFor

Mid-March, 2003
Public officials from the Ministry of Human Development visit Monte Azul

March 18, 2003
Summit in the Government House to discuss the use of agrochemicals in the province

March 26, 2003
Roadblock in Monte Azul organized by MoCaFor
Judge orders the cessation of fumigations

End of March – early April, 2003
Public officials attempt to make a deal with peasants

Early August, 2003
Soybean growers spray herbicides in spite of the judge's order

August 12, 2003
The judge extends the order prohibiting fumigations

November 11, 2003
Audience in the Court of Appeals between peasants and the lawyer of soybean growers

FIGURE 3.1 Timeline of peasants' collective actions and elites' reactions

responses elicited by the protest: whereas drivers from other provinces showed support, those from Formosa mostly reacted with insults, saying the peasants were lazy people who did not want to work—an issue I will return to below when I analyze the ambiguities of protesters seen as troublemakers.

"They Called Us Dirty": Health Problems and Disrespect

After this direct action, the provincial government acquiesced to peasants' demands for healthcare and an assessment of the environmental problems in Monte Azul. A "whole army" (*un ejército,* as peasants repeatedly told me) of public officials and medical doctors arrived in the community, unexpectedly. They settled into the small healthcare center and summoned locals, from whom they obtained blood samples to be tested for the presence of agrochemicals. Likewise, they took water samples from reservoirs and collected cassavas, sweet potatoes, and grapefruit to test.

Some days later, public officials released the results: there were no organochloride or organophosphate agrochemicals in either the blood samples or the water. The studies revealed, however, that the water was contaminated with pernicious bacteria, and was thus not potable, but officials gave no indication of whether they were going to take action to address this problem. The results raised skepticism among locals for several reasons. First, the samples were tested for agrochemicals *different* from the ones Hispano's report identified as responsible for the environmental damage. Second, as Hispano explained to peasants in a follow-up meeting, several agrochemicals are rarely detected when analyses are performed more than 15 days after the exposure. And third, an intense rain after the initial contamination could have washed away the presence of herbicides in the plants.

What troubled the peasants most—more than the subtleties of chemical analysis—were the diagnosis and proposed cure offered by the public officials from the Ministry of Human Development and publicized on provincial radio. Officials suggested that skin rashes and eye and throat soreness should be cured by washing with water and lye soap, arguing that these symptoms were due to contact with dirt and the use of winter clothes in the summer. They also distributed antiparasitic drugs to everybody in the healthcare center, saying the pills would solve their problems of diarrhea and other ailments. Horacio provides insight to how peasants sought the support of the government but were soon disappointed:

HORACIO: We trusted in the Ministry of Production and the Ministry of Human Development, they let us down . . . the Ministry of Human Development was a disaster.

PABLO: Why?

HORACIO: For all the things they did here. Because not only did they not do anything positive, but we felt insulted by these people . . . As soon as they came here, without even getting close to the people, from two meters [away], they saw pimples and attributed them to the hygiene of the people, without analysis, without review, without examining or touching the patients.

In every interview I conducted in Monte Azul, the answer given to locals regarding their health problems came to the surface. "Our skin problems were a matter of lack of hygiene," said in an ironic tone, or "officials said it was the dirt and the clothes we used; as if we weren't born and raised here and in permanent contact with dirt, or as if we didn't know how to dress ourselves." An interview with Juana and her husband Don Cura, on their Monte Azul farm, captures people's feelings about the incident:

DON CURA: And those people from the Ministry of Human Development . . . they called us dirty.

JUANA: Ah, that too, those from Human Development who should have come to see what was really going on with the people, they called us dirty . . . I remember we started itching, we had pimples, and they say it was because of dirtiness. They say it's because we didn't know how to dress . . . They treated us badly. And that gets you down—besides all the loss, that someone is telling you that you don't know how to dress yourself, that you don't know how to take a bath . . . It's like they were crushing us, worse than we had been before.

PABLO: And what did you feel when you were told that—

JUANA [CUTTING ME SHORT, ANGRY]: To me, I wanted to hit them in the mouth. Because I think that an educated person, supposedly more intelligent than us, should know how to respect people, no matter how dirty we may be . . . And they thought "We'll tell them anything, so they just go away." That was the feeling I had. That they were telling us, "Go away, stay at home and if you have to die, die." I think that's mistreatment . . . things that made us feel worse than we were. We were feeling bad, but they made us feel worse.

Emilia expressed similar thoughts, but focused on the ways in which the distribution of medicine reinforced feelings of subordination and disrespect:

We were in a meeting and we asked each other: "what did they give to you?" And then we realized that everyone had the same pills . . . even though one was there for diarrhea, another for headaches, another for nose bleeds . . . And we got all the same thing! Some symptoms were repeated, but how is it possible that all of us received the same pills? . . . They were making fun of us . . . We all took the anti-parasitic pills, for everything . . . for vomits, for hemorrhaging . . . [Long pause, she remains pensive]. And I think that people were making fun of us; they treated us as if we didn't have any culture, since we're peasants, and most of us are illiterate.

When rumors about another visit from the Ministry of Human Development reached Monte Azul, Horacio prepared a basin with water and lye soap with the idea of asking public officials to show them how to take a proper bath. However, the officials did not show up and so the peasants could not enact their sarcastic performance.

The events pitting peasants and authorities against each other were about the recognition of the health and environmental effects of agrochemicals, but also about the status of peasants. Nancy Fraser defines misrecognition and status subordination as those situations where "institutionalized patterns of cultural value constitute some actor as inferior, excluded, wholly other, or simply invisible, hence as less than full partners in social interaction" (2003: 27). Claims for recognition seek to overcome subordination and "establish the subordinated party as a full partner in social life, able to interact with others as peers" (Fraser 2003: 28; see also Schlosberg 2007). These claims rarely emerge spontaneously: by definition, a subordinate group encounters obstacles in its attempts to articulate its quest for recognition. The conflict involving peasants, authorities, and agribusinessmen entwined demands for recognition with struggles for economic redistribution; it was about agrochemical exposure but also about the disrespect of peasants.[4] The roadblock triggered a "battle of meanings" illustrating that peasants were not only putting forward material claims but also, in the words of Javier Auyero (2003), expressing a "quest for recognition."

Roadblocks and Lack of Recognition

In late March, three weeks after the first road blockade, peasants organized another road blockade shortly after a judge determined that fumigations ought to be suspended for six months and a study of environmental impact carried out.[5] The order brought relief to locals, but they still could not sell their produce in the farmers market (because it was contaminated), and the cotton they were planning to sell was either destroyed or severely damaged.

A new blockade pitted Monte Azul's *campesinos* and *empresarios* of CEFA against each other, exposing the institutional power wielded by the latter. Peasants of MoCaFor obstructed the entrance to Monte Azul and therefore to the soybean plots, at a moment when entrepreneurs needed to apply more herbicides. The businessmen met a judge in Formosa, the province's capital, who issued an order tailored to meet the needs of the soy growers: it commanded the police "to guarantee free circulation . . . especially the entrance and exit of agricultural machinery, and to evacuate any person obstructing the normal transit." With the written order in hand, the businessmen showed up on the road with more than 60 policemen. The massive presence of police-men enraged rather than deterred the peasants: "When we asked the police to come and see the contamination, they wouldn't, but when they [the soy growers] needed them, of course they showed up," said one peasant woman. Horacio showed the police officers the judiciary decision ordering a suspen-sion of fumigations, arguing that the judge issuing that order (and not the judge from Formosa) had jurisdiction over the area. Without being able to refute this argument and to avoid a situation of open violence ("there were women and kids; it was going to be a disaster," a representative of the busi-nessmen told me), soybean growers withdrew from the scene.

After the road blockade, representatives of CEFA and the provincial gov-ernment arrived in Monte Azul; their intentions and attitudes reinforced their lack of recognition of peasants. The company's representatives first tried to make individual deals and offered compensation for the destroyed cotton at a rate far below the market price. Yet they refused to pay for the losses of produce the peasant families sold in the farmers market. The offer denied recognition of peasants' strategies for survival and their alternative channels of commercialization (i.e., the farmers market) by only recognizing the value of products sold on large-scale, commodity markets. Furthermore, the sense of disrespect was underscored by the way in which the offers were made. Augusto, one of the affected peasants, summarizes how *empresarios* dismissed his concerns telling him: "Okay, I'll give you 100 pesos for each hectare and that's it; shut up; that is that; sign here" (*Bueno, te doy 100 pesos por hectárea y arreglate, callate la boca, termina todo ahí, firmame acá*).

Representatives of CEFA then tried a different strategy to overcome peas-ants' resistance. They attempted to make deals with the most active members of the protests (Horacio, Nélida, and Facundo), but the peasants remained firm, saying the company had to compensate *all* of the affected families, not only the leaders. The minister of production, acting on behalf of soy grow-ers, made one last attempt. He convened a meeting in Monte Azul, request-ing the presence of all of the affected families under the condition that no journalists be invited. The meeting was tense, and, according to the peasants' lawyer, the minister was very defensive; "Rather than acting like a public servant in charge of taking care of inhabitants' security regarding the use of agrochemicals, he [the minister] acted like the manager of the company," the lawyer wrote.

The minister recognized that the company should compensate the fami-lies for their losses, but he also expressed that the claims were "exaggerated."

His attitude triggered a furious reaction from Nélida who, agitated, raised her voice and gesticulated nervously when recalling the scene during our conversation (I use italics to highlight Nélida's emphasis on certain words):

They said it was a lie what we were saying, that everything was burned, that it wasn't like that! So in that meeting, the Minister was there and I told Cortello [the agrarian engineer working for soy growers], "Why don't you say the truth?" [I told them] that if they said the truth maybe we could come to an agreement, but because they were such *liars* we wouldn't make any deal. We are not the liars, you are! And I said to Cortello, "you know perfectly well what I'm saying and what you're doing." And they obviously wanted to play a trick on us, and to mistreat us; because we are farmers [*agricultores*], they think we are *so dumb*, that we'll accept anything they say. "Because the Minister used to work with you, and you know exactly what poisons you used to mix. How can you dare say we are liars?" I told them . . . "You didn't tell my son to use gloves when getting inside the tank to clean it up. Are you not a father? Why don't you tell the truth? Did you mix [the agrochemicals] or not?" "Yes," he told me, in front of everybody. "And *why* are you telling everyone we're lying? We're not lying. It *was* mixed; you put in the 2,4D." Because it was their orders . . . First he stayed quiet, but then he accepted it. What could he say? He cannot tell me something like that. My son was working with them that night and another kid. And that day he accepted it, but in front of a judge he will never do it. He will always lie . . . they were always saying that nobody would be affected, that [the problems caused by agrochemicals] weren't true, that they [the soybean growers] work everywhere and nothing happens . . . They kept saying things like that. How come nothing happens?! All our chickens, our ducks got killed; the horses got sick, the plants all withered.

Nélida's emotional narration of this meeting reveals how the conflict was *as much* a matter of recognition as an economic issue. Peasants were furious over being treated as liars and being blamed for the ailments from which they were suffering. Their reactions illustrate that the conflict went beyond the narrow demands for fumigation cessation and compensation for lost crops. Granted, peasants wanted to recover their sources of food and income, but at the same time they strived to reverse the mistreatment they felt and what they sensed as disrespect by public officials, moved by the anger created by the public denial of the contamination and the attempts to cast blame on affected families. In doing so, they also were redefining their relationship with powerful authorities and expressing their right to speak up.

Building Up the Rage: Contention in Moreno

A group of MoCaFor members from Moreno participated in the Monte Azul roadblocks. When the conflict subsided, they returned to their town. The experience of seeing the deleterious consequences of agrochemical exposure firsthand and the controversies aired in the media had a crucial role in agglutinating the grievances of peasant families in Moreno. As Benito García, a leader of MoCaFor, expressed it in the judiciary report:

> [We] noticed that in other towns of the province these kinds of fumigation have damaged agricultural production in various ways, affecting the inhabitants' health and the environment; this is the reason why concern prevails and it is feared that that same damage could be caused in our jurisdiction since people in charge of the fumigations are using the same agrochemicals that have already brought harm elsewhere.

Nelson is a skinny yet strong-looking man, with pronounced crow's feet framing his vivacious eyes, and he speaks with a thick country accent, often interjecting Guaraní words. He reveals the connection between the support for the conflict in Monte Azul and the lead-up to the conflict in Moreno:

> I remember everything, we endured cold, heat, hunger, exhaustion . . . We had the opportunity to go [to Monte Azul] to fight alongside them to strive, to block roads, to make demands. And between protests, we came back on a Thursday; we got here very tired and realized that an airplane was also fumigating nearby.

Kiko Martínez is a stocky man always wearing a cap, a sort of mandatory accessory for the people working in the sunny fields of Formosa. People regard him as a hard-working man, knowledgeable about agricultural production and committed to the care of his farm. While talking with him in the warehouse that doubles as the MoCaFor offices in Moreno, I asked him about the seizure of the fumigating plane in February 2003. Kiko suggests that the effects of contamination witnessed in other areas demonstrated a threat to peasants' survival.

PABLO: How was the plane seized? How was the day to day . . . ? How did the idea of doing something first come to mind?

KIKO: It was due to the need to stop the harm that all this was bringing about, the kind of fumigation that was carried out. We realized we needed to bring this to a halt at all costs. We had seen in other areas of the province that there were bad consequences to the fumigation. So in our area, we decided to seize the plane to defend the people and the production, that is, the families' subsistence. Because if we didn't act and let everything go on as it was happening, people may have not been able to survive. In general, poor people live on what they produce on their farms. Those fumigations would make waste of everything. People wouldn't be able to subsist.

These anxieties motivated peasant leaders to organize meetings and make contact with local authorities. MoCaFor members initially presented a request to Violeta Paloza, the mayor of Moreno, a former councilwoman who took office as mayor when her husband resigned from the position. MoCaFor members presented a formal note to the Municipality, demanding a stop to the fumigations. Nelson described the attitude of Paloza in the following terms: "She told us she didn't know what soybean growers were doing . . . So she was erasing with one hand what she was writing with the other" (quería borrar con el codo lo que hacía con la mano). Dismissed by the mayor, peasants decided to file a complaint with the police, yet to no avail. As Kiko explained to me:

We went there and they told us, "You have to decide what to do. We cannot do anything. We have sent the message to the people at the top, but nothing happened. You will have to make your own decisions." And we've always sought to avoid conflict or doing anything wrong. We've only tried to solve the problem.

The mayor knew the peasants were uneasy and that direct action could take place (the contentious events in Monte Azul were, by then, common knowledge). To avoid losing face with provincial authorities if a contentious event erupted, the mayor left town, leaving the president of the city council, Nancy Valente, in charge. Valente did not belong to the Peronist party and was receptive to the peasants' claims. She received the complaints of

MoCaFor members and decided to issue a municipal note using respectful and measured language, ordering a suspension of fumigations until further notice.[6] Soy growers, however, continued with the aerial fumigations.

I interviewed Valente in 2008, in the bodega she opened in Moreno after she retired from politics. It is worthwhile to quote her at length, since her description of the situation highlights the sense of disrespect and misrecognition that prompted peasants to turn to transgressive contention:

> They [soybean growers] didn't respect the note, or the police or anything. Because for sure they thought, "she's not from the [Peronist] Party, we are fine with the government," and they went on doing their thing. That enraged the peasants. They told me, "*Señora*, they keep fumigating, we already listened to the radio, and we saw the note you signed." Because I had given them a copy of what I had submitted to the police, asking for the fumigation to be suspended until the misunderstanding was clarified, if it was a misunderstanding at all, so that at least they explained what they were using, what poison they were spreading. Then the soy growers said "no" and kept doing it, they said they couldn't stop ... The peasants took the plane because fumigations never stopped, not caring if somebody else was concerned or if the authorities allowed them ... Besides, they [the soy growers] went to the local radio station and they were aggressive, treated us as ignorant. We were told to modernize, to leave the Old Age in which we were stuck, that things were currently done this way.

Isaías, whose farm and family were repeatedly sprayed with agrochemicals, connected the sense of disrespect and being dismissed with the feelings of anger motivating peasants' actions:

ISAÍAS: The police and the mayor were notified, everyone was, so that they [the soy growers] wouldn't go on [with the fumigations], but the soy growers replied that they couldn't do anything. Then, since they didn't respect us, we took action.

PABLO: How did you participate in the seizing of the plane?

ISAÍAS: We held a meeting to figure out how to stop the plane. They had told us they couldn't stop it, since they had received orders from the Ministry. The engineer said he had come to work and that nobody would stop him. And this made the people angry.

PABLO: What was the meeting like?

ISAÍAS: Well . . . we didn't want the plane to work in the area, because it was causing damage. They wouldn't, so to speak, respect us willingly. We talked nicely: to the police, to the mayor, and they kept fumigating, kept doing what they wanted. So we decided to seize the plane.

A police note also expressed the soy growers' disregard of the order putting a halt to fumigations and the anger felt by peasants: "The representatives of the company were notified of the request for suspension. However, the fumigation went on, enraged by this, the people decided to occupy the place in question, demanding the presence of the Minister of Production and a qualified person in the matter."

These excerpts express what peasants were thinking and feeling at the time: dismissed by authorities, disrespected by soy growers fumigating indiscriminately, and only recognized as a vestige from the past doomed to disappear, they decided to act collectively and address the problem on their own.

After a meeting where a representative of the soybean growers told peasants that fumigations would not stop, peasants attempted to organize a new meeting with soy growers. When the latter did not show up, and another representative of soy growers appeared on the local radio denying that herbicides were harmful and acting "with arrogance" (as several interviewees put it), peasants decided to march to the local airstrip and stop the fumigating airplane.

On the evening of February 28, MoCaFor members and peasant families affected by agrochemicals walked from Moreno to the airstrip used by the fumigating airplane located on the outskirts of the town. There, they found one of the employees of the soybean growers seated in a pick-up truck. An activist from MoCaFor got into the truck and told the employee to stay calm, while other activists secured the entrance to the airstrip with a chain and a lock. Shortly after, the airplane landed on the airstrip and the crowd descended on it. They removed the pilot from the cockpit, escorted him to the truck, and locked both employees inside, while others slashed the airplane's tires. Peasants created a bonfire and improvised tents preparing to spend the night there. At nightfall, a group of policemen showed up on the scene. The protestors received them with a firm and adamant attitude, saying that if the police attempted to break into the place to evict them, they would set the airplane on fire. Some hours later, demonstrators got in touch with their lawyer, who recommended letting the employees go. They followed this advice, but remained camped at the site, demanding the presence of provincial authorities and representatives from the soybean growers.

That same night, councilwoman (and interim mayor) Valente paid a visit to the airport escorted by the police and her aids to negotiate a peaceful resolution to the conflict, framing her intervention in terms of reciprocity: "I went to talk to the people . . . to ask them to stop the airplane but not to do anything else. To ask them, personally, because I took the risk of stopping the fumigations." Members of MoCaFor and supporters remained in the airport for a week, waiting for a confirmation that fumigations would cease if they returned the airplane. They organized a soup kitchen with food donated by supporters, and entire families, including women and children, stopped by to get plates of food. Valente contributed by organizing a breakfast with *mate cocido* (a kind of tea made of *yerba mate*). Indicative of the importance of food provision during poor people's demonstrations, Valente explained to me that she provided food

> so they could eat breakfast and be more calm, so that dialogue could be restored (*para que se amansen, para que se dialogue*) . . . I could not add more fuel to the fire. And because of that, they said I supported the peasants. No one can dialogue with an emboldened group or person if you confront them. So they calmed down, understood, people talked, and the fumigation was over.

When visited by councilwoman Valente, demonstrators clearly stated their commitment saying: "We won't give up, even if we get killed, because what's the point? We will have to suffer throughout the whole year [because of the lost crops]. We will die on our feet."

Upon the return of the mayor, representatives of the provincial government and the soy growers approached the airport to negotiate with the peasants. Under the agreement reached the peasants would vacate the area and return the airplane, while soy growers signed a document reassuring demonstrators that they would suspend the aerial fumigations. The owner of the airplane verified the state of the machine, under the attentive vigilance of MoCaFor members who pushed the airplane outside the airport and left it there. After these events, peasant leaders and activists were accused of kidnapping and destruction of private property, but were ultimately acquitted.

Authorities' Reaction: Denial and Disrespect

The escalation of the conflict also prompted a firmer resistance to peasants' claims. As the protests brought the agrochemical drift under public scrutiny, it also set the stage for the emergence of counterdefinitions among powerful actors. The views put forward by the provincial authorities can be summarized in three points: denial of contamination, dismissal of demands, and vilification of protesters.

The denial of the contamination by the Ministry of Human Development (when arguing that ailments were due to the peasants' hygiene) was taken a step further by important provincial figures. On March 1, a month after the drifts, a press conference was convened by the minister of production along with other members of his staff and the president of the provincial association of agrarian engineers. The main province's newspaper quoted the minister in its headlines, asserting there were "interests beyond agricultural production" in the events of Monte Azul and that

> the accident [the agrochemical drift] with the treatment of products in a specific crop . . . was used to misinform and create concern in the community, since [the agrochemicals] are products that passed strict controls and do not affect human health, neither animals nor the soil, as some want us to believe . . . There are people interested in creating discord and a confrontation that does not benefit society nor the agrarian sector, but instead terribly damages the province's image.[7]

Similarly, the company CEFA issued a public statement accusing "unscrupulous politicians" for the "alleged effects on human health, animals or soil deterioration" and admonished those making such evaluations:

> [They should] refuse to make such accusations, because we retain the right to sue for the felony of libel and slander and for civil damages caused.[8]

Reinforcing these points of view, the representative of one of the landowner associations qualified the actions of the peasants as "dangerous," stating that "as lay citizens we cannot act outside the law, as if trying to take justice into our own hands,"[9] because the protests "put us in a very hard situation, as producers and as a province."[10] Along similar lines, the president of the Rural Society of Formosa, a powerful and traditional organization of landowners, declared that "some people, journalists, and even a legislator" were "adding an element of disintegration," stating that

> to see this accident as a conflict between small farmers and landowners, to make imputations as to growers contaminating, without any

proof and showing the utmost ignorance on the matter, are distortions of the facts, that do not seek to solve any problem but rather to bring chaos and confusion.[11]

Taken together these statements deployed a vilification, that is, "a rhetorical strategy that discredits adversaries by characterizing them as ungenuine and malevolent advocates," casting opponents under an exclusively negative light and magnifying an opponent's power (Vanderford 1989: 166–167). In so doing, landowners and political figures were not creating a completely new depiction: the equation "dissent = social disintegration" was a common trope in the discourse of Argentina's military dictatorship of 1976–1983. Unsurprisingly, provincial elites were among the stronger supporters of military rule in Formosa (see chapter 2).

Peasants disputed this vilifying frame although without the publicity achieved by elite members. During one of our conversations, Emilia, one of the affected peasants, interpreted the situation in very different terms and concisely expressed the combination of disrespect, disparage, and dismissal peasants felt during the controversy:

> They say we were being treated [medically] by them, that we were *well* treated by them, that we received medicines, that we got all we needed . . . They said that in the media, and they said that we were against the government, that that was the reason why we were complaining . . . And I really don't know, Pablo . . . A movement, an organization, always makes its claims about rights to the government, isn't that so? That's why we get organized. Well, then they see us as belonging to the opposition. And it's not true! They said we were demanding ridiculous things; that we were just making things up. Maybe they took it that way . . . it wasn't like that. It was the moment to make claims through the movement, through the organization . . . But they sure treated us as dirty, as scum, like nothing.

What this dispute shows is that a definition of a given situation goes well beyond a simple depiction; actors do relational work when they understand the same events in contrasting ways. As Marc Steinberg rightly observes, "discourse never neutrally conveys meanings . . . as an ideological process, discourse therefore is a terrain of conflict, and not simply the medium or messenger" (Steinberg 1998: 853). Hegemony is achieved when monologic discourse becomes authoritative and suppresses alternative understandings

(Steinberg 1998: 855). The war of words between peasants and authorities was not only about what happened, but also about their relationship and the right to speak up and make claims.

By defining the contamination as a mere accident, elite members were attempting to discourage further debate on the matter and attribute the events to fate rather than human action. As Jill Harrison argues: "As long as the problem of pesticide drift is conceived as a series of accidents, the everyday exposures to pesticides remain invisible and naturalized" (Harrison 2004: 296; see also Harrison 2011, Wright 2005). The contamination resulting from the careless management of agrochemicals was a *foreseeable* consequence rather than a fortuitous event. But by using a convention along the lines of "it was just bad luck," elite members not only offered an explanation of the events but also defined their relation vis-à-vis peasants. When people provide answers to the question "Why did X do Y?" they give rationales for behavior, but they also offer statements about the social relationships at stake (Tilly 2006b).

Members of the provincial elite intervened in the conflict, offering technical accounts while also vilifying demonstrators and reinforcing the subordinate position of peasants. Probably reacting to an earlier newspaper headline stating "Hemorrhagic diseases reported in Monte Azul,"[12] the president of the provincial association of agrarian engineers declared that

> we are hearing really dangerous opinions, like people saying that some neighbors may have hemorrhagic fever; to make such a big claim is to show that you don't know anything.[13]

The president of the Rural Society similarly stated that the issue should be treated only by "trained technicians" to avoid "biased opinions and the search of spurious profits" while the aforementioned representative of a landowners association stressed that the agrochemicals were authorized by the SENASA (the equivalent of the FDA). Providing a strong institutional endorsement to these discourses, the Ministry of Production organized a meeting in the Government House with the presence of SENASA representatives on March 18, 2003. The official policy, expressed by the provincial minister, was

> To put the matter on a technical level, which is the level where it should be, with institutions related to those issues ... The idea was to redirect the matter to the areas where it should have always been.[14]

What do these appeals to technical accounts do? The appeals to "keep the discussion on a technical level" implied that peasants and their organizations should not have a say in matters of agrochemical use and contamination; only people invested with the proper knowledge should opine on the issue. Furthermore, even when demonstrators in Monte Azul were not protesting against the use of agrochemicals per se but against its effects on their health, animals, and crops, the issue veered to a discussion of its lawfulness. In this context, the focus of the discussion moved from the negative effects of agrochemicals on peasants' farms to questions about its harmlessness and the authorization of its use by the federal administration.[15]

The dispute between peasants and elites revealed, in short, that those who are more easily exposed to the suffering created by agrochemical exposure have to face invisible but powerful barriers to make themselves heard and to be taken into account in public debates about environmental hazards.

In August, soybean growers disobeyed the judge's order and fumigated the fields yet again. Shortly after, they harvested the soybeans and left the area. They relocated their investments in Paraguay where, as a person linked to the company told me, "they have better perspectives . . . here they had all those little problems of insecurity" (*esos problemitas de inseguridad*), in reference to the protests. The suit for damages against CEFA and the Ministry of Production has been sitting in courts for years now and there is no agreement or decision in sight.[16] "When people go to court," Charles Tilly observes, "they seek to fix blame on the authors of their hardships, and to punish them appropriately. Yet they also seek recognition of their own merit . . . They ask for vindication" (Tilly 2008: 33).

The conflicts drove some soy growers out of Monte Azul and Moreno (what at first glance may be seen as a success for MoCaFor), but other soybean growers arrived or remained in the area. As we will see, however, the protests induced changes in the way soybeans are produced. The agrochemical drift had a direct impact on peasants' agricultural practices and impaired them economically while also affecting MoCaFor's mobilization base. Some peasants abandoned the farmers market and did not grow staples again, afraid of investing monies and work in crops that could be destroyed by another agrochemical drift. The loss of production during the 2003 agricultural campaign also prompted some peasants to migrate in search of work. Augusto is a good example:

> We used to go to meetings with organizations that were with us . . . But then I got out, because I went to work in Las Lomitas [120 miles west of Monte Azul]. I had to leave everything . . . I needed work, and all my produce was destroyed. I didn't have anything, and I had to

feed my family. They [MoCaFor members] kept dealing with the issue but I left. Then I totally lost touch with them . . . Because once you've lost, excuse me, but you're fucked the whole year. Then the next year, you grow everything again . . . Or you get lost, like we did; we went to work, to somehow get by. Left our families, our homes; [you need to] get a job so you don't starve.

Augusto's account captures the effect of agrochemical drifts on the subsistence of peasant families while also highlighting, paraphrasing Marx, the dull compulsion of economic relations that plays a key role in creating pressures on social movements (as we will see in the next chapter).

Contentious Language: Mothers and Picketers

When I began analyzing ethnographic data to reconstruct the 2003 conflict, I noticed suggestive discrepancies between public discourses (deployed by leaders during moments of open confrontation and presented in written accounts) and face-to-face conversations with and among peasants. The ways in which leaders and rank-and-file members understand GM crops, agrochemical drifts, and contention overlap in certain respects but also presented crucial differences. In addition, the interpretations of active *and marginal* members of MoCaFor, and those of Monte Azul inhabitants who did not participate in the movement suggested subtle lines of vision and division regarding the identities involved in contentious collective action.

How do people make sense of their contentious actions in a province where patronage is the norm, where peasants occupy the lower echelons of the social and symbolic order, and contentious actions are seen as out of place? I answer this question by exploring two identifications that emerged during the contentious events: women justifying their actions as mothers, and people referring to demonstrators and movement members as "picketers," *piqueteros*. In examining the "vocabularies of motive" surrounding contentious events, I follow C. Wright Mills in assuming that these utterances "do not denote elements 'in' individuals" but rather "stand for anticipated situational consequences of questioned conduct" (Mills 1940: 905).

Exploring the ways in which people justify their actions and evaluate the actions of others provides two insights. First, it sheds light on the meaning-making processes that take place *within* social movements, interrogating the ontological coherence and unity that is often ascribed to actually loose networks of leaders, activists, members, and sympathizers (Edelman 1999,

Rubin 1998, Burdick 1995, Wolford 2010). In this case, making sense of contentious participation as stemming from motherhood exposes the gendered lines of hierarchical division within movements and the available scripts from which women draw. Second, paying attention to the concerns of being seen as *piqueteros* offers access to the ambiguities of transgression and the symbolic barriers people in Formosa (and elsewhere in Argentina) need to overcome to engage in contentious collective action. As such, this latter exploration bridges this chapter on contention with the next two on processes of demobilization, offering a first glimpse as to why people *did not* react contentiously when facing environmental problems in 2009.

Benito García, the main leader of MoCaFor, is a man in his early thirties who speaks softly but firmly and rarely smiles. During one of my visits to Moreno, we sat down for a conversation and talked about the conflicts brought about by GM soybean production: "The struggle is very hard; the agribusiness model is being imposed at any price . . . Soybean production is the imposition of agribusiness and the appropriation of natural resources." As the spokesperson of MoCaFor, he presented similar ideas to journalists: "We see transgenics as the invader displacing us, taking the soil from us, poisoning the environment, producing the concentration of wealth in the hands of a few." He linked the advance of GM crops to a broader agricultural system dominated by transnational corporations: "We are against this system of concentration, genetic manipulation, this way of production, the transnationalization of companies that commercialize the supplies for agricultural production." In Benito's view and public statements, the conflict pitting peasants against soybean growers was framed as an environmental problem and the expression of agribusiness marginalizing the rural poor.

When examined more closely, however, this interpretation contrasts with the views of the rank-and-file.[17] The women in the movement expressed their participation in terms of an environmental struggle but mostly using motherhood as an idiom for protest. As we have seen, the first reactions against agrochemicals took place when women's sons were affected (as in the case of Emilia). Nélida was particularly adamant when she saw agrochemical exposure affecting the health of her children and future grandchildren, and "we the mothers," as Juana said, prompted the initial local collective actions.

This deployment of "contentious motherhood" can be seen as a consequence of the active politicization of gender since the 1990s fostered by the *Equipo de Mujeres Campesinas* (Peasant Women Group) introduced in chapter 2. Furthermore, this "contentious motherhood" extends beyond

MoCaFor as expressed in other cases of agrochemical exposure like the Madres de Ituzaingó from Córdoba province (see chapter 1) and the noticeable mobilization of women during Argentina's crisis of 2002–2003 (Borland and Sutton 2007). As Shannon Bell aptly put it, "the well-being of family and community are often inextricably linked—even undistinguishable—in many women activists' minds" (2013: 7). The use of motherhood also harkens back to the Madres de Plaza de Mayo and their struggle for human rights in Argentina. As Diana Taylor wrote about the Madres de Plaza de Mayo: "The role of mother . . . offered the women a certain legitimacy and authority in a society that values mothers almost to the exclusion of all other women . . . among the few roles open to Argentine women, the suffering mother is the most popular and certainly the most socially rewarding" (Taylor 1997: 235).[18]

The effects of corporate agriculture or concerns as mothers as rationales for protest are not mutually exclusive. Yet it is still important, I believe, to take note of the disjuncture between the public presentation of the movement and the ways in which their members interpreted their participation in their own terms. As Wendy Wolford argues, "presenting a coherent and unified picture of social movement means choosing some subalterns over others. If we do not pay attention to alternative or multiple subjectivities within movements, we have selected for those voices we wish to hear and, as a result, we are likely to miss (or misunderstand) broader movement trajectories" (Wolford 2010: 12).

When analyzing interviews and fieldnotes taken from everyday conversations, I also noticed another common pattern: a negative connotation associated with the term "*piqueteros.*" The word refers to the organized unemployed in Argentina, who during the second part of the 1990s resorted to pickets blocking roads and streets as their main form of protest.[19] The meaning assigned to roadblocks (pickets, *piquetes*) was initially unknown to many peasants of Monte Azul in 2003. During an extensive interview, Nélida narrated how she learned what a picket was:

NÉLIDA: Once I went to a meeting of women in La Plata [near Buenos Aires]. And I remember that a woman went [to the stage] and said [mimicking a person screaming], "For the next year, more women at the picket!" And I didn't know what a picket was. Here we call picket a place where we take the animals [to graze]. I did not know what a picket was.

PABLO: You had never held a roadblock before?

NÉLIDA: No, we knew nothing about roadblocks. For us, that's what we thought a picket was.

The identity attached to those participating in roadblocks (*piqueteros*) became a derogatory expression even among Formosan social movement leaders, reproducing its use by elite members who equated the term with "troublemakers." During my fieldwork, I noticed that "picketer" was used with an apologetic tone when uttered by activists and one of disgust when used by people not involved in the movement. For instance, a peasant told me that she heard a manager of a soybean plot say, "I'm going to make those picketers cry" when he was preparing to fumigate a soybean field in 2007.

But not only those opposing MoCaFor used the terms "picket" and "picketer" with scorn. While staying at the MoCaFor offices in Sarambí, I participated in several meetings of the organization. In one of them, Julio said to three youngsters and prospective members of MoCaFor that "some call us picketers, and some call the [unemployed welfare] subsidy 'the picketer subsidy' [smiling]. It's not that we *like* to blockade a road, but we do that so people from other provinces, or from Buenos Aires, get to know what's going on, to make ourselves heard." When the meeting was over and I was sipping mate with Julio, he told me that one of the more talkative girls from the meeting once told him: "I agree with you [the MoCaFor], but I don't like when you block the road," to which Julio replied, "No, I understand, we don't like it either!" Isidoro, a local leader in Sarambí, told me: "This [welfare] program is called 'the picketer program,' mind you [laughing]." When recalling the roadblock, people several times remarked how they did it because "nobody was hearing us." The term used in the legal demands to soy growers also reflected these feelings: "Facing the government's utmost indifference to the sufferings of inhabitants affected by indiscriminate fumigations, they were *forced* to blockade the road" (emphasis added).

"We looked like picketers," was the expression I heard several times, used by activists of MoCaFor in an apologetic tone and echoing the public statements of officials saying they were "troublemakers." Others in Monte Azul also provided glimpses of this perception. The principal at the local elementary school, who is not sympathetic toward MoCaFor, told me, "Even when people in the colony [Monte Azul] say that they are troublemakers, that they are *piqueteros*, I'm proud of my colony [Monte Azul]." During an interview, Nélida's daughter spontaneously offered her view on the topic:

And here, this colony is criticized. It is criticized because the people from here always, always protest; they say what they don't like. So they are marked, the peasant movement as well. And you notice it, for instance, when the fumigation started, there was Mom, Horacio, all of them, and even at my work, they called me "the daughter of so-and-so, of Nélida, the picketer."

The multiple views on what it means to participate in a roadblock harken back to what Marc Steinberg calls "the multivocal nature of discourse," that is, that "actors over time within a movement or actors from different movements can create distinctive meanings from the same words and phrases" (Steinberg 1999b: 750). As a signifier, the charged and changing term *"piquetero"* shows that certain identifications invoked in the course of contention "alter the array of actors, identities, and actions that appear in routine politics and further contention once the particular episode of contention has ended" (McAdam, Tarrow, and Tilly 2001: 56). Similarly to peasants' views of patronage discussed in the previous chapter, these identifications (*piquetero*) and actions (roadblocks) express a "sociological ambivalence." MoCaFor leaders were being pushed and pulled toward acceptance and rejection "not because of their idiosyncratic history or their distinctive personality but because the ambivalence is inherent in the social positions they occupy" (Merton and Barber 1976: 8). Leaders are both representatives of their organizations and members of their communities, and as such they interact with people outside their movement that see them as troublemakers. In addition, leaders of a social movement are also pushed and pulled by, on the one hand, the views of current and potential constituents (who may see *piqueteros* and roadblocks in negative terms) and, on the other hand, by their allegiance to their national allies, the FTV, whose leaders and members identify as *piqueteros* at the national level. The ramifications of these ambivalences will become even more apparent in the next chapter, when examining processes of demobilization.

Conclusion

The events in Monte Azul and Moreno presented in this chapter allow provisional conclusions regarding the "dark side" of the agricultural boom prompted by the expansion of GM crops and the meanings involved in popular contention.

On the one hand, scrutiny of GM crop production problematizes the interpretation of agrochemical drifts as mere "accidents" (Harrison 2011, Wright 2005). From a sociological standpoint, the concrete instances of managers of soybean fields privileging economic gains over environmental damage and provincial elites dismissing peasant claims can be seen as the expressions of a neoliberal approach to agriculture and power inequalities. After all, as James Scott nicely put it, "no abstract force, collectivity, or system, ever arrives at the door of human experience, except as it is mediated by concrete, particular human 'carriers.' Not the landed aristocracy in general, but a particular lord of the land, with his own family history, his own personality, in this particular place. Not capitalism, in general, but this money lender, this trader, this factory boss, and this foreman, each with his or her own personality, ethnicity, and routines" (Scott 2005: 398).

The cases also underscore that biotechnology applied to agriculture is embedded in social relationships, since technologies are not neutral, but carry implications in terms of the kind of society they foster (Kinchy 2012; Levidow 1998). As Jill Harrison argued about agrochemical drifts in California, they must "be understood as a social problem as much as a technical one, and the intersections between these social and technical dimensions explain the continuation and invisibility of pesticide drift" (Harrison 2011: 9). In the case of GM crops, its inexorable use of toxic agrochemicals and its orientation toward large-scale feed production pose a difficult coexistence with small-scale, locally oriented food production (Altieri 2005, Levidow and Boschert 2008).

It is true that these negative environmental impacts can occur with either GM crops or conventional mono-crops. Yet some of the characteristics of GM soybeans favor their geographical expansion and create the conditions for the agrochemical drifts suffered by rural populations. GM soybeans can be sowed without harrowing the soil and can be grown following standardized procedures of herbicide application and harvesting. GM soybeans are thus easier to grow and require less monitoring than conventional crops; these two factors explain their geographical expansion in Argentina. Furthermore, when GM soybeans are sowed on plots where other GM soybeans were previously harvested, other herbicides besides Roundup, which the plants are engineered to resist, need to be used to eliminate the plants emerging from seeds that fell during the previous harvest because all of the plants have to be the same height for the combine harvester to work properly.

Put in other terms, growing soybeans in marginal lands like the ones in Formosa only makes agronomic and economic sense if the soybeans are GM. Indeed, herbicide drifts could have occurred in Formosa with the production of either GM or conventional soybeans, but soybeans would not have been grown in Formosa (or, for that matter, in other marginal lands in Argentina) if it were not for the advantages of GM soybeans. The outcome of these agronomical and environmental processes is that GM crops perpetuate—and geographically expand—the shortcomings of mainstream, agrochemical-dependent agriculture (see the introduction for the changes and continuities between "conventional" and GM crops).

On the other hand, when analyzed in terms of popular mobilization and social development, these contentious events of Monte Azul and Moreno underscore the entanglement of material and symbolic processes. The literature on GM crops (either celebratory or critical) overwhelmingly focuses on their economic implications. While techno-productivists praise GM crops for the gains they may bring to farmers and agribusinesses, scholars adopting a critical perspective on GM crops focus on its implications for peasant agriculture in terms of economic marginalization. The Argentine context exemplifies that GM crops may bring about economic development *for some*, namely capitalized farmers and the owners of large plots of land. For peasants and small farmers, in contrast, GM crops present dubious benefits, to put it mildly. What this book seeks to underline (and this chapter exemplifies) is the importance of considering the interests but also the *ideas and feelings* of the people living in the territories where GM crops have social and environmental impacts.

The events analyzed in this chapter suggest that recognition, disrespect, and dismissal of peasant life inform contention about GM crops. Taken together with the next two chapters, the events presented above suggest the interpenetration of emotions and interests, of material and symbolic concerns. As Deborah Gould argues: "Attending to affect rather than assuming rational actors or rendering emotion in cognitive terms illuminates a great deal by forcing consideration of the multiplicity and indeterminacy of human needs and desires; the often ambivalent and contradictory nature of our feelings; our more bodily and nonconscious forms of knowing and sense-making; inconsistencies and noncoherences within our thoughts and between our cognitive and felt responses to the world . . . all phenomena that have political consequences" (2009: 26).

The conflicts scrutinized in this chapter, in short, show that poor people's protests intertwine the defense of their economic survival with their need to be recognized as legitimate actors in public life. During the contention over agrochemical exposure, Formosan peasants simultaneously put forward their material interests, defined and defended their identity, and asserted their worthiness when facing powerful actors denying them due recognition. Elites' rebuttals prompted morally charged protests because peasants sought not only to recover their material losses, but also to restore a sense of justice and to demand recognition of their right to be peasants and speak up.

Now, what happens if authorities *recognize* social movements and *acknowledge* the effects of agrochemical exposure? In the next chapters, we will continue scrutinizing issues of recognition, language, and emotions, but focusing on the flip side of contention: processes of *de*mobilization.

4

DEMOBILIZATION

PEASANTS, GOVERNMENTS, AND CONSTITUENTS ACROSS POLITICAL SCALES (2004–2013)

"[Néstor] Kirchner gave a lot of things to the [social movement] organizations, and they neutralize you," shared Raúl, the leader of a peasant movement of Northern Argentina. We met at a bar in Buenos Aires in 2011. During our conversation, he said that the rural policies of the Kirchners "do not have a place for the small farmers" (*no tiene un lugar para los pequeños productores*), and that the national minister of agriculture and other national authorities "say one thing but then do another; they have a double standard." Raúl sees the Kirchner administrations as "typical of Peronism: they don't have an anti-capitalist politic, but [promote] a capitalism with a human face." From his perspective, the goal of the Kirchners is to make the situation "a little less unequal," to maintain business as usual and avoid social unrest (*para que todo siga funcionando igual, sin conflictividad social*).

Given Raúl's stance, you may think that he is part of the political opposition to the Kirchners. On the contrary, he is a staunch supporter of the Kirchner administrations. Furthermore, since 2008 Raúl held a position in the national agency in charge of land titles. He took the job with the goal of helping the constituents of his movement and also to be closer to the place where decisions are made (as I repeatedly heard during my fieldwork, "God is everywhere, but His offices are in Buenos Aires"). Raúl travels to the North periodically, bridging the provincial peasant movement with national authorities and activists based in the Argentine capital. When Raúl talks to his movement's constituents in the North, he emphasizes that the Kirchner's is *their* government.

Raúl embodies the dilemmas and contradictions that I tackle in this chapter. At an individual level, he exemplifies the frictions and paradoxes that exist between social movement leaders and members, national and provincial governments. This chapter turns from the examination of resistance in the previous chapter to a close analysis of *processes of demobilization*. I pivot between three levels of analysis—the social movement organization, authorities' responses, and subjective understandings—to capture the connections between *material concerns and symbolic interpretations* in the active production of demobilization. The analysis hinges on the articulation of multiple political scales, as movement leaders navigate the vexed scenario of answering to local constituents and dealing with a hostile provincial government, all the while supporting a national administration that supports *both* the movement and the governor.

To explain processes of demobilization, I propose two concepts that illuminate these dynamics: "dual pressure" and "institutional recognition." First, I introduce the concept of dual pressure to scrutinize the relationship between MoCaFor and its national allies: the national government and the national social movement FTV (Federación de Tierra y Vivienda, Land and Housing Federation). I argue that the relational field in which social movement leaders and members are embedded is dominated by an entrenched clientelism, and social movements are seen, in part, as "problem-solving networks" (Auyero 2000). I show that demobilization is less a function of co-optation than the result of dual pressures from members and political allies of MoCaFor; in other words, demobilization is a product of relationships *within and between* movements.

Second, I analyze the impact of rural development policies on local organizations, a process that I call institutional recognition. Unlike the situation of 2003, when peasants were disrespected and dismissed by provincial authorities, starting around 2004 but crucially after 2008, the national government recognized peasant organizations as a valid social actor in agrarian life. This created opportunities for social movements but also engendered friction among them. Moreover, I argue that along with institutional recognition, MoCaFor spokespeople experienced a closing of discursive horizons as they participated in government initiatives. The inclusion of peasant organizations in rural development policies exposed the tensions that Gianpaolo Baiocchi (2005: 4) identified in projects of participatory democracy in Brazil; namely, the pulling forces of "disruptive, rowdy, and contestatory" social movements and the expectations of "virtuous, civil, and cooperative" participation. Taken together, dual pressure and institutional recognition shaped the organizational dynamics of MoCaFor (and arguably, similar movements throughout Argentina). MoCaFor's alliances with other social movements and its participation in governmental policies, I argue, helped to keep the organization running while posing obstacles for contention.

Dual pressure and institutional recognition reveal the complex scenario in which a social movement seeks to address the material demands of its constituents and, in doing so, compromises its autonomy. Issues of scale and location cut across all of these processes. Rather than focusing on global or national scales alone, I seek to incorporate the *articulation of multiple scales* into my analysis. Thus we will see how dual pressure results from the connection of national and provincial political actors, and how performative governance (introduced in the next chapter) generates diverse effects across national, provincial, and localized scales.

I propose the concepts of dual pressure and institutional recognition with the goal of eschewing other labels that may be more familiar but less nuanced (i.e., "co-optation"). I understand demobilization as an active process, an achievement involving the agency of subordinate actors, something that the patronizing and pejorative label "co-optation" poorly conveys. Put differently, I believe the term "co-optation" says more about what an analyst is expecting to encounter and finds lacking rather than addressing the situated actions of subordinate actors "on their own terms." In the case of Argentina, by 2003 popular social movements had already gone through more than a decade of neoliberal policies (ca. 1990–2000), and they were adjusting to the aftermath of one of the deepest social and economic crisis in the history of the country (during 2001–2002). In that context, cooperation with a government could have brought concrete material benefits to social movement members while supporting a political project that sought, at least discursively, to break away from neoliberalism.

Social movement leaders, particularly among popular movements, voice their rights and make demands but also need to deliver. They need to respond to the concrete material demands of their constituents. To see compromise and collaboration as co-optation, in my view, privileges a top-down understanding of the relationship between the polity and social movements and glosses over relational and interpretative processes. It may be shortsighted to see the relationships between a social movement and a sympathetic government in terms of the latter manipulating the former, or to assume that leaders can easily control their constituents. As I show through ethnographic evidence, the term co-optation overlooks the pressure that leaders face and the multiple relationships that explain social movement trajectories. In contrast,

I argue that dual pressure and institutional recognition hold the analytical promise of better capturing these multilayered dynamics.

Peasant Social Movements and Dual Pressure

Peasant life is a life committed completely to survival. Perhaps this is the only characteristic fully shared by peasants everywhere.

—*John Berger (1992: xi)*

The first piece of the puzzle that explains the demobilization of Formosan peasants is a process of dual pressure that began circa 2004. Social movement leaders experienced twofold pressures, stemming "from below" and "from above." I derived this spatial metaphor from the expressions explaining relationships between social movements and the national government that I heard repeatedly during my fieldwork. Resources "come down" (*bajaron recursos*); information or negotiations that leaders have with authorities need to be "brought down" to the people (*bajamos la información a la gente*); and the state is conceived as being "up there."[1]

The process of dual pressure can be summarized as follows. In Formosa (like other places in Argentina and Latin America), patronage is pervasive and poor people develop survival strategies relying on clientelistic arrangements based on expectations of reciprocity.[2] As I will show, poor people participate in social movement organizations and volunteer their time to voice their rights, but they also do so to address pressing survival needs by gaining access to resources. In other words, they provide movements valuable resources while expecting something in return. These expectations of constituents, I argue, create pressure from below for leaders of social movement organizations (SMOs) like MoCaFor, which respond by securing and distributing resources obtained through alliances with national political actors. In turn, these alliances create a pressure from above for MoCaFor and its leaders, ultimately creating obstacles to contentious collective action. The corollary of this process is that when acting as brokers, local leaders reciprocate the support given by their national allies by eschewing the organization of collective actions.

Pressures from Below

After Néstor Kirchner took power in 2003, MoCaFor began to receive resources from the national government: these included unemployment benefits (*planes* in the jargon of popular movements), scholarships for youth attending high school, food, and agricultural machinery for a cooperative created by MoCaFor in Moreno. In the administration and distribution of these resources, the relationships between MoCaFor leaders and constituents began to resemble those of political brokers and their clients. The administration and distribution of *planes* made MoCaFor akin to a "problem-solving network" (Auyero 2000), blurring the lines between the practices of a social movement and those of patronage politics. Leaders continuously derided clientelism, but nonetheless they (and their constituents) could not escape the determinants of their social milieu.

This excerpt from my fieldnotes illustrates the topic of MoCaFor as a problem-solving network; in this case, with a group of prospective MoCaFor members. On a Sunday afternoon in 2008, a meeting was held between two MoCaFor leaders (Julio and Isidoro) and a dozen women in the office of MoCaFor in Sarambí, a warehouse on the outskirts of town. After the meeting, four young women stayed to talk with Julio and Isidoro about the possibility of joining the movement.

> The women want to join the organization, so Julio begins to explain that they acquire *planes* and distribute them "according to the needs of the people." . . . They privilege those who participate more, "because sometimes you get a *plan* for someone, and then they don't come anymore, or they only appear when their *plan* gets cut, or their *plan* gets cut and they don't even show up then." They ask for a contribution of 10 pesos for those who get the *plan*, because that's how they pay for their computer, internet, and the "costs of the paperwork, supplies, trips that have to be made, if we need to go to Formosa for something, if we need to go Buenos Aires, for the gas for the vehicle when we have to go to the rural communities to talk to people or have meetings." . . . One of the women says, "We want to participate, and if later there's some *plan*, great, I hope you will keep us in mind." Isidoro tells them to come to the meeting Tuesday and Wednesday [referring to a two-day gathering with peasant organizations of the northeast] (October 26, 2008).

The passage encapsulates two dimensions of the movement: first, that people join the organization to participate, but also, in a context dominated by patronage, to eventually obtain something in return. ("We want to participate, and if later there's some *plan*, great, I hope you will keep us in mind.") Second, the distribution of *planes* contributes to the organization's survival (through the collection of dues) and recruitment efforts ("come to the meeting Tuesday and Wednesday").

Some of the quotidian practices I witnessed in the offices of MoCaFor in Moreno resembled the workings of a patronage network even more closely. During the several days I spent in the warehouse that doubles as the MoCaFor office, I witnessed a continuous procession of people coming from the poorest areas of town asking for *mercadería* (food). MoCaFor members wrote down people's information and gave them a bag with milk, cacao, and peas. The resemblance between these practices and the ones of a patronage network did not go unnoticed by MoCaFor members. When I asked Armando, a member of MoCaFor in Moreno, if a lot of people had come asking for *mercadería* in the days before my visit, he said "no, but last time [they received and distributed food] it was a ton . . . It was like a political rally!"

In the management of *planes* MoCaFor not only distributes these benefits among their constituents, but it also helps people to solve problems they encounter as beneficiaries (payments in arrears, paperwork, etc.). The following excerpt from my fieldnotes exemplifies this situation:

> We are in Nélida's house/farm with her son Julio [also a MoCaFor leader]. An older man arrives asking about his son's *plan*; he says he got paid but they haven't paid his son yet. Julio explains how to solve a series of problems with the paperwork and says that for some people the paperwork goes through quickly, because of politics. The man thanks him several times and leaves (June 19, 2009).

A year earlier, in 2008, I interviewed Benito García, the leader of MoCaFor in Moreno. I was seated with Benito in his office when I witnessed the following situation:

> Someone knocks on the door, it's Nelson [a MoCaFor member]. He walks in and recounts a problem he had in the mayor's office (he's presenting some projects there) and says that he wants to present another letter. Benito tells him, "Bring what you've written tomorrow and we'll look at it." Two women enter the office and say that they went to get their scholarships from the Ministry of Education but couldn't; they were told that the school wasn't registered. Benito says that's not it; they get paid through MoCaFor and not through the school. Two men enter and recount how they were not able to get paid either. Benito says to Nilda [who works as an ad hoc secretary for

Benito]: "Give them five pesos to buy bread . . . and the Spam in the kitchen. Because you didn't eat anything today, right? Go and make breakfast" (November 11, 2008).

In casual conversations, some leaders complained to me about continuously having to attend to people's demands. Returning to MoCaFor offices after having dinner, Tito (who is in the offices day and night) bitterly complained that "people come asking for anything and everything: medicines, help with a legal issue, food." As Benito told me: "People think you are the priest, the police captain . . . You end up in a personalized situation, when the matter should be collective." In spite of this, the distribution of food in a context dominated by patronage inevitably resembles the workings of clientelism, as Armando noticed in the quote above. In fact, in contrast to Moreno, MoCaFor leaders in Sarambí refuse to distribute food because, as Julio told me, "that is *asistencialismo* [a synonym of clientelism]; that is what politicians do, we don't want to do that." Furthermore, the *personalized* way in which some goods were distributed in Moreno also suggested a clientelistic dynamic. During my fieldwork, I noticed that when people wanted access to the tractor or the scholarships MoCaFor received from the national authorities, they had to wait in line and have individual meetings with the leader.

An SMO receiving and distributing resources does not necessarily translate into a reproduction of clientelist practices. However, the type of resources, its personalized distribution, and the demands of constant problem solving have strong parallels with patronage. An additional example underlines this point by showing the expectations of reciprocity embedded in exchanges. During a long interview on his farm, a grassroots member of MoCaFor told me that he wanted to criticize the organization's leadership, but he kept his "mouth shut" because his daughter was studying with a scholarship she received through MoCaFor. Just as the exchange of goods and services may eschew collective contention (as we will see in the next section), expectations of reciprocity may also subdue internal dissent.

The ethnographic data presented so far illustrates the pervasiveness of patronage in Formosa and how the distribution of resources obtained by MoCaFor mimics certain clientelistic practices. MoCaFor fulfills the expectations arising from the ubiquity of patronage in Formosa by addressing the pressing material needs of its constituents. At the same time, the interactions involved in such exchanges tend to reproduce the pervasiveness of patronage politics in the province. When MoCaFor leaders need to obtain resources, however, they move from the role of distributors to the role of clients in a process that creates pressures from above.

Pressures from Above

A series of events that took place in 2004 shed light on how the allegiances and alliances that involved MoCaFor in the Kirchners' administration contributed to a process of demobilization. On June 15, 2004, MoCaFor had planned a march to Formosa's capital to present a series of demands to the provincial government. On the day of the scheduled march, Luis D'Elía, the head of the FTV (the national social movement Federación de Tierra y Vivienda, the Land and Housing Federation) arrived in Formosa and arranged a meeting with Benito García (the head of MoCaFor) and Governor Insfrán. Both the FTV and Governor Insfrán were allies of the national government of Néstor Kirchner. During the meeting, the three men agreed that the provincial administration and MoCaFor would create a commission to negotiate peasants' demands.

As a result of the meeting, MoCaFor's mobilization to Formosa was suspended. D'Elía expressed in a local newspaper that the policies of the provincial government "strongly support the province's development" and noted that "there was a good amount of dialogue and willingness from both sides, to initiate a new phase . . . and to try to support the project put forward by President Néstor Kirchner." The newspaper also stated that "the leader highlighted that the national project of President Néstor Kirchner is absolutely identified with the Formosan governor." Benito was quoted in the newspaper, saying that the meeting "was an opportunity to begin a new phase between the province's government and a sector of organized society. It has been fruitful in terms of reaching an agreement to work together and beginning to look for effective solutions."[3]

The signing of the agreement was scheduled for a month later on July 16, 2004. MoCaFor peasants mobilized en masse to go to the capital of Formosa to make sure their demands were addressed. However, when the time came to sign the agreement, the minister of production declared that peasants' demands were exaggerated and that they would consume the province's budget, ultimately blaming the peasant organization for not reaching an agreement. MoCaFor peasants still marched to Formosa's capital to demand the signature of the agreement, but the official response was that the governor was negotiating with D'Elía in Buenos Aires. MoCaFor rank-and-file members then blocked a road on the outskirts of Formosa's capital, demanding that the governor receive them and accept the agreement that had reached in June. "As soon as we blocked the road, I got a call from D'Elía telling me we would be repressed, that we should stop the blockade," a MoCaFor leader told me. Despite the pressure of the mobilizations, the provincial government never fulfilled the promises reached in the agreement. MoCaFor leaders remember these events as the demise of any possible collaboration with the provincial government. Some months later, in September 2004, MoCaFor organized another march when President Kirchner visited Formosa. The movement considered blocking a road, but D'Elía got in touch with them to ask them to reconsider the blockade and offered his support to negotiate on behalf of MoCaFor's demands. MoCaFor accepted D'Elía's offer, and leaders then held a meeting with the president's secretary and established new contacts with the national government.

The alliance between the FTV and MoCaFor provided the latter with resources (welfare *planes*) to be distributed among its members and constituents in addition to contacts within the national administration. These resources and connections were necessary to ensure the organization's survival, in terms of maintaining its support base and independence from the provincial government. In the process, MoCaFor leaders became not only distributors of resources among their constituents but also receivers of resources from the national government. Accordingly, the reception of these resources created certain (unspoken) obligations. For instance, MoCaFor members participate in rallies in Buenos Aires supporting the president. They are not *forced* to do so, but rather feel the *obligation to reciprocate* the support of the national government by taking part in its activities. This is similar to the way that MoCaFor members receiving *planes* are expected to participate in the activities organized by MoCaFor in Formosa, as shown in the previous section. In short, obtaining and distributing resources creates a field of reciprocity with multiple points of reference and pressures that influence processes of demobilization.

Seated at a table in the patio of his humble house in Moreno where we just had lunch, I asked Oscar, a local leader of MoCaFor, about the roadblocks of 2004, the intermediation of D'Elía, and why they decided to suspend the mobilizations against the provincial government. Oscar's answer clearly connects the mobilization of people to their access to resources in both that instance and for MoCaFor's actions in general:

Our concern was always to maintain the economic component. To sustain the people. So this was one of the factors affecting why we had to suspend the roadblocks. Because to mobilize the people from here to

Formosa, it's 300 km [186 miles], from San Martín, it's 800 km [497 miles], and if you don't have resources, how can you mobilize the people? We also had the issue of food. This was always a factor for our organization. Not just that time [in 2004], but in many roadblocks that we did, it was hard to sustain them, because of the economic component. Because most of us are poor. So when we went to Formosa, there were groups that made empanadas, sold raffle tickets, got some pesos together to cover our transportation round-trip. And if there were peasants who wanted to go, we covered the cost of the trip. That was our system. But we couldn't sustain this for very long; we didn't have the resources. This was always the problem, resources. Not because we don't work, but because of where we live, [we've] scarce resources, the crops we have aren't worth much, people have large families . . . There is a series of factors, that if you say "let's go, x days, on the road" it's very difficult to sustain.

When I went back to Sarambí, I sat down in the warehouse/office of MoCaFor to talk to Nélida and Isidoro, two leaders of MoCaFor. They elaborated on their relationship with the FTV and the concomitant restrictions it posed to the movement. Nélida explained:

Lately, we have gotten closer to a politician that helped us, but also conditioned us, not directly, but we knew that that was his intention. We had to join the people from Buenos Aires so that our *compañeros* could have a bit more help. If no one gives us anything, the organization will crumble, it will fall down; people are not doing fine, and if they don't get some help . . . We realized that through the organization we could negotiate and obtain welfare *planes* for our *compañeros* . . . Lately, I've seen that if we don't do anything and if we cannot give anything to our people . . . nothing at all can be done. We are all poor and with some help, we are joined together. It's not that much, but we are keeping up and growing. Lately, many people have become [MoCaFor] members, now we are even bigger.

Isidoro chimed in, connecting the need for external resources in a context of economic crisis and how welfare benefits contribute to the organization's survival:

If the provincial or national government had given us the help that every small farmer deserves, we would have been in better shape and the people of the organization wouldn't have needed even one peso from anyone. Because the people need certain things to live . . . We knew as leaders that the *planes* were not the solution, they weren't what we were looking for. We were searching for something else. But we took these things [*planes*] to maintain the organization.

MoCaFor leaders are aware that being an oppositional group in the province puts the movement in a difficult spot, since the provincial government complains to national authorities about their actions. Thus, MoCaFor leaders express concerns about alienating the national government. As Benito said to me:

It bothers Gildo [the governor] that the national government supports us . . . The provincial government always tells the national government that they got 75% of the votes, and that all those votes went to Cristina [Kirchner, the president and ally of the governor]. So they [the provincial government] tell them [the national government] "don't tell us what we ought to do in our province."

A last interview excerpt from a conversation with Telma, a local leader in Moreno, brings the process full circle. She provides insight in to how MoCaFor leaders navigate the complex field of alliances in which they are embedded, and how they might privilege negotiations over contentious action, given the constraints the organization and poor people face:

The thing is, we sometimes confront the government and we don't obtain anything, but we just make our people suffer . . . We will try other means, for example, in this case presenting projects to the [national] ministry, or working more at a national level than at the provincial level . . . Gildo [Formosa's governor] won't change his system, so . . . I don't want to tell you that we've been defeated or that we've dropped our guard either . . . I think we should avoid confronting the governor and try to find alternative means to get what we want, which is what we are negotiating with the national government. They are allowing more participation from the organizations.

What these voices suggest is that open, defiant, and disruptive contention may be *one* of the means of popular movements to achieve their goals. Involvement in clientelism, although usually expressing an exploitative relationship, may also be a strategy to achieve a movement's goals (Hilgers 2012b). And, similarly to the poor tenants studied by Michael Lipsky (1970) in the early 1960s, leaders in Formosa have to address different constituencies including members and authorities. In doing so, an SMO may demobilize (privileging negotiation over direct contention) to avoid alienating allies and to satisfy the pressing survival needs of members.

Social Movements and Institutional Recognition

What is at stake in the struggles about the meaning of the social world is power over the classificatory schemes and systems which are the basis of the representations of the groups and therefore of their mobilization and demobilization.

—PIERRE BOURDIEU *(1984: 479)*

The adamant reactions of peasants against agrochemical drifts in 2003 were in great part motivated by the lack of recognition of their pleas, as we saw in the previous chapter. This lack of recognition changed in the ensuing years. Since 2003, the governments of Néstor and Cristina Kirchner developed alliances with social movements involving the distribution of resources that nurtured the dual pressures described above. This new approach to social movements also involved symbolic and institutional recognition. In spite of these favorable political opportunities and access to resources (two conditions that established social movement theory deems as conducive to mobilization), MoCaFor and many other social movement organizations in contemporary Argentina have demobilized sharply.[4] Why?

An examination of the policies of the national government toward peasant movements shows the ways in which recognition can create obstacles for contentious collective action. One of the national policies involves the intervention in the agrarian sector via the expansion of the taxation of soybean exports since 2003. As described in chapter 1, this export tax was at the heart of the conflict that pitted the national government against soybean growers in 2008. In the midst of this conflict, popular social movements mobilized in support of the national government, among them, several peasant movements and the FTV. This support was reflected in a "roundtable" (*mesa coordinadora*) created in June 2008 by peasant and indigenous peoples organizations, demanding "effective participation . . . in the design of agrarian policies" (in addition to the suspension of land evictions and a new land legislation).[5]

In this context, the national government launched a series of initiatives directly aimed at garnering support from small farmers, peasants, and rural workers. One of these initiatives was the transformation of the Social Agricultural Program (PSA), a program that was renewed annually, into a permanent office. The PSA was upgraded and turned into the Sub-Secretaría de Desarrollo Rural y Agricultura Familiar (SSDRAF, the Sub-Secretary of Rural Development and Family Farming).[6] Below, I present a description of the ceremony launching the SSDRAF in October 2008 to underscore three points: first, to illustrate how the government recognizes popular actors in symbolic and institutional terms. Second, I pay close attention to the views of social movement leaders, clearly showing that they are not government dupes. Third, I zoom in on the effects of these policies at the local level, stressing the dilemmas and risks they pose for peasant and indigenous movements.

The launching of the SSDRAF was staged in the sports center of a union, located in a working-class suburb of greater Buenos Aires. The streets were filled with buses that brought people from all over Argentina, paid for by the SSDRAF and the FoNAF (*Foro Nacional de Agricultura Familiar*, National Forum of Family Agriculture), a network of rural organizations created to underpin the work of the SSDRF (more on this below). I bumped into leaders and members of several peasant movements; every peasant organization of Argentina seemed to be in attendance. I chatted with an activist of a peasant organization from Chaco province, and he told me that "the government sometimes gives money, but instead of uniting us to reach agreements about land, water, and other important issues, no, they give us money to divide the organizations. For the public officials, those issues are not a priority."

In the packed stadium, I met the members of MoCaFor and we listened to a speech from the head of the SSDRAF. He repeatedly mentioned the "small producers and indigenous peoples" (*pequeños productores y pueblos originarios*) and elicited spontaneous applause when offering Peronist slogans ("our aim is to achieve social justice, political independence, and economic sovereignty"). When he announced programs that would be developed by the SSDRAF, a MoCaFor leader whispered in my ear: "If only half of that would come true."

President Cristina Kirchner closed the event, mentioning the "rural workers, peasants, and the rural family" (*trabajadores y trabajadoras rurales, campesinos, y la familia rural*) and prompting enthusiastic applause and ovations from the crowd. "I feel a *great* honor being here today, with those who work the land from sunrise to sunset, *from sunrise to sunset!*" said the president, emphasizing the latter phrase in the midst of the applause. "And with the men and women who, throughout the country, contribute every day to building food sovereignty for the Argentine people." She mentioned the importance of creating the SSDRAF in order to have "an institutional area within the state that takes into account the small producers of our country." The president closed her speech with a remembrance of her grandfather, "who had a dairy farm, and worked from sunrise to sunset."

For anyone reading between the lines, the celebratory reference to people "working the land from sunrise to sunset" was a not-that-subtle critique of soybean growers, which during the conflict with the government were depicted by public officials as absentee proprietors who did not want to contribute (via taxes) to the rest of the nation. Furthermore, the concept of food sovereignty that she mentioned several times during the speech was a nod to peasant organizations: the term had been promoted by the global peasant organization Via Campesina, to which many of the organizations at the event were associated.

The comments made to me by the peasant activist and MoCaFor leader suggest that the peasant movements do not take the words of the government at face value. For instance, I traveled to Formosa some weeks later and listened to the president's speech with Nélida. "What she's saying is very nice . . . we'll see if she delivers what she promises," was her reaction. In short, it would be a mistake to think that peasants uncritically support the government. At the same time, the government's institutional recognition can redirect time, energy, and resources from contentious collective action, as my ensuing field-work in Formosa suggested.

Some weeks after the launching of the SSDRAF, I traveled to Formosa, heading to Sarambí. On the night of my arrival, I had dinner with Julio, a local leader of MoCaFor. While catching up, he told me that the PSA "was a bandage, it really didn't solve anything, it never worked," and that MoCaFor was participating in a provincial roundtable organized by the FoNAF (*Foro Nacional de Agricultura Familiar*, National Forum of Family Agriculture). Still, all the resources coming from the national SSDRAF (the former PSA) were channeled through provincial and regional roundtables organized by the FoNAF. "Even though we aren't Kirchneristas, it's better to change things from within," Julio said, justifying their participation in the roundtables. He complained that the Formosan representative of the PSA (still using the old denomination) had invited some organizations to the provincial roundtable that were like "a rubber stamp . . . like the MAF, totally coopted by the government," in reference to the Movimiento Agrario de Formosa (Formosan Agrarian Movement; see chapter 2). MoCaFor and the MAF compete for the resources from the national government; thus MoCaFor leaders fear that they may be sidelined, since a portion of these resources is first allocated to the provincial government.

A few days later, the MoCaFor offices in Sarambí were abuzz; representatives of several organizations of small producers, peasants, and indigenous peoples were arriving for a meeting of the ACINA, *Asamblea Campesina Indígena del Norte Argentino* (Peasant and Indigenous Assembly of the Argentine North, see Figures 4.1, 4.2, and 4.3). Isidoro, a leader of MoCaFor and the main organizer of the event, told me that the organizations linked to the FoNAF wanted to present the event as a FoNAF assembly, "but that belongs to the government, and we want to have an independent meeting" (*nos queremos reunir por afuera*). Two NGOs linked to the Catholic Church had provided funds, and the goal of the meeting was to determine how to gain access to the resources of the SSDRAF channeled through the provincial roundtable. "We don't want to be excluded from the distribution [of resources], or to have the MAF be the only organization of small producers at the roundtable," Isidoro said. They were also expecting presentations by national public officials to explain how the SSDRAF would work and how the funds would be distributed. The next day, nearly 70 people gathered to discuss

FIGURE 4.1 Women cooking for the ACINA

FIGURE 4.2 People gathered in the ACINA

these issues, and then we broke into small groups of seven for further discussions and to create posters. Several posters summarized concerns about the
SSDRAF and the need to be recognized by the government (see Figure 4.3).

A month later, I traveled from Sarambí to the city of Formosa with two
MoCaFor members to attend the meeting of the provincial roundtable organized by the FoNAF. We met other members of MoCaFor at the house of
Elisa, who lives in the city. While we sipped mate on Elisa's sunbathed patio,
Oscar, a member of MoCaFor in Moreno, complained that "the nation [the
national government] hasn't given us even one peso yet, but we're already busy
thinking what [agricultural] machinery we're going to buy, how are we going
to spend the money coming from the sub-secretary [the SSDRAF], and that
distracts us from the struggle."

The next day, we gathered in a building owned by the Catholic Church
to discuss MoCaFor's strategies for the FoNAF roundtable. Most of the
conversation revolved around resource concerns and debates about which
organization would have the right to represent family farmers at the roundtable. A back-and-forth dialogue between Arturo (a leader of MoCaFor near
Moreno), Isidoro, and Julio (both leaders of MoCaFor in Sarambí-Monte
Azul) encapsulates these concerns.

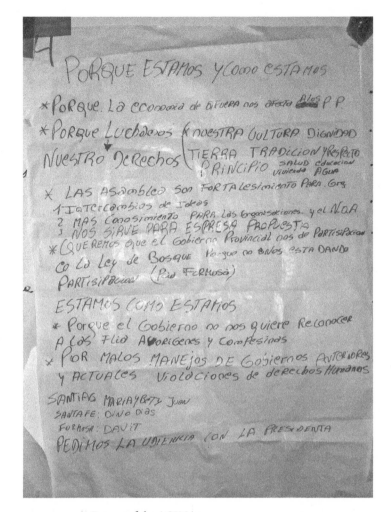

FIGURE 4.3 Posters of the ACINA

ARTURO: We don't want the guys from the PAIPPA or the MAF at the [provincial] roundtable. The roundtable has to work well [representatives of the provincial roundtables gathered at higher-level regional roundtables]. And we have to aim for that at the regional roundtable, because if the regional [roundtable] is strong, we'll be stronger. If we slack off [*si aflojamos*], they [PAIPPA and the MAF] will get in because they're skillful.

ISIDORO: And they have money.

ARTURO: They have economic power.

JULIO: They have mobility; they have economic power.

ARTURO: And they can talk, they can really talk [*mucha lengua tienen*]. We have to be aware that the roundtable is a political decision. And the national government doesn't want to lose face with the provincial government; it will be a big struggle.

JULIO: We have to have a representative at the regional [roundtable].

ARTURO: The provincial roundtable is weak, let's be realistic. Because there wasn't any money. And the same thing happened with the regional. If we have a strong position within the provincial roundtable, we'll also be strong at the regional [roundtable].

I joined MoCaFor representatives at the FoNAF provincial roundtable the next day. We gathered with representatives of several provincial organizations at another Catholic Church building on the outskirts of the city of Formosa from morning until late in the afternoon. Most of the hours were spent discussing the bylaws of the roundtable, who had the right to represent small farmers, and the next steps to ensure that resources would "come down" (*que bajen*) from the national government (a discussion, as Bourdieu's epigraph suggests, involving classificatory schemes, the representation of groups, and their mobilization and demobilization).

In summary, the creation of the SSDRAF was a powerful sign from the national government in terms of recognizing peasant families as a valid actor in food production and rural life. Nevertheless, as the up-close analysis of the effects of this recognition at the local level suggests, symbolic and institutional recognition also has its perils. The funds that had been promised to strengthen local organizations through the FoNAF roundtables were, as of 2011, arriving very slowly or not at all. Furthermore, as hinted by Oscar's comment in Elisa's house, the endless meetings and the constant bickering distracted peasants "from the struggle."

When I traveled to Formosa in 2011 to present my research to MoCaFor activists, I further registered the dilemmas of institutional recognition. I took these fieldnotes at an internal meeting of a peasant social movement while Nélida and Silvio, two vocal rank-and-file members, debated participation in the institutional spaces opened by the national government.

NÉLIDA: We went to countless forums in Buenos Aires and it was useless. We only went to eat and travel . . .

SILVIO: The organizations are useless because they [the government] have the power.

NÉLIDA: Because Kirchner used it. We were like animals they brought to Buenos Aires; I've lost track of how many forums I have gone to in Buenos Aires.

SILVIO: Okay, fine, but you knew that when you went there. You're the first culprit.

NÉLIDA: No, sir. I went to learn and to see what was going on.

SILVIO: On one hand, that's okay, but at the same time, it serves them [the authorities].

These bittersweet tones also emerged when discussing the role of organizations and their participation in and influence on government policies.

SILVIO: You know, the movement says, "The nation [the national government] says that we must organize to access things, we have to organize in order to have a voice and vote." But the truth is that you have neither a voice nor a vote, not anything.

NÉLIDA: I saw that the nation [the national government] at one time gave lots of attention to organizations in many places. They allowed them to participate, to talk. And afterwards, they faded when they did what they wanted, they solved one thing, they fixed another thing, and it is a strategy they have to win you over. In Buenos Aires, we met with the people from the Secretary of Agriculture and we took part in the Ministry for Social Development. We are still there today, but they conditioned you.

Members of the peasant movement, in short, came to feel sidelined and see their participation in public events as a self-serving strategy of politicians. Yet they also believe that it was hard to disengage from their connections to the government, lest they be isolated, lose their voice, or be left without resources. The conversation between Nélida and Silvio shows that peasants are keenly aware of the pitfalls of institutional recognition, but they also find it hard to turn their backs on an influential ally. The ambiguous relationship with authorities surfaced again in 2009, when Monte Azul peasants suffered the consequences of yet another agrochemical drift (which I present in the next chapter).

Conclusion

To ignore the self-interested element in peasant resistance is to ignore the determinate context not only of peasant politics, but of most lower-class politics. It is precisely the fusion of self-interest and resistance that is the vital force animating the resistance of peasants and proletarians ... "Bread-and-butter" issues are the essence of lower-class politics and resistance.

—JAMES C. SCOTT (1986: 26–27)

Some people see things that are and ask: why? Some people dream of things that never were and ask: why not? Some people have to go to work and don't have time for all that.

—GEORGE CARLIN *(quoted in Gould and Lewis 2014)*

This chapter stands in contrast to the previous one. Whereas in chapter 3 I argued that a lack of respect and recognition fueled protests, here I claim that, somewhat paradoxically, the recognition of peasant organizations created barriers for contentious collective action. To capture this process, I used the terms dual pressure and institutional recognition instead of resorting to old labels like "co-optation." I refrain from using this term for two reasons.

By implying that leaders and members are sell-outs or easily duped—that is, that people are corrupt or dumb—the term "co-optation" becomes sociologically thin. Co-optation is a term that usually comes "from the outside in"; it gives short shrift to the situated agency of both leaders and constituents. It would be shortsighted to explain demobilization as a direct result of authorities and national allies manipulating local leaders of MoCaFor or to assert that local leaders control their constituents. "Co-optation" overlooks the pressures that leaders face and the multiple relationships that explain social movement trajectories. It also fails to capture the political significance of the pressing survival needs of subordinated actors (misunderstanding, as James C. Scott argues, the key elements of lower class politics). The etymology of "co-optation" ("mid 17th century, from the Latin *cooptare*, from *co*-'together' and *optare*-'choose'") actually conveys the agency in demobilization that I am proposing here,[7] but in political parlance, the term is ridden with derogatory connotations.

With the concepts of dual pressure and institutional recognition, I unraveled the dilemmas faced by popular organizations and the relational field they navigate. In situations where social movements compete with other organizations for resources and political allegiances, leaders need to respond to the material demands of their constituents while trying to maintain a certain level of autonomy (Fox 1994, Hellman 1994). I kept normative and judgmental labels at bay and instead, concentrated on the multiple relationships between national and provincial authorities, national social movements, provincial social movement leaders, constituents, and local populations. In doing so, I paid close attention the dynamics of mobilization *within* movements (Wolford 2010), which in turn help to eschew a romantic view or the idealization of "resistance" (Abu-Lughod 1990).[8] In other words, informed by my ethnographic fieldwork, I showed that demobilization processes resulted from a series of relational mechanisms linking leaders, constituents (both mobilized and not mobilized), allies, and authorities at different scales (from local, to provincial, to national). Paraphrasing Belinda Robnett's argument that "movements mobilize leaders as much as leaders mobilize movements" (Robnett 1997: 8), here I argued that leaders *de*mobilize movements (as conventional wisdom would have it), as much as movements *de*mobilize leaders. In the next chapter, I further scrutinize these processes by zooming in on the reactions (or the lack thereof) to an agrochemical drift in 2009.

5 ACCOMMODATION

PEASANTS NEGOTIATING GM CROPS AND AGROCHEMICAL EXPOSURE (2009–2013)

In February 2009, I received an email from one of the younger members of MoCaFor in Sarambí telling me that on the coming Monday, they would distribute pamphlets for the anniversary of the 2003 contamination. On Tuesday, I sent an email asking how it went. This was his response:

> We first suspended the pamphleting because of the rain, and yesterday we suspended it again; it's raining again. My dad [a MoCaFor leader] just came back from the countryside, and I don't know when we'll do it. Another thing: my aunt has welts, as if she was burnt; we think it's the poison again. Also ducks, chickens, and geese are dying throughout [Monte Azul]. We made a complaint to the police, the policemen stopped by, and as usual, the hospital didn't give my aunt an answer. It looks as if it was on purpose, right when we thought about doing something. But here we are, as always.

In the ensuing days, I continued exchanging emails with him and other members of MoCaFor, eager to hear more about what was happening. The message below from Elisa, an active member of MoCaFor living in the capital of the province, encapsulates the worrisome scenario people were facing.

> Hello Pablo,
> It's incredible how cruel and inhuman this system is, and its followers . . . I really don't have words to describe them . . .

they cause so much damage and pain, they make you feel so impotent; you have no idea. Nobody dares confirm that the agrochemicals are the cause, or say what we should put on the painful welts that Nélida is suffering from. [It's] as if she was burned. The kids have irritated eyes. And Doña Marta has a headache and has been weak in bed, but she had to leave her five sick kids so she could work at the farmers' market. No, it's indescribable what you come to feel . . . We all complain but nobody does anything.

But to surrender would be to die. We'll keep fighting with the strength we have left. We are working on notes to send to national organizations, and preparing documentation to present as evidence.

Anyway, the struggle goes on.

I traveled to Formosa some weeks later. When I arrived into the rural communities and met with peasants, I confirmed what the emails from MOCaFor members suggested: no disruptive protests had occurred following what looked like an agrochemical drift very similar to the one of 2003.

This gap between what I was somehow expecting (the emergence of a protest in reaction to the agrochemical drift like in 2003) and the lack of contention is at the core of this chapter. I zoom in on the relationship between social movements and government actors in the aftermath of the agrochemical drift of 2009, paying special attention to the interplay between the *responses and discourses of authorities* and peasants' views and actions, which I understand as an instance of "performative governance." Drawing on Erving Goffman's concept of "impression management" (1959), performative governance applies to situations "in which impressions of committed governance are staged and maintained by officials, yet effective inclusion of citizenry in the decision-making process is negligible" (Futrell 1999: 495). I understand performative governance as a composite of authorities' impression management and "performative speech acts" (Austin 1962). J. L. Austin elaborated the concept of performative utterances to indicate those speech acts that, rather than merely describing the world, intervene in it and remake it (for instance, "I now pronounce you husband and wife" in contrast to "the sky is blue"). I build on this concept to indicate that authorities can "do things with words" by deploying performative actions that create effects in their audiences (in this case, social movement constituents).

In the second part of the chapter, I scrutinize the *subjective understandings* of contention, GM crops, and agrochemical drifts. I seek to unpack the meaning-making processes that contribute to the flattening out of contention by examining the role of rumors, processes of blame-assignment, and the reproduction of elites' views regarding contention. I also explore the local views on GM crops and agrochemicals, showing the accommodations and adaptations developed by peasant households (for instance, the adoption of GM cottonseeds promoted by the provincial government) to better understand the ways in which peasants *negotiate and adapt* to the social and environmental impacts of GM crops.

Authorities and Performative Governance

In February 2009, six years after the contentious events of 2003, peasant families of Monte Azul experienced dèjá-vu. Nélida had a burning sensation in her neck, blisters on her skin, and dry and sore lips; a neighbor got blisters all over her back. Hundreds of chickens, which peasants of Monte Azul let roam freely, died suddenly (see Figure 5.1). Nélida went to the hospital in Sarambí, where she told the director that they were having the same problems as in 2003: "He told me that it was possible [that they were affected by agrochemicals] but that no doctor in Sarambí was prepared [to diagnose it]."

FIGURE 5.1 Dead chickens

The people of Monte Azul took their children to the hospital to cure the sudden eruption of pimples on their skin. The children and people suffering from skin rashes were told they had scabies. Nélida and her brother Isidoro went to the hospital (an institution they see as the turf of political brokers) and talked to "the guy that runs the whole hospital, he's like the hospital's dog, guarding it." Nélida told him that the tanks with "poisons" (agrochemicals) were being cleaned near people's houses and the community health center. "The hospital is not in charge of agricultural matters," was the response they received. MoCaFor wrote a communiqué denouncing the situation but, unlike 2003, no contentious collective action took place.

Shortly after peasants visited the nearby hospital and complained about the effects of agrochemical exposure, provincial authorities unexpectedly arrived in Monte Azul. Dozens of doctors, employees, and authorities from the provincial Ministry of Human Development gathered Monte Azul's inhabitants in the local community health center. Authorities told the people there was no reason to be alarmed, that they would take blood samples to determine if they had traces of agrochemicals in their bodies, and proceeded to distribute antiparasitic drugs to everyone.

Authorities did not allow people to ask questions, but Nélida and Horacio spoke up to say that the reason for their ailments was not parasites but the agrochemicals used in the soybean fields. A heated debate ensued, with authorities insisting that soybeans were grown around the world and that the government authorized the use of agrochemicals.

Nélida and Horacio replied that soybeans also created problems around the world and that the poisons may be harmless, but the government was not controlling agrochemical use.

The employees from the ministry administered surveys, took blood from 140 people, and sent the samples to be analyzed in Buenos Aires. The people in Monte Azul never received the results.

After the contamination, people in Monte Azul "were growing *very* anxious," as Mario Hispano told me. Hispano did an environmental assessment for peasants in 2003 while he was working as field technician for the PSA. By 2009, he had three years of experience as head of the PSA in Formosa, and he was reappointed as provincial representative when this federal program was promoted to the SSDRAF. The newly created SSDRAF, the Secretaría, received a note from small farmers of Monte Azul listing how many chickens each peasant had lost (700 in total). Hispano organized meetings with the affected peasants and told them that the Secretaría was going to compensate them for their losses. He also brought peasants to the city of Formosa (the province's capital) to be tested for the presence of specific agrochemicals, although he was skeptical about the results: "I knew the tests would turn out negative ... and they did." The tests that can be done in Formosa are for insecticides, not the herbicides that are used in GM soybean production. "And back then, it was not the season when insecticides would be used. But even if I explain that, they won't hear me [the people of Monte Azul]. They are very anxious." Throughout our conversation, he repeatedly mentioned people's anxiety, "And we needed to do something ... Peasants told me, 'we are tired of seeing people coming, taking blood samples, and then nothing happens.'" The Secretaría also organized meetings to discuss the provincial environmental laws because, according to Hispano, "a lawyer needs to train them on what to do in cases of contamination; because peasants always take the wrong path: they go to the police, or to the mayor, or they want to burn the fumigating machine."

In 2009, the peasants of Monte Azul did not try to burn the fumigating machine, but rather appealed through the institutional channels recently created by the national government. Peasant leaders sent a note to the national Secretary of Environment requesting a study of the environmental impact on the community. Horacio, a leader of MoCaFor in Monte Azul, sent a note to the Ministry of Health asking for the intervention of the *Comisión Nacional de Investigación sobre Agroquímicos*, the CNIA (National Commission of Research on Agrochemicals), closing the note saying he was "confident in the prompt response of the Minister." The CNIA had been created in January 2009, in the aftermath of the conflict between soybean growers and the national government. Its purpose was to investigate cases of agrochemical drifts, in large part motivated by the publicity of cases in the province of Córdoba (see chapter 1).

In March, Monte Azul families received a visit from a representative of the CNIA. He wrote a report that clearly backed up peasants' complaints about the contamination, mentioning that provincial authorities did not do a study of environmental impact and pinpointed a series of environmental hazards affecting local families.[1] The conclusions and recommendations of the report closely followed the demands that had been made repeatedly by peasant leaders, specifying that there were "enough elements to assert the existence of problems of environmental contamination due to the use of pesticides resulting in a risk for the local population" and that "local inhabitants should not demonstrate the poisoning but instead the State should create proper and impartial institutional procedures to assess health damages, to prove there is no environmental contamination, and to demonstrate that the local habitat does not pose a health risk." The report also recommended the suspension of pesticide use, closer control of the soybean companies, and the creation of "instances of participation for the control of pesticide management." The report even recognized the clash between the peasants' mode of production and that fostered by soybean growers, saying that "the coexistence between a productive model for self-consumption and an extensive industrial agriculture is very hard" and asserting that the introduction of soybean production had disrupted the lifestyle of peasant families that had been developed in "close connection to the environment."[2]

Performative Governance as an Obstacle for Contention

The reactions of the provincial authorities, the support of the SSDRAF, and the report of the CNIA acknowledged the health problems of the local population and the environmental hazards created by soybean production and the use of agrochemicals. Combined, the actions of provincial and national authorities showed peasants that "something was being done" about the health and environmental problems affecting them. Unlike in 2003 when peasants blocked the provincial roads because they were "not being heard," in 2009 the government was paying attention to their complaints. In terms of popular contention, the actions of public offices curtailed local leaders' abilities to frame the situation as a denial of the contamination.

I use the term performative governance to refer to the actions of authorities (in Formosa and elsewhere) that respond to people's demands without addressing the underlying causes motivating those claims (Futrell 1999). I draw on the idea of performance in a twofold sense. First, I understand performance as it was defined by sociologist Erving Goffman (1959) in terms of "impression management," not as cynical or manipulative action but as a means of managing the ways others interpret interactions and characters in public life. Second, I see the official reports as performative utterances; that is, speech acts that "bring about or achieve *by* saying something, such as convincing, persuading, deterring, and even, say, surprising or misleading" (Austin 1962, 108, original emphasis).

In the events presented above, I define the responses of the authorities as an illustration of performative governance for two reasons. First, the results of the analyses of blood samples taken by the provincial Ministry of Human Development were never shared with local inhabitants. As Hispano underscored, the SSDRAF administered blood tests mostly due to the pressure of peasants, which suggests the interplay between actions and audience

(Alexander and Mast 2006, Mische 2008). Moreover, provincial authorities never attempted to regulate soybean production or created a more systematic or efficient control of the use of agrochemicals. Despite the clarity of the CNIA's report, it never translated into concrete actions to stop fumigations or enforce regulations of agrochemical use. The report, however, was a way of "doing things with words" (Austin 1962) since it sent the message that the government was dealing with the peasants' demands.

Some months after the report was issued, the national minister of health was replaced due to disputes within the government. As a result, the public official in charge of the CNIA was replaced as well. The newly appointed official continued the Commission's meetings, but the language about agrochemicals became even more industry-friendly and no concrete actions were taken to curb the indiscriminate use of agrochemicals at the national level. In 2012, the *Auditoría General de la Nación*, the office that audits the federal government, issued a report concluding that the work of the CNIA has been stalled since 2010.[3] In short, even when the deeds of street level officials seem animated by the best intentions, their actions ultimately convey the sense that the problems were being addressed and there was no need for a fight (i.e., staging a contentious performance) in order to solve the issue.

The Subjective and Discursive Constraints of Contentious Collective Action

Compliance does not consist of conscious rule following or straightforward exchange, but of pursuing personal agendas by maneuvering among obstacles, obstacles put in place by other people and past experience. Often people share agendas, maneuvers, and obstacles; those people are ripe for collective action. The exercise of power consists of placing obstacles and of offering rewards for completing the course. These lessons hold for compliance, passive resistance, and open revolt. They hold for individual action and for collective action as well.

—CHARLES TILLY *(1991: 601)*

Taking heed of studies on environmental suffering among the destitute in Argentina (Auyero and Swistun 2009), in the ensuing sections I zoom in on the subjective understandings creating obstacles for contention. Specifically, I focus on the processes of blame assignment, the role of rumors, and symbolic violence, which refers to those instances when the subordinated accept definitions of the situation put forward by more powerful actors (Bourdieu 1991). In what follows, I present diverse points of view, including those of people actively participating in the movement, those who are marginally involved, and those who *do not* participate in MoCaFor. These views are *subjective but not individual*, in the sense that the sources of these interpretations are *social*: their origins hearken back to power inequalities, the ambiguous results yielded by previous contentious events, and a history of social movement organizations tainted by suspicion—the obstacles of Tilly's epigraph above.

A first example of these constraints is the shifting assignment of blame for peasants' suffering. The excerpt below, taken from my fieldnotes, exemplifies this issue by capturing a disagreement between Nélida, a representative of MoCaFor in Monte Azul, and her sister Nina, who participates in the movement sporadically.

It is a Sunday mid-morning and Nina, Nélida's sister, and her husband Mariano pay a visit to Nélida's farm and house where I am staying. We bring some chairs and gather to chat and drink mate. Mariano says that a neighbor rented his field, adding that they "will surely grow soybeans" and he says the soy growers brought a "mosquito" (the fumigating machine) that is taller than the one used before. "They are going to fill the grass with poison," says Mariano, concerned because his animals will not be able to eat the grass.

Nina says that neighbors who rent their fields to grow soybeans are to blame: "if you invite a thief into your home, then you cannot complain if you are robbed."

Nélida retorts eagerly, arguing that *the government* is to blame and not the people; "they [the government] allow the *empresarios* to come and grow soy without controlling the use of poisons." Nélida was nonetheless cautious about the rights of soy growers: "You can't go there and tell them how they should work, that's their right." But she added: "the government should control them."

"Now people are not willing to work, they just want money, a little salary (*un sueldito*)" adds Nina. She goes on to say that in the past, local people were more willing to work: "everybody had their corn, their manioc, their vegetables, but not now, no, they don't work the land."

Nélida gets riled up again: "but people have no tools to work, the government does not give them anything!"

Nina stands her ground, remarking that the neighbors are guilty because if everybody got together and blocked the soy growers, they would not have problems. "But people prefer to rent their land rather than work it themselves, so *they* have to be blamed," Nina concludes.

"No, that's not true, the *government* is to blame," Nélida replies, shaking her head and leaving the room to bring more water for the mate we are sipping (July 2, 2007).

As my fieldwork developed, I began to notice that many peasants recalled the roadblocks of 2003 with bittersweet undertones. People remembered that they had to endure high temperatures during the day and chilling cold at night, without getting any concrete compensation for their loss. Others, especially those living in dire poverty, hinted that *any* compensation for the lost crops would have been better than ending up empty-handed. Among peasants only loosely associated with MoCaFor, the lack of concrete solutions inspired suspicion: some, expressing mistrust, suggested that the leaders might have reached a deal for their own benefit. Paula and her brother Luis brought up this last point in 2008. I interviewed them in their very modest house, which was made of adobe clay and wood and built next to a large soybean field. After expressing their frustration with losing their crops in 2003 but not receiving any compensation, they spontaneously began to talk about the role of MoCaFor leaders:

PAULA: And after that time [in 2003], they didn't mobilize again. That's why we thought that they were benefitting themselves and we were just supporting them [during the protests]. I think their families [of the local MoCaFor leaders] were the only ones who profited.

LUIS: And they got some *pesos* . . .

PAULA: . . . and they were fixed.

PABLO: But . . . who told you they were fixed? Because it depends who says that.

LUIS: Well, you know, here everybody knows me. Somebody told me.

Toward the end of the interview, I asked them if they wanted to add anything. As Paula talked to me, she contrasted her situation to that of social movement leaders in terms of access to resources and information.

It's good that you come here, to know, because when one is poor, and one doesn't have [the means] to travel far, one doesn't know anything. And if someone comes from another place, at least we know what's going on. Through conversation, you can understand [*Conversando se entiende*]. In those cases, we didn't know anything. They [MoCaFor leaders] went to Buenos Aires, Resistencia, Formosa, Salta [cities in Argentina] . . . They went as far as they could! But if we are poor and we don't have much, we cannot go to those places. And we are just left with what they come back and tell us.

As far as I know, these rumors were not true, but they nonetheless had real consequences. Paula and Luis's beliefs show the negative effects of the endless waiting.[4] Rumors and gossip are an everyday occurrence, but the histories of other peasant organizations also help explain why Paula and Luis gave credit to the rumors they heard. Recall the history of the Movimiento Agrario de Formosa, the MAF, described in chapter 2. The leaders of MAF organized a peasant movement in the mid 1980s, and a decade later, they made a pact with the governor. Throughout my fieldwork, people told me several stories about sell-out politicians and community leaders. The rumors about MoCaFor leaders, although inaccurate, rang true in a social context marred by stories of using leadership in organizations as instruments for personal gain.

Obstacles to mobilization were also suggested by the views expressed by Monte Azul peasants not affiliated with MoCaFor. In 2009 I approached some Monte Azul peasants who were not affiliated with MoCaFor to hear their ideas about GM crops, agrochemical exposure, and the 2003 protests. The following fieldnotes suggest that many peasants endorsed the interpretations put forward by local elites.

I go the farmers' market that does not belong to MoCaFor, on the main boulevard of Sarambí. I approach one of the stands selling vegetables that is attended by a middle-aged man with a thick moustache and callous hands. I introduce myself, saying that I am a sociologist interested in the production of soybeans in Formosa and the 2003 conflicts. He introduces himself using his surname, Pérez. Two other peasants join us for the conversation: a woman wearing a floral dress and a slender man wearing worn jeans and a baseball cap (which in the area is a sort of marker of being a worker). When I brought up the road blockades, Pérez says that many people "saw the opportunity and joined in, expecting to get some money out if it. Everything was politics, all politics." The other man adds that agrochemicals are harmless: "that's why the government approved them." He continues, saying: "If you are on your plot and you use something that affects me, I have to make my claim to *you*. Why should you ask the government to pay if the damage was done by someone else?" Pérez adds a comment about the manager of the warehouse where soybean growers keep their machinery: "They *say* that he died because he was manipulating poisons [agrochemicals] all the time" [stressing the "say" as if not trusting what he heard]. "They say that many chickens died due to the chemicals used on soybeans," the woman chimes in. She mentions a kid in Monte Azul who suddenly got many pimples, to which Pérez retorts that the skin rashes were "because of a lack of hygiene; the doctors went to the community and they did the analyses, they took blood samples, and it turned out that everyone is healthy. I have a lump in my back, but I don't pay attention to it, you have to die from something, right?" (June 20, 2009).

The lack of consensus on who should be blamed for the agrochemical exposure, the discourse of peasants repeating the views of provincial authorities, and the rumors about social movement leaders combined to create doubts regarding the effectiveness of contentious collective action. Paula's recollection about the situation in 2003 encapsulates this mistrust:

PAULA: And because they couldn't reach an agreement in a good way, they were going to do it the hard way. [One MoCaFor leader said] that we should . . . either die or save ourselves.

PABLO: What do you mean?

PAULA: Well, they [the soybean company] sent a group to reach an agreement the good way or the hard way, answering what we asked for. And Nélida said: "If they come, you have to be alert, we have to confront them." [But] what we have to do is to chat, to explain, to talk to them. And make them understand, they have to understand . . . [MoCaFor leaders] wanted to agree the hard way. We are not going to challenge them [the authorities and the soybean company], but talk to them properly. Talk. Because by talking people can agree, not by fighting. They [the MoCaFor leaders] got mad and they didn't want to reach an agreement, they wanted to solve it the hard way . . . We didn't go to fight, but to solve things properly. And that was that. They got mad, and came to fight . . . We have to talk to them nicely.

Paula's views suggest a dilemma that became a centerpiece for MoCaFor leaders, who were increasingly torn between confronting and negotiating. The following excerpts culled from my 2009 fieldnotes reflect these dynamics, involving the relationships between MoCaFor and other organizations of the province, and between MoCaFor and public officials. The excerpts show how, in the everyday activities of peasant life and social movements, MoCaFor members increasingly felt that the discursive space was narrowing, particularly for expressions of dissent.

We ride Julio's scooter to the farm of his mother, Nélida, in Monte Azul. While sipping mate, Julio briefs Nélida about the meeting on rural policies that he attended a few days ago in Formosa. The provincial minister of the community, Zorrilla, praised the provincial welfare program for the rural poor, called the PAIPPA, in front of Braulio, the president of the provincial roundtable of peasant organizations.

"Zorrilla said that the issues of the small farmers were solved by the PAIPPA," Julio explained, "that we should leave personal ambitions aside and not raise any flags . . . I don't know how much bullshit he said; that we should join the PAIPPA, and that the PAIPPA was being discriminated against because it wasn't allowed to join the roundtable."[5]

"If I was there, I would have told him to his face that he was lying," Nélida replies, upset.

"And Braulio sat there, not saying anything" Julio continues. He adds, angered: "I understand him, he has a salary of 2500 pesos for being the chair of the roundtable. I wouldn't criticize him because everybody needs a salary, but why didn't he say anything! He was just sitting there, his mouth completely shut. And I'm not going to say anything, because he is the representative of the roundtable. It won't look good if I say something, because I'm not the roundtable representative" (June 18, 2009).

The next day, Julio recounted the meeting in Formosa to Isidoro, another MoCaFor member, nurturing the tensions between peasant organizations:

[I am on Nélida's farm in Monte Azul and I just witnessed Julio, Nélida's son, and his brother in law, Germán, butcher a pig that Nélida will sell in the farmers' market on Saturday.] Julio and Germán bring

a table outside and place the dead pig over it. We chat as Julio pours
boiling water over the pig and he and Germán peel off its hair. Some
minutes later, Isidoro joins us and Julio tells him what happened at the
meeting in Formosa [he repeats the story from the day before]. While
Julio describes the situation, Isidoro snorts and shows his disapproval
with a tsk-tsk. "If Braulio is not up to the task, he should resign,"
Isidoro says. Julio adds that Braulio told him that they shouldn't fight,
that if they barked, they wouldn't get anything, "But it isn't fighting,
it's telling it as it is!" says Julio (June 19, 2009).

Some days later, I was at the warehouse that doubles as the MoCaFor offices in Sarambí, typing fieldnotes on my small laptop. Nélida, Isidoro, and
Horacio were preparing for an upcoming meeting with the representative of
the national SSDRAF and they invited me to join their discussion on the
best strategy to implement.

Horacio says that they have to be more diplomatic, that the way they
talk may sound aggressive to other people. "I'm uncouth [*bruta*],
I don't know how to say things," says Nélida apologetically. I add that
is a matter of saying the same things but in a different way. "We won't
stop saying the things we want to say," Isidoro chimes in, "but, as Pablo
says, we should think about the way we say them." [They briefly talk
about the roundtable.] "And they see us as the troublemakers" (*como
los que hacemos quilombo*), continues Isidoro. "At the roundtable they
think discussing is fighting" (June 25, 2009).

The following week, this discussion was amplified from the local to the
provincial level, when representatives of MoCaFor from different regions of
Formosa gathered to discuss the best approach to take in an upcoming meeting scheduled with the representative of the SSDRAF.

"We need to be more diplomatic in the way we talk to the PSA. We
have to make clear that we want advice, but we don't want them to tell
us what to do. And if they tell us what to do and we don't want to do
it, we are not discrediting or attacking them; they just have to accept
that we don't want to do it . . . We need to propose to the PSA that
we want to be sincere. They should tell us what they don't like about
us, but they also should respect our decisions. And this while being
diplomatic, without fighting." "So we need to put a gag on Isidoro,"

intervenes Nélida, at which we all laugh. "I'm going to shut up," Nélida continues in an apologetic tone, "sometimes I say things badly and then I regret it." When Mario Hispano arrives with two aides and joins the meeting, Horacio takes the lead, saying: "Sometimes we are not diplomatic, we don't talk in a nice way, but that's the way we talk, is not that we want to clash with the PSA" (June 29, 2009).

At a general level, this situation can be seen as an instance of what social movement scholar James Jasper calls the "naughty or nice dilemma." As Jasper explains, "Naughty actions—those of which most players disapprove—pay off if you can obtain a quick and irreversible victory, but if such engagements are prolonged, your reputation will suffer ... The risk is that some powerful player or alliance will decide to punish your transgressions" (2006: 107). In this case, what these interactions amount to is the perception among MoCaFor leaders that a discursive field was closing in on them; some of the grassroots members of their movement, the leaders of other organizations, and public officials were suggesting that they subdue their discourse and be less confrontational (the sociologist, i.e., myself, included).

"They Are Killing Us With a Wooden Knife": Accommodating GM Crops and Agrochemical Exposure

In much of the global south, agriculturalists live perilously close to the margin of subsistence. They have little or nothing in the way of reserves or savings that could serve as insurance against a run of bad luck ... An incapacitating illness during the work season, a crop failure, or a large drop in the price of the crop they grow can send them over the edge ... This means, in brief, that farmers in this situation are particularly risk averse; they strive to minimize the danger of a life-threatening economic failure.

—James C. Scott (2012: 5)

The literature on GM crops is vast and includes a variety of approaches, from studies considering them as a further commodification of nature, to their role in the global governance of science and intellectual property rights and their environmental impacts, just to name a few (Stone 2010). When it comes to critical perspectives on what GM crops mean for the future of peasants, however, two main narratives tend to dominate the conversation. One focuses on transgenic crops as an expression of how dominant actors marginalize peasants and increasingly gain control of the global agro-food system. A second narrative positions the latter as a backdrop for peasant resistance to these forces. Both highlight important social implications GM crops have for agriculture, yet we know much less about those situations that do not fit either of these narratives.

Below, I inspect a phenomenon that is infrequently explored: those instances in which peasants *accommodate and adapt* to GM crops and its consequences (rather than resisting them). In other words, I do not analyze how peasants *resist* power but actually how they *negotiate power relationships* from their subordinate position. If we agree with Lila Abu-Lughod that "we should use resistance as a *diagnostic* of power" (1990: 42, original emphasis), then I would argue that the same point can be made about accommodation. In what follows, I present ethnographic data on the relationship between peasants, agrochemicals, and the adoption of GM cotton to show how peasants "minimize the danger of a life-threatening economic failure," as James C. Scott argues.

My fieldwork among peasants in Formosa suggests that they do not object to the production of GM soybeans or the use of agrochemicals in and of themselves. Rather, they are troubled when they both affect their own crops and pose a threat to their daily survival. As Elizabeth Fitting describes in her investigation of GM corn in Mexico, transgenics "may not be a topic of conversation or debate in the countryside, and when it is, the debate is often framed in distinctive ways" (2011: 5). Formosan peasants usually discussed GM crops in the context of their own worries about making ends meet, and their views were informed by their experiences with agricultural production in general. This should not come as a surprise, but I underline the point because research on GM crops sometimes sidesteps a basic ethnographic lesson: paying attention to the localized understandings of social processes that may differ from the researcher's point of view.

In several interviews and everyday conversations with Formosan peasants, for instance, I repeatedly heard the phrase, "I reckon they're working," referring to soybean growers and their use of agrochemicals. In so doing, peasants recognized the right of soybean growers to work their lands as they please and seemed to express certain empathy for people (like them) making a living from agriculture, an always uncertain activity highly dependent on the weather, where timing (for plowing the land, sowing, and harvesting) is key to ensuring a proper yield.

Furthermore, peasants in Formosa regarded transgenic crops as a menace only when it threatened their daily survival. For instance, I asked Isaías (a member of MoCaFor in Moreno) when he decided to file a complaint for the damage to his crops, and he replied that he did so "when the flowers began to fall, and the cotton bolls withered. Just then. Why should I do it before that? If I wasn't affected, I wouldn't make the complaint." He went on to compare the situation with previous years when fumigations were done using a mosquito, the tractor-drawn spray rig:

> In previous years, a mosquito arrived in the area. No one bothered it. It did not bother a single farmer. The job was done correctly and it left. Soybeans are being sowed there, behind those woods: the owner goes with his tractor and he doesn't bother anyone. I am not against farming, but the fumigation cannot be done in the fields with an airplane in a community.

I asked him what happened to the soy growers after the demonstrators forced the crop duster to leave the town (described in chapter 3):

> They harvested their soy. No one interfered with their work. The only problem was the plane. It is said that soy ruins this, or that it has ruined that, but that, at least personally, has not happened to me. If someone rents his soil, he's the owner; he ought to know what he's doing.

Other members of MoCaFor expressed similar views. For example, in the following excerpt, Nelson connects his views on how fumigations should be done with the subordinate position of peasants:

> It was confirmed that the fumigation affected the animals, the humans, and the plantations, and that was the problem. The thing is the soy growers *did* stop. We could stop them in this area. We let them work as long as they use a [fumigating] backpack correctly, not too much; but they weren't respecting anything. The plane would sprinkle [agrochemicals] everywhere; a *compañero* would have his cistern and his house all sprayed with poison. We also denounced this but . . . you see, we are peasants, we are useless, and they are the ones in charge. The one in power is the one who controls, the one at the wheel, who does whatever he wants. The one working the soil only screams.

Nelson clearly stated the point of not being bothered by GM crops per se by saying, "What we are asking them is to sow in the country, far from the populated areas. But they came to spray the town, the farmhouses. That was the battle we had to fight." He went on to say, "I don't care if they grow soybeans, but I'm bothered when they contaminate."

When I visited Monte Azul in 2013, Cintia, a local elementary teacher, was concerned that soybeans growers were regularly burning the agrochemical containers in a field close to the elementary school. "They were burning the containers the whole night, and they were still burning in the morning. The smoke lingered in the air. The kids and the teachers had headaches; the kids asked permission to return to their homes, because they start to have headaches," she said. To get to the school, the kids had to walk by the warehouse where soybean growers keep their machinery and prepare the herbicides. "They get water [for the fumigating machine] from a place next to the school, and their faucets leak all the time . . . We don't say that they shouldn't fumigate, but not in such a way. They have a right to work, but we also have the right to live," Cintia said.

Although peasants expressed that they were mostly bothered by the damage caused by agrochemicals (and not by the production of GM soybeans per se), this does not necessarily mean that their views do not have an environmental aspect. Environmental conflicts can be defined as "any conflict having at its center the dispute for resources or the externalities derived from its use" (Soto Fernández et al. 2007: 64, my translation). The understandings of Formosan peasants may be seen as an instance of the "environmentalism of the poor"; that is, an environmentalism that does not respond to "postmaterialist values" but rather "grows out of distribution conflicts over the use of ecological resources needed for livelihood" (Martinez-Alier 1995: 70). It is also important, however, to be wary about essentialisms that may be implied in labels such as "environmentalism of the poor."

The experience of Formosan peasants is intertwined with the production of cotton, an activity that demands the use of a myriad of often highly toxic agrochemicals. They attempted to transition to more environmentally friendly agriculture by growing vegetables and selling them in the farmers market, but the agrochemical exposures they have suffered since early the 2000s cut this experience short (see chapters 2 and 3). In other words, the practices of Formosan peasants are not necessarily compatible with the idea of a "good peasant in harmony with nature" (on this point, see Fitting 2011: 13–15 and 21–25). This is hardly an idiosyncratic characteristic of Formosan peasants but rather applies to peasantries reliant on monoculture; for instance, activists of the Landless Movement in Brazil face similar problems in promoting agro-ecological practices among peasants in areas of sugarcane production (Wolford 2010). This argument should not be overstated to the point of cynicism, but I discuss the matter to avoid the all-too-common idealization of environmental struggles, which particularly pervade narratives about GM crops in the so-called global South.[6]

When I visited Sarambí in June 2010, I participated in a meeting at MoCaFor offices where representatives of the movement and the members of an NGO were organizing a public presentation to raise awareness about the dangers of agrochemicals. One of the NGO members proposed inviting medical doctors "who know a lot about agrochem—agrotoxics," changing the word mid-sentence to replace "agrochemicals" with "agrotoxics," a term favored by environmental activists. Isidoro, a MoCaFor representative, proposed to have the presentation before the sowing season, "so maybe they will be more respectful" (*así tal vez respetan más*), suggesting that the presentation could induce soybean growers to be more careful when spraying agrochemicals. In the document written after the discussion, they identified two goals for the event: "To put the issue on the table (to inform, clarify, sensitize), so the state takes up the issue. From the citizen's perspective: to propose and construct, to show that many of us are concerned." Nearly a month later around 50 people gathered for the presentation in downtown Sarambí, which was sponsored by the provincial office of the national Sub-Secretary of Rural Development and Family Farming (see Figure 5.2). The effort put into organizing this presentation indicates that the issue of agrochemical exposure is

FIGURE 5.2 Presentation about agrochemicals in Sarambí

still important to MoCaFor and peasants. The public discourse against agrochemicals, however, is still contrasted with what peasants say during quotidian conversations. Julio, for instance, a middle-range leader of MoCaFor told me in 2008 that "the glyphosate wasn't so terrible like the 2,4-D . . . or the aztrazina was even worse! If you touched that, you get burned right there. But the glyphosate . . . if you have a thousand hectares, you can't work it with a hoe, you have to use something [an agrochemical]."

In my latest visits to Monte Azul, I perceived a sense of faltering on the part of MoCaFor members. During conversations and interviews, peasants conveyed a mix of despair and resignation, particularly when talking about their future and agrochemical exposure. Emilia, one of the peasants affected by agrochemicals in 2003, encapsulated people's feelings in a telling metaphor: "They are killing us with a wooden knife; they don't kill you at once but little by little." Similar thoughts were expressed by Artemia, who lives with her husband Elio on a small farm next to a large plot of soybeans. Both of them are seniors, but they still manage to keep their farm producing. In a conversation we had in 2009, after saying that her garden and fruit trees were slowly withering, Artemia added, "Because [the agrochemicals] don't kill the plants at once, they die slowly. And the same will happen to us . . . My kids want me to move away from here, but I don't want to. I like to be here . . . I'm stubborn." In one of my many conversations with Nélida, she saw the future in similarly bleak terms:

> It may be that the government wants all the poor people out of here. Maybe they want to buy all the land, to make people tired, and to see everybody leave. Sooner or later you have to do something. Because if you can't work, if they fumigate and burn all your plants, you can't do anything. You have to leave. Or you have to fight again to make them leave . . . And if you don't do anything, you have to grow the same things they grow if you want to keep living here. So they are getting us used to what they produce.

The phrase uttered by Nélida about "getting us used to what they produce" has a clear referent: the adoption of GM cotton among some of the local peasant families.

On Adoption and Adaptations: GM cotton

In 1990, Emilia's father gave her seven hectares of land he owned in Monte Azul and she started farming it with her husband. He had lost his job in 1987 when the company where he was working as a woodcutter went bankrupt. Emilia shared: "[My husband] is illiterate, he is Paraguayan, and there's no way around it [*no hay para entrarle por ningún lado*]. He cannot find work, neither in politics; if you have an education you may find something in politics, or a [welfare] plan, or anything. But he was already a bit old, and the sawmills didn't want to hire him either." They initially moved to Sarambí, where her husband found some gigs (*changuitas*), and she made some money washing clothes. But after a while, they moved back again: "I said, I'll go to Monte Azul to grow pumpkin, sweet potatoes, cassava, and have milk to feed my children."

Emilia was a vocal activist of MoCaFor when I first met her in 2003, but she has since become less and less involved in the movement, becoming more occupied with the activities of her evangelical church and taking care of her and her family's fragile health. When I visited her in 2010, her grand-daughter had died a few months before. "She was full of life, but then we took her to the hospital because she was having respiratory problems; they told us she died of the H1N1 flu." A feedlot (also known in the US as a CAFO, Concentrated Animal Feeding Operation) had been built near her home a few years prior. "You should see it Pablo, when the wind comes from there, it *stinks*, we cannot breathe. And my daughter lives next to the feedlot," Emilia explained forlornly.

In December 2011, I paid Emilia another a visit at her farm in Monte Azul. As we sat under the shade of a tree next to her humble house, I asked her what she was growing now. "Cotton. I know that it uses poisons and it's bad for us, but we have no choice. Everybody is doing it except Nélida and Isidoro. As they say, *la necesidad tiene cara de hereje* ["necessity knows no bounds" or "beggars can't be choosers"]. The big [farmers] do it because they make money, and the small ones because of necessity, there's no choice." She enumerated the reasons why they were growing GM cotton on six hectares of their farm: they did not have to pay for supplies upfront; the government gave them seeds, and a company linked to the government sowed, fumigated with agrochemicals, harvested the cotton, and took it to the selling point (also managed by the provincial government). Once the process was over, they received whatever money was left, minus the cost of the agrochemicals and the services. "They use an herbicide when the cotton plant has four leaves, then a growth regulator so all the plants are the same height [so the harvest-ing machine works better], then they use a defoliant to let the cotton boll grow alone, and then they harvest. The government doesn't charge us for the poison against the *picudo* [the boll weevil, a beetle that feeds on cotton], and they fumigate every week."

The government sent a mosquito to fumigate, the same type of machine used in 2003 by soybean growers. "But we prefer using a lower fumigating machine, because we have cassava and beans and we don't want them to be affected." Her husband had recently undergone a hernia operation and was now experiencing prostate problems. She had arthritis and had been recently diagnosed with lupus. "And that is an incurable disease . . . I'm being monitored, but I'm ready to depart," she told me in a broken voice and on the verge of tears.

In 2012, in one of my periodical phone calls to Formosa, I was sad to hear that Emilia's husband had passed away. When I visited Emilia in November 2013, she was still growing GM herbicide-resistant cotton and was upset that the local middle farmers hired by the provincial government were rarely showing up in time for the harvest. "And when they take a while to harvest the cotton, the boll gets dry and it weighs less," Emilia said. "And if we complain, they tell us 'What are you complaining about? You didn't do anything'" (because the work is done by contractors, as explained above). In 2013, Emilia also planted pumpkins, but she could not find a buyer, so she left the pumpkins to rot in the field. "With the transgenic seeds, they shut us up, we cannot complain [about GM crops encroaching on peasants], since we are also planting them," Emilia told me haggardly.

The story of Emilia and her family reflects the multiple hardships that Formosan peasants face. Her experience also illustrates the ironic twist I registered during my latest visits to Formosa; namely, that many peasants started adopting GM cotton when the provincial Ministry of Production began to give away glyphosate-resistant seeds.[7] The initiative was part of a broader agreement between Monsanto Company and provincial governments launched in 2008 (van Zwanenberg and Arza 2013). Formosan peasants say they adopted GM cotton as a sort of "insurance policy": since the variety of GM cotton promoted by the government is glyphosate-resistant (just like GM soybeans), a potential agrochemical drift like the one of 2003 would not affect their plants.

Artemia and her husband Elio, a senior couple, provide further insight on why peasants resort to letting the government produce and sell their cotton, and to the expectations of reciprocity embedded in that relationship. The cotton can be classified as I, II, or III (in decreasing level of quality), but Artemia and Elio explained that at the government-managed buying point, "they always pay you quality II, no matter if it's a beautiful, super white cotton." Confused, I asked them if they couldn't sell the cotton to private dealers. "Yeah, but you have a commitment with the agronomists; they gave you the seed, the chemicals . . . And to sell it privately you have to ask, walk around, and sometimes the price is lower." The government only buys cotton from the peasants registered as receiving GM cottonseeds; thus, in order to have access to the more stable official price and the conveniently located buying point, peasants need to first adopt the GM cotton. Facundo, for instance, also planted GM cotton, "and when I took my harvest to the government they weighed the cotton and came up with a lower weight. I complained to the agronomist, but she told me that if I wasn't happy with the weight they calculated, I could take my cotton elsewhere."

"We asked the government to include other products at the buying point like cassava, beans, and corn so people could produce them knowing that they would have a place to sell it. But the request didn't go through," said Isidoro, a leader of MoCaFor in Monte Azul. "A lot of people got into the GM cotton program . . . They don't have to do anything, just open the gate to their farms, then close it." He was concerned because many people think that they signed up to get "help" (*ayuda*, a subsidy) in the form of GM cottonseeds and agrochemicals, "and now they're finding out that it was actually a credit; they have to pay it back. And they put their lands down as collateral." He confirmed what I heard about planting GM cotton as a sort of insurance policy: "The people planting transgenic cotton now don't have problems with the [GM] soybean fields being next to their farms; on the contrary, the agrochemicals drifting from the soybeans help their cotton . . . The government does it on purpose, so they don't have any trouble like in 2003."

Isidoro was also troubled by the consequences of a widespread adoption of GM cotton in terms of the availability of food: "The people planting transgenic cotton don't plant anything else, they cannot plant sweet potatoes or cassava next to it, because they will be affected by the agrochemicals. And lately, you cannot find cassava branches [to replant]. You go to people's farms and they don't have any beans, sweet potato, cassava, they don't have anything!" He connected these issues to a decay in rural life, saying, "The communities around here are less and less populated; the elementary school of [a nearby community] has only six students." While we were having this conversation at the gate of Facundo's farm, I noticed that a tractor came and went twice, carrying a tank with faucets to fumigate the GM cotton.

When I presented the ideas of this book in front of an audience of MoCaFor leaders and members in 2011, their reactions reflected both their worries about agrochemical exposure and peasants' concerns about providing for their families. As Julio, a local leader of MoCaFor, put it during the collective conversation: "I don't get angry with people who are planting transgenic cotton. If you have to eat, I am not going to say, 'don't grow cotton; grow pumpkins.' You have to do what you have to do; they have to eat. So I'm not going to get mad at people, because the people know that it is harmful ... I think that the people minimally know that it's killing them, they know that the poison is bad—any poison is bad—but still, they have to make ends meet [*de algo tiene que vivir*]." One of the local leaders argued that many people were growing GM cotton because of a lack of awareness (*falta concientización*). Nélida rejected this idea, echoing the sense of despair mentioned above:

NÉLIDA: About awareness, I disagree, because Facundo knows exactly, Chiche knows exactly, Emilia knows, there is no need for me to go to Emilia's, Chiche's, Facundo's, Mimi's or Mariano's house to tell them. They know exactly; there isn't a reason to tell them again. The people are aware of what is happening. We got together and talked, they know everything. And they are doing what they want to do, knowing what they are doing.

SARA: Because there is no alternative.

JULIO: There's not an alternative; it's true.

SARA: There isn't anything else we can do.

JULIO: MoCaFor doesn't have the ability to give credit or subsidies, so people have to take whatever there is.

Conclusion

This chapter elaborates the argument initiated in the previous one concerning processes of demobilization. Here I delved into the subjective aspects of demobilization and the survival strategies that peasant households devised to negotiate the advance of transgenic agriculture. My goal was to capture the transition from contention to adaptation, from adamant reaction against GM crops and agrochemical exposure to processes of accommodation. In understanding these processes of demobilization, I also sought to take concrete material problems seriously and avoid seeing them as spurious interference in the political aspect of a social movement. My goal in this chapter was thus to understand these two intertwined sides of the lives of peasants and their movements, heeding anthropologist Sherry Ortner when she argues that "the impulse to sanitize the internal politics of the dominated must be understood as fundamentally romantic" (2006b: 49). In short, I inspected the nitty-gritty realities and dilemmas of social movements by adopting a basic ethnographic stance of seeing normative interpretations with suspicion while keeping local experiences in focus.

I need to stress, however, that demobilization is a phase of popular mobilization rather than an endpoint. Just like peasants in the 1990s reignited mobilization and resuscitated the collective organization of the 1970s, the demobilization of the late 2000s served as an experience that illustrates the benefits and drawbacks of collaborating with a sympathetic national government. In the conclusion, I discuss the theoretical underpinnings of demobilization processes and further explore the implications of agricultural biotechnology.

CONCLUSION—COMPANION PLANTING

THE CRUCIBLE OF GM CROPS, GLOBAL PROCESSES, AND SOCIAL MOVEMENTS

"I was with Monsanto, which announced a very important investment in corn ... And besides, they were very happy because Argentina today is—shall we say—at the forefront in matters of biotechnological events ... Here I have—and the truth is that I want to show you all because I am very proud—the prospectus of Monsanto [which made] a very important investment in a new, transgenic corn seed in the province of Córdoba," said President Cristina Fernández de Kirchner in June 2012 during a meeting in New York with the Council of the Americas, a US business organization. She went on to say:

> Monsanto's investment is incredibly important and is going to help in the realization of our Agro-Food 2020 industrial plan. And today, the head [of Monsanto] told me that they were very impressed by the support that our government is giving to science and technology. You should all be certain that we are going to continue in the same line ... We are 40 million inhabitants [in Argentina] and we have a territory that is the eighth [largest] in the world. This places us in a "pole position" [sic] in terms of food generators and biotechnology ... the people of Monsanto recently explained to me that this corn is going to permit a seventeen percent increase in soy production when you rotate it in the soil. And besides, and this is the most interesting part, it is going to practically demand that we use no insecticides, thus it will not only increase productivity but also improve the environment.

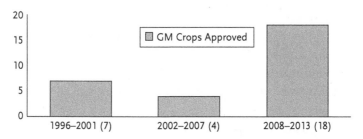

FIGURE C.1 GM seeds approved in Argentina 1996–2001, 2002–2007, and 2008–2013.

Coincidentally, the same week that President Kirchner announced Monsanto's investment in Córdoba, environmental groups mobilized in that same province for the trial brought by the Madres de Ituzaingó against soybean growers accused for health issues caused by agrochemicals (see chapter 1). The mobilization of environmental groups and the Madres de Ituzaingó ultimately stalled the construction of Monsanto's seed facility that had been so enthusiastically announced by President Kirchner.[1] In her speech the president referred to the Strategic Agro-Food Plan 2020, an initiative launched in September 2011 aimed at increasing agricultural production and expanding the area used for agriculture in Argentina. She also made reference to new GM seeds, which were increasingly supported by the government during her two terms. To wit: between 2008 and 2013, 18 new GM crops were released in Argentina—in contrast with the eleven transgenics approved between 1996 and 2007 (see Figure C.1).[2]

As I discussed in the introductory chapter, and as these 2013 events suggest, Argentina is an important global player in agricultural biotechnology. What does Argentina tell us about GM crops? What lessons about the globalization of agriculture and social movements can we draw from this book?

GM Crops' Broken Promises

Argentina offers a unique context to evaluate the social and environmental impacts of the expansion of GM crops, particularly herbicide-resistant soybeans. Only in the United States have GM crops expanded so quickly and widely. Transgenic seeds, as I argued in the introduction, have two intertwined lives: one as crops that transform rural landscapes, and another in the discourses and projects of both promoters and critics. How can we evaluate this dual life after reviewing the impacts of GM crops in Argentina?

The typical techno-productivist discourse promoting transgenic agriculture goes as follows: GM crops can uplift the rural disadvantaged from poverty, and, in a win–win scenario, also contribute to sustainable growth by offering environmentally friendly techniques for agrarian production. The impacts of GM herbicide-resistant crops in Argentina belie this argument on at least two points.

First, any potential environmental gains that may result from GM herbicide-resistant crops are contradicted by the realities of agrarian production. Promoters of GM crops argue that they can benefit the environment through no-tillage techniques and by replacing more toxic agrochemicals with other, less dangerous ones (e.g., Cerdeira and Duke 2010). These hypothetical advantages contrast with the realities of the sweeping expansion of GM soybeans in Argentina, where the use of agrochemicals has increased exponentially. As agribusiness companies and relatively well-off farmers grew soybeans over several consecutive seasons, they resorted to the use of toxic herbicides like 2.4D (see chapter 2). This, in turn, resulted in a sort of "transgenic treadmill" (Binimelis, Pengue, and Monterroso 2009); that is, the appearance of weeds that resist the standard glyphosate, which in turn result in the use of more toxic herbicides.[3] In the face of weeds that resist the same herbicides endured by GM crops (i.e., glyphosate), the response of the industry has been the promotion of new crops that "stack" genes, making plants resistant to additional agrochemicals, namely, herbicides that are more toxic than glyphosate. For instance, Dow AgroSciences in the United States obtained approval for a GM soybean that simultaneously resists glyphosate, glufosinate, and 2,4D.[4] In addition to the problem of escalating agrochemical use, GM crops have also aggravated problems of deforestation in Argentina (see chapter 1) and South America more broadly (Austin 2010, Gasparri, Grau, and Angonese 2013).

Despite the hype they received during their launch in the mid-1990s, GM herbicide-resistant crops fall short of offering solutions to the environmental problems created by the green revolution. Rather, they actually perpetuate some of its problems—particularly, dependence on agrochemicals. It can be argued that these negative impacts have more to do with the way that GM crops are grown in Argentina than with transgenic crops per se. I readily accept this point, and contend that this only strengthens my argument that GM crops cannot be disentangled from the social contexts in which they are adopted and thus showing the blind spots of the techno-productivist discourse that sees GM crops as a disembedded technology.

Second, the pleas of small farmers and peasants in Argentina suggest that the gains that GM crops may bring to the rural poor in the abstract techno-productivist scenarios are overwhelmingly countered by their actual negative social impacts. Scholars focused on the global scale and studying corporate strategies have shown the shortcomings of discourses presenting GM crops as a tool to "feed the poor in the developing world" (Glover 2010a, 2010b). The experience of Formosan peasants illustrates, at a localized scale, the limitations of presenting GM crops under a developmentalist light. In Monte Azul, peasants organized a local farmers market seeking to overcome the economic constraints imposed by neoliberalization—in their case, the difficulties of surviving in a deregulated cotton market. Furthermore, they also began changing agricultural practices, switching from fiber to food production while reducing their use of synthetic pesticides in the process. This experience was devised out of necessity, but still provided cheap and healthy food for local communities and allowed peasants to diversify their agricultural production and improve the food security of local consumers. The agrochemical drift of 2003 cut this experience short by destroying the produce of peasant families and instilling a lack of confidence in the nearby town of Sarambí about the safety of consuming locally grown foods.

At least in northern Argentina, GM crops did not provide economic alternatives to the rural poor, but rather benefitted medium to large landowners and export-oriented agribusinesses, with the negative corollary of discouraging locally based and more environmentally friendly food production. Moreover, and as we saw in chapter 5, Formosan peasants have been returning to cotton production because they do not see other economic alternatives and, in part, because they feel pressured by the provincial government to adopt GM cotton. Beyond Formosa, in chapter 1, I discussed how the expansion of the agricultural frontier through the production of GM soybeans has resulted in evictions of peasant families and indigenous peoples from their land and spurred an increase in rural violence. When seen from the perspectives of peasants and the rural poor, rather than offering solutions to social problems, transgenic crops aggravate some of them.

The Argentine scenario raises questions about the claims put forward by discourses touting the benefits of GM crops, particularly regarding herbicide-resistant crops. Does this mean that critical approaches to GM crops offer a precise picture of agricultural biotechnology and its discontents? In this book I drew from critical approaches, but I also sought to improve the ways in which they conceive the globalization of agriculture and social movements that emerge in response to this trend.

Putting Food Regimes in (Their) Place

By examining the role of GM crops in the current neoliberal food regime from an up-close and long-term ethnographic perspective, I was able to incorporate some of the insightful critiques that human geographers have made to the food regime perspective (Goodman and Watts 1994, Le Heron and Roche 1995, Le Heron 2009, Moran et al. 1996, Woods 2007). Scholars characterizing the current moment as a "third food regime" (McMichael 2009) stress the role of transnational corporations as the leading actors of agricultural globalization. A sympathetic critique of this conception proposed the idea of a "neoliberal food regime," arguing that we need to pay attention to not only corporations but also to national states in the promotion of agricultural biotechnology (Otero 2008b, 2012, Otero, Pechlaner, and Gürcan 2013: 10). In this book I complemented these perspectives that privilege global and national scales by incorporating into my analysis the role of subnational, regional, and localized scales and their articulations. I inspected the scalar and spatial dynamics of GM crop expansion, showing how a social movement forges alliances, engages in conflicts, and negotiates transgenic agriculture at localized, provincial, regional, and national scales, while also drawing from global discourses. I showed that the national state can simultaneously oppose certain global neoliberal institutions and ideas while effecting little change in the neoliberalization of agriculture at subnational scales. In doing so, I reconstructed the vexed scenario faced by a peasant social movement when navigating different political scales (e.g., supporting the national government and opposing the provincial government, while both governments support each other).

This importance granted to the state at its various scales does not mean, of course, that corporations do not play an important role in the current neoliberal food regime and particularly in the expansion of GM crops. Yet my close range observations also led me to argue that this expansion relies on the collaboration of national and subnational agribusinesses in order to diffuse spatially and take root in concrete places. This approach, in turn, allowed me to incorporate into my analysis the uneven geographies of GM crop expansion and argue that its impact is asymmetrical in social and spatial terms. I argued that if we take the internal variation of countries and regional inequalities into account, we might paint a more precise picture of the social and environmental impacts of agricultural biotechnology. Moreover, by taking the complex relationship between spaces, places, and scales seriously, we can circumvent a series of conceptual shortcomings; for instance, the unreflective use of a category like "the Global South," which tends to homogenize entire countries with the risk of missing meaningful internal variations.

An ethnographic perspective on GM crops that is attentive to spatial and scalar dynamics can also offer a more nuanced picture of social movements than the prevalent view in food and globalization literature. Studies of the globalization of agriculture have paid attention to social movements, but they have done so by privileging global and national scales from an overly structuralist perspective. Food regime scholars have paid attention to trans-national movements, mostly focusing on the role of a global movement like Via Campesina (Desmarais 2007, McMichael 2006). In this book I expect to make a modest contribution not only by spreading the word about peasant movements in Argentina, but also by arguing for more focused attention on the challenges faced by small, localized social movements (Blee 2012, Voss and Williams 2012) and for an integration of the material interests of social movements with their emotional rhythms (Summers-Effler 2010). Scholars have looked for alternatives to the dominant food regime by examining ini-tiatives emerging "from below." I assert that this view also reinforces the ar-chitectural imagination of structural forces "up there" and alternatives cre-ated from below, which may obscure inequalities and power struggles that are also present *within* and *between* social movements (Wolford 2010).

The agrarian and environmental politics of GM crops in Argentina pro-vide an invitation to reexamine the relationship between neoliberalization and contentious politics, showing that mobilization is not a prerogative of subordinate actors but can also be used as "weapons of the wealthy" (Radnitz 2010). By and large, scholars in the food regime tradition tend to assume that protest is the tool of the powerless and that social movements follow a progressive agenda. However, contentious mobilization can also contribute to *maintain* a neoliberal food regime, as shown in the collective actions of agribusiness actors in Argentina in 2008. This point is crucial if we are to approach agro-food politics from a relational perspective; that is, by paying attention to the relationships within and between movements and also the impacts of countermovements. Specifically, as we saw in chapter 1, the agri-business lockout of 2008 in Argentina created political ripples informing the state's actions, which in turn shaped the actions of localized peasant social movements (in the events presented in chapter 4, for instance, creating con-straints for contentious collective action). This broadened view involves "stra-tegic action fields" in which collective actors "vie for strategic advantage in and through interaction with other groups in what can be seen as meso-level social orders" (Fligstein and McAdam 2011: 2).

My criticism of the understanding of contention and social movements within the food regime scholarship is that the emphasis on transnational movements, the fascination with "alternatives from below," and the favoring of the national state as an arena of contention may miss the paradoxes that emerge during up-close and long-term participant observation (Rubin 1998). As long as we look at social movements "from the outside in" and fail to incorporate their contextual, situated logic of action (with all its frictions, dilemmas, and contradictions), we run the risk of misplacing our hopes by "sanitizing politics," glossing over the internal politics of the dominated (Ortner 2006b). In so doing, we may easily fall for "the romance of resistance" by being "more concerned with finding resistors and explaining resistance than with examining power" and therefore not fully exploring the implications of resistance (Abu-Lughod 1990: 41). In doing so, the symbiotic relationship between dominant and subordinated actors and the "everyday forms of peasant collaboration" may be overlooked. Peasant collaboration is as present and relevant as peasant resistance, particularly during periods in which regimes seek "normalization" after a phase of heightened contention (White 1986), like Argentina after the 2001–2002 crisis.

In this book, I crossbred critical perspectives on the globalization of agriculture with social movement scholarship and debates on peasant resistance. In doing so, my contribution lies in showing how global ethnography can enrich both food regime scholarship and social movement studies. In what ways have I moved the conversation on social movements forward by using an ethnographic approach to contention and demobilization?

Agency, Culture, and Demobilization

This book examines the dynamics of mobilization and demobilization by looking at institutions, social actors, and their interpretations. In other words, in order to explain contention and its decline, I examined the sinews connecting: 1) authorities and institutional politics; 2) social movement organizations and leaders; and 3) subjective views of social movement members and constituents. I did not look at these three factors in isolation or statically, but rather adopted a longitudinal and relational perspective, reconstructing the ways in which each influenced each other and considering how their relationships changed over time.

In 2003, peasants reacted to an agrochemical onslaught by organizing transgressive and disruptive protests, within the context of a historically undemocratic province. They were able to carry out several contentious collective actions in large part thanks to the fact that leaders and members were strongly unified in their demands and means of action. The authorities denied that contamination due to agrochemicals was even taking place, and they disrespected the people protesting in Monte Azul and Moreno, blaming them for the ailments they were suffering and arguing that the protests were politically motivated. The collective actions of 2003 were not only a function of organizational strength, but also stemmed from the rage and indignation of peasants, two emotions that were germane in triggering and escalating contention.

In contrast, in 2009, an agrochemical drift similar to the one that occurred in 2003 motivated a different reaction among the affected peasants and authorities, which I captured with the concept of performative governance. Authorities' use of "impression management" (Futrell 1999, Goffman 1959) and their capacity to "do things with words" (Austin 1962) through their discourses and reports resulted in obstacles for contention. The recognition of the contamination and of peasants' demands, and the interactions between peasants and authorities, created a very different context than that of 2003. At the organizational level of the social movement, between 2003 and 2009 MoCaFor became ensnared in what I called institutional recognition and a process of dual pressure, resulting from alliances with a national social movement, the support of the national government, and the expectations of its constituents, which combined to create subtle but powerful barriers for contentious collective actions.

In addition, the views and emotions of social movement members, sympathizers, and peasants also changed. While some were discouraged by the meager results of the 2003 conflict, others were convinced by the negative interpretations that the provincial government put forward at that time. Meanwhile, the consistency regarding blame assignment had also changed by 2009. These changing meaning-making processes informed the localized understandings of politics, reciprocity, and collective action—in other words, the relationships with allies and authorities and the views on contention were influenced by the prevalence of patronage politics in the province.

I gained access to these cultural interpretations by scrutinizing the interactive and communicative processes conveyed in discourses. By analyzing the language of politics and contention, I delved into the ways in which struggle is understood, trying to go beyond the dichotomy of consent/resistance. I thus built on the work of James C. Scott and, more specifically, of anthropologist William Roseberry when he observed that "languages of protest or resistance must adopt the forms and languages of domination in order to be registered or heard" (1994: 363–364). I heeded the insight that "words, images, symbols, forms, organizations, institutions and movements used by subordinate populations to talk about, understand, confront, accommodate themselves to, or resist their domination are shaped by the process of domination itself" (Roseberry 1994: 361).

I tackled the dynamics of mobilization and demobilization arguing that agency is not only exerted through resistance and collective action, but also through processes of accommodation and negotiation (for instance, analyzing how clients understand their own subordination, showing that they are aware of their position and actually struggle to maneuver it to their own advantage).[5] Following anthropological research, I did not consider agency ("the socioculturally mediated capacity to act") as a synonym of freewill or resistance, since "oppositional agency is only one of many forms of agency" (Ahearn 2001: 112, 115). Whereas the term agency "calls to mind the autonomous, individualistic, Western actor," agents are always embedded in contexts that are culturally and historically constructed and shaped by relations of solidarity, on one hand, and "enmeshed within relations of power, inequality and competition" on the other (Ortner 2006a: 130–131). In this sense, "if power and the subordination of others is always in the service of some project, so too is resistance; the entire domination/resistance dialectic makes sense as the clash of people's projects, their culturally constituted intentions, desires, and goals" (Ortner 2006a: 151).

E. P. Thompson famously wrote that the "working class did not rise like the sun at an appointed time. It was present at its own making" (1991 [1963]: 8). Paraphrasing Thompson, I contend that peasant social movements in Argentina did not disappear like a setting sun, but they were active in the making of their own demobilization. In scrutinizing agency in demobilization and the role of emotions in that process, I sought to contribute to social movement studies by taking into account that "the dynamics of demoralization is rarely the focus of social movement theory ('political opportunity' is the focus, not political 'foreclosure'; 'abeyance,' but not defeat)" (Fantasia and Stepan-Norris 2004: 560). Building on research that incorporates culture, context, and temporality into the study of social movements and contention (Blee 2012, Sewell Jr. 2005), I analyzed the decade-long processes within which a peasant social movement moved from contention (chapter 3) to demobilization (chapter 4), while paying attention to the broader historical context (chapter 2) to underline that the current state of demobilization is not an endpoint, but rather a phase in the ebb and flow of popular social movements in Argentina.

Social Movements and the Polity

This book examined the dynamics of mobilization and demobilization in the context of the expansion of transgenic agriculture, paying particular attention to meaning-making processes informing relationships within and between social movements and their interactions with authorities. While I emphasize the relevance of situated meanings to understand these dynamics, I also believe that it is important to indicate how my findings speak to research that may not be directly interested in GM crops in Argentina. Zooming out from the specificities of my study, this book intersects with two issues: the contemporary commodity boom in Latin America and the relationship between social movements and the polity.

First, the impacts and implications of agricultural biotechnology are relevant beyond Argentina (De Sousa and Teixeira Vieira 2008). Considering that GM soybeans have expanded to southern Brazil, Uruguay, and the Paraguayan countryside, some of the social and environmental phenomena analyzed here also have regional implications. In addition, the widespread expansion of GM soybeans is an expression of the broader commodity boom that has fueled economic growth throughout South America since the late 1990s, with extractive industries (oil, gas, mining) and agriculture as its engines (Bebbington 2012, Haarstad 2012, Levitsky and Roberts 2011). The concepts offered in this book (for instance, institutional recognition and performative governance) will hopefully resonate with researchers investigating the dynamics of mobilization and demobilization around these socioeconomic, political, and environmental processes.

Second, the role of patronage politics as the cultural logic mediating the relationship between social movements and the state also has implications beyond Argentina. Patronage politics is an enduring phenomenon in Latin America that survives (and even thrives) in the context of leftist popular governments; for instance, in Bolivia (Albro 2007, Shakow 2011), Uruguay (Alvarez Rivadulla 2012, Canel 2012), Venezuela (García-Guadilla 2002, Penfold-Becerra 2007, Smilde 2008), and Ecuador (Bane 2011, Becker 2013). This overlap between post-neoliberal governments and clientelism invites us to further explore an understanding of social movements and patronage politics that sees them not as opposite phenomena but as salient characteristics of popular politics that often overlap and can, in turn, allow social movement organizations to survive—although at the cost of sacrificing their disruptive potential.

During the last decade many a South American social movement has allied with the government, with leaders facing the enticing opportunity of becoming public officials—creating dilemmas that, for instance, have been insightfully analyzed for the case of Mapuche activists in Chile (Park and Richards 2007, Richards 2013). As social movement activists move from the streets into offices, they become embedded in policies and programs as public officials after years of fighting "on the ground." This situation confronts social movements with "the paradox of collaboration"; that is, when "movement objectives may be subsumed by the goal of ongoing access in the bodies that are beginning to regulate the partial policy changes that the movement has won" (Coy and Hedeen 2005: 417). Attention to this paradox and to the overlap between social movements and patronage politics in Latin America offers the opportunity to refine our understanding of the relationship between contentious and routine politics, considering that this issue has been overwhelmingly investigated in the United States and Europe (Aminzade 1993, Banaszak 2010, Goldstone 2003, Heaney and Rojas 2011, McAdam and Tarrow 2010, Meyer 2007, Tarrow 2012).[6] Scholars of Chinese politics have examined mechanisms of "bureaucratic absorption," patron–client relationships (Lee and Zhang 2013: 1480–1481), and the blurring boundaries between contentious collective action and institutionalized participation (O'Brien 2003); and social movement studies have taken notice of the role of patronage politics in contention (Jenkins and Eckert 1986: 34–35, Tarrow 2012: 41). Yet more research is needed to elucidate the interfaces between institutional and contentious politics in a variety of cultural contexts.

Companion Planting

A common custom among peasants around the world consists of combining the crops they grow. Unlike the monoculture of large-scale agriculture (planting only one crop in large land extensions) peasants use a technique known as "companion" planting: for instance, they plant beans next to maize so each one supports the other and both grow stronger. I learned this lesson doing fieldwork among peasants and, in my own peculiar way, I heeded that wise practice while writing this book. In order to inspect the social and environmental consequences of GM crops and processes of popular demobilization, I combined literature on the globalization of agriculture and social movement research, complementing the weakness of one perspective with the strengths of a different one, and bridging different disciplines that often talk past each other.

I addressed some of the shortcomings of food regime scholarship (e.g., its lack of attention to spatial dynamics and subnational scales, the dichotomous understanding of mobilization, and the top-down view of neoliberalism) by drawing from social movement concepts, the insights of anthropological studies of resistance, and the interest of human geographers in space/place dynamics, uneven geographies, multiscalar analysis, and processes of neoliberalization. Accordingly, I drew heavily from social movement scholarship but I also sought to overcome its northern biases and extend its recent interest in cultural dimensions of contention to Latin America, inspecting the weight of patronage politics to explain demobilization. In addition, by situating the cases of this book in the context of agrarian capitalism and approaching neoliberalization as a cultural process (Edelman 1999: 40), I also made a modest contribution toward reuniting social movements scholarship with its original interest in capitalist formations (Buechler 2000, Hetland and Goodwin 2013).

In summary, I have been eclectic and applied a sort of disciplinary polygamy, drawing from sociology, anthropology, human geography, and Latin American and development studies. As C. Wright Mills lyrically put it when explaining the ways of exercising the sociological imagination: "You try to think in terms of a variety of viewpoints and in this way to let your mind become a moving prism catching light from as many angles as possible" (1959: 214). In this sense, my interdisciplinarity grew from an omnivorous appetite for ideas but also from an ethnographic approach to global and political phenomena that I applied in this book. A microscopic perspective allowed me to see processes that are otherwise invisible using the wide lenses of food regime scholars, and to tame their overly enthusiastic faith in social movements when seen from afar. In making this point I am combining Michael Burawoy's (2010) critique of overly optimistic approaches to transnational movements, and the argument that ethnography's value may reside "not in its commitment to 'the local' but in its attentiveness to epistemological and political issues of location" (Gupta and Ferguson 1997: 39). Global ethnography, in other words, may better serve the purpose of capturing the complexities, tensions, and paradoxes of global forces and the resistances and accommodations they inspire at a localized scale.

As I explained in the preface, this book flourished from my political and scholarly motivations to understand the actions and suffering of Formosan peasants. As I delved deeper into this research, I kept precooked answers at bay and allowed myself to get lost in the maze of ethnographic fieldwork, exiting from it with some answers and a new set of questions. I am certain that GM herbicide-resistant crops, at least in Argentina, do not solve environmental problems (rather they create new ones) and do not offer solutions for the needs of the rural poor (but instead contribute to new forms of suffering).

At the same time, I cannot help but harbor doubts about wishful proclamations regarding the inherently democratic power of social movements. Paraphrasing Gramsci, I would say that I entered the field carrying the optimism of the will, and after the journey I emerged imbued with the skepticism of reason. To put it bluntly and broadly, I do not take pleasure in cynicism or embrace a postmodern nihilism, but rather believe in the political and analytical value of exploring the ambiguities, tensions, and contradictions created by contestation and power relationships (Rubin 1998). My goal is to express respect for resistance "not just by arguing for the dignity or heroism of the resistors but by letting their practices teach us about the complex interworkings of historically changing structures of power" (Abu-Lughod 1990: 53). I do hope, however, that the concepts and analyses presented in this book will stand as cautionary tales for social movement members while inspiring other researchers inspecting processes of mobilization and demobilization.

As Marc Edelman noted, "Books have an end, histories do not" (1999: 184). In this case, the lesson is twofold. It remains to be seen if popular social movements in Argentina will rekindle contentious collective action under different circumstances. As I finished writing this book on the demobilization of a peasant movement in Formosa, the contentious mobilization of environmentalists and grassroots activists against Monsanto in the province of Córdoba was again on the rise.[7] Regarding agricultural biotechnology, I hope that this book provides food for thought to problematize a techno-productivist narrative in the current understanding of agriculture and development, which portrays GM crops as a silver bullet to uplift the rural poor. The discourse that currently dominates policy and the mass media may eventually incorporate the insights of social sciences in assessing agricultural biotechnology, understanding that its impacts are highly dependent on the socioeconomic context and mediated by national and subnational politics.

ON THE ETHNOGRAPHIC CRAFT

Back in the city he felt homesick for those first evenings out in the desert when, a long time before, he had felt homesick for the city. He made his way to his adviser's office and told him that he now knew the secret, and that he had made up his mind not to reveal it.... "The secret, I should tell you, is not as valuable as the steps that brought me to it. Those steps have to be taken, not told." The professor said coldly: "Very well, I shall report your decision to the board. Are you thinking of living among the Indians?" Murdock answered: "No. Maybe I won't be going back to the reservation. What I learned there I can apply any place on earth and under any circumstances."

—JORGE LUIS BORGES, "*El Etnógrafo*"

Unlike the character in Borges's short story "The Ethnographer," also translated as "The Anthropologist" (1974), I feel that I did reveal certain secrets that I learned doing fieldwork. While finishing this book, I distilled two lessons from rereading Borges's story. First, that scholarship is a process where the search is as important as the finding: Eureka moments are less frequent than the iterative back and forth between data, analysis, fieldwork, and writing, resulting in similar doses of drudgery and satisfaction. In that process (as any ethnographer knows), not only the field changes, but also the researcher. Second, what we learn from ethnographic research is particular and situated, yet it holds the promise of generalization and the key for understanding places beyond the ethnographer's site.

My involvement with the people that lend their voices to this book harkens back to my work as a rural sociologist at the University of Buenos Aires, and my activism with friends and colleagues that I briefly described in the preface. I first visited Formosa in March 2003, a month after the events discussed in chapter 3. I traveled north with two friends who were also researchers and teachers at the University of Buenos Aires. We had heard about the Monte Azul protests because Formosan peasant activists had gotten in touch with the Land and Food Forum (*Foro de la Tierra y la Alimentación*), an activist network in which we participated (see preface). Doubling as rural sociologists and activists, we recorded interviews with a digital camera, helped to make the situation known among other activist networks, and published a book chapter analyzing the case.

In September 2004 Diego Domínguez, Pablo Sabatino, Patricia Digilio, and I returned to the province to present a documentary we had made. Through peasants' testimonies, the documentary outlined the agrochemical drifts and the protests organized by MoCaFor. With the support of professors from the University of Formosa, we co-organized a screening of the documentary and a presentation by Monte Azul peasants. After the event, we shared a long table with more than a dozen people in downtown Formosa, dining on empanadas and wine on a warm spring night. "You know, here we say that once you've touched Formosan dirt, you're going to keep coming and coming to this province," a man sitting across the table told me. Folk saying or not, after those initial visits in 2003 and 2004 I returned to Formosa every year between 2007 and 2011, doing fieldwork for my PhD dissertation for a total of 12 months (divided into periods of one- to two-week visits, to longer stays of up to four months). I also revisited Formosa in 2013 and met with Formosan informants in Buenos Aires in 2012, 2013, and 2014.

The way I gained *entrance* to my research site created both opportunities and challenges for my ensuing fieldwork. While I believe that it gave me credibility with the peasant organization and their sympathizers, it also created some obstacles for interviewing other relevant actors including politicians, agribusinessmen, and agronomists working for soybean growers.

In terms of *data collection*, I used semistructured interviews, archival research, and ethnography. I conducted 45 semistructured interviews with social movement leaders (N = 10), social movement members (N = 15), peasants and local inhabitants (N = 9), public officials (N = 4), agronomists (N = 2), lawyers (N = 3), and agribusinessmen (N = 2). I relied on "snowball" sampling and also interviewed peasants by simply approaching their farms and asking for an interview after explaining my doctoral research project. With these interviews I did not aim to obtain a representative sample in the statistical sense (Small 2009), but rather I followed the principles of theoretical sampling, seeking to develop or contrast emerging themes (Corbin and Strauss 1990, Hammersley and Atkinson 2007). On several occasions, I avoided formal interview appointments and preferred to sit down, drink mate, and start interviewing more informally, while taking notes on the notebook that I carried everywhere. That is why many interviews only involved one interviewee, but I did not shy away from talking to two or three people at the same time. These group interviews, rather than "contaminating" the setting, proved to be extremely useful in terms of enriching the depth of the conversation (see the interview with Rafael and Julio in chapter 2), and suggesting points of disagreement between social movement members.

During fieldwork I greatly benefitted from the generosity of peasant families, particularly the siblings I call Nélida and Horacio, and their extended family (following a standard ethnographic practice, I used pseudonyms in an effort to avoid potential problems for my informants). Julio, Nélida's son, slowly became a research assistant and, eventually, a friend. Traveling in the Formosan countryside is not easy, and we did many trips on his scooter. As a result of these entanglements (and as you can tell from reading this book), my reconstruction of events, interactions in the field, and the significance of processes and politics in Formosa are read through the prism of the ideas, feelings, and voices of Nélida, Horacio, and their family. This close relationship with a group of activists in the field, however, did not prevent me from seeking to diversify my sources. To further capture the interactions between spokespersons and rank-and-file members of MoCaFor, and to avoid portraying the movement monolithically, I also organized activities called "the barometer of values." For this exercise, I proposed an ambiguous statement and asked participants to place themselves alongside an imaginary scale ranging from "total agreement" to "total disagreement." This tool helped to uncover, for instance, the diversity of ideas about politics, clientelism, and leadership *within* the movement. The presentation of my PhD dissertation at the end of 2011 also proved informative in terms of elucidating differences within the movement and seeing peasants' reactions to my findings. Drawing inspiration from Alberto Melucci's "sociological interventions," these tools allowed me to go beyond the discourse of leaders and individual opinions, and to gain access to a "system of interactions in its making" (Melucci 1996: 60).

I took extensive notes on interactions and dialogues while participating in the quotidian activities of MoCaFor offices in Moreno and Sarambí (where I slept on some of my trips), and also while living in the farmhouses of Monte Azul families and participating in meetings and activities held by MoCaFor in the capital of Formosa and in Buenos Aires. I also reviewed three provincial newspapers for the period 2003–2006, collecting 78 news stories about MoCaFor, and compiled documents (communiqués, bulletins, leaflets, pamphlets).

To analyze my data, I coded and analyzed interview transcripts, fieldnotes, and documents after each round of fieldwork, using open and focused coding (Emerson, Fretz, and Shaw 1995). Provisional findings guided my subsequent rounds of data collection. In the initial stages, the goal of focused coding was to reconstruct the grievances and contentious events of 2003, peasants' views on authorities and allies, relationships between participants in the social movement organization, interpretations of agricultural changes, and perceptions of the environment. While I was working on this focused coding, unforeseen language tropes emerged as well as the pressures of members and allies on leaders. These topics thus became open codes, and I recoded interviews, fieldnotes, and documents using them. It was in this back and forth between data collection and analysis that innovative concepts were formed and unexpected findings emerged.

While writing this book, I strove to present my data in a way that allows readers to assess whether my conclusions and analyses are valid. Following Jack Katz, I presented in the text "empirical materials showing variations in the lives of subjects that are directly relevant to the theory offered" (Katz 2004: 282). Throughout this book, I thus tested my readers' patience presenting extended quotes from interviews and several fieldnote excerpts. In presenting evidence in this format, as Katz notes, "the key issue is pragmatic, whether the reader is disempowered by presumptive interpretation or is enfranchised to participate in the discussion by being given access, to the extent the researcher can provide it through quotations and in situ field notes, to the subjects' realities as they experience it" (2004: 289).

With regard to the sites where I conducted fieldwork, readers may ask how representative they are or the criteria for their selection. The rural communities of Formosa where I conducted fieldwork cannot be considered representative in the statistical sense of the term, since qualitative studies "call for logical rather than statistical inference, for case rather than sample-based logic, for saturation rather than representation as the stated aims of research" (Small 2009: 28). To address the perennial question "What is this a case of?" I provided an overview of agrarian neoliberalization and the expansion of GM crops and their socioenvironmental impacts in chapter 1—processes that affected not only Formosan peasants, but also several other rural communities in northern Argentina.

During the iterative process of collecting and analyzing data, writing preliminary results, and returning to the field, I managed, in a methodological judo maneuver of sorts, to turn constraints into opportunities. Sociologist Pierre Bourdieu said that sociology is like a martial art: you use it for self-defense and not for unfair attacks. I adapt this metaphor to argue that, like a judoka, I wrestled with my research project using the strengths of my opponent to my advantage. I took the constraints imposed by academic life and the theoretical categories that obfuscated my sight and turned them on their heads.

First, due to my obligations as a graduate student in the United States, I was not able to follow the standard ethnographic protocol of spending an entire continuous year immersed in a community. Yet this limitation eventually became a source of rich evidence, since I stretched data collection and analysis over a decade (from my first contact with Formosan peasants in 2003 to the final writing of this book in 2013–2014). These points will resonate with researchers arguing for "an account of the ethnographic process that recognises the structural context of the fieldwork setting and the academic environment, which has been somewhat marginalized as greater attention is given to personal identity and active participation" (Roberts and Sanders 2005: 296).

As I was working on the research project, I thus realized that I was adopting a form of longitudinal qualitative study (e.g., Hermanowicz 2013, Holland 2011, McLeod and Thomson 2009, Saldaña 2003) and applying a variation of the "extended case" method (Burawoy 1998). My "ethnographic returning" (O'Reilly 2012) was also motivated by ethical concerns inspired by the inquisitive Formosans who asked, in my initial visits, "So, are you coming back or will we not see you again?" In other words, my revisits were equally inspired by a commitment to the people that opened their homes and volunteered their time to help me in my project.

Second, this prolonged engagement allowed me to use negative cases as opportunities to extend and reconstruct theory. My research began as a study of the resistance against GM crops but evolved into a comparative study about the dynamics of mobilization *and* demobilization following the lack of collective action in 2009. I saw that MoCaFor was increasingly demobilized while it was gaining access to resources in the national context of favorable political opportunities. This situation contrasted with the established social movement wisdom that access to resources and favorable political opportunities facilitate contentious collective action. As a sociologist trained in social movement theories, this situation was initially disorienting. My confusion was eventually illuminated by "negative case methodology." I adapted the arguments that Rebecca Emigh and other historical sociologists have used for situations "in which an outcome that had been predicted by theory did not occur," and began to see the lack of protests in 2009 as an opportunity to expand "the theory's range of explanation" (Emigh 1997: 649).

In short, I used paradoxical evidence to contribute to the reconstruction of social movement theory (Burawoy 1998). In doing so I used a tool of analytical ethnography, connecting theory and data through theoretical extension; that is, I did not develop a whole new theory but extended "preexisting theoretical or conceptual formulations to other groups or aggregations, to other bounded contexts or places, or to other sociocultural domains" (Snow, Morrill, and Anderson 2003: 187). Specifically, I was able to refine social movement theory by proposing mechanisms of demobilization (i.e., dual pressure and institutional recognition) that connected organizational and meaning-making processes. And I extended social movement theory to better understand the relationship between social movements and patronage politics, since (in Latin America and elsewhere) the latter pervades relationships within and between social movement organizations, and informs engagements between social movements and the state at different scales (national, provincial, and local).

Taken together, longitudinal qualitative studies and negative case methodology can enrich our understanding of path dependent processes among social movements. Kathleen Blee, in an insightful book on small and sporadic groups of activists, articulated the value of granting importance to "what doesn't happen and what isn't said," reminding us that activism "isn't made only by what groups decide and what actions they take. Equally as significant is what they fail to do or say—and what they fail even to consider. It is a mistake for scholars to focus only on visible events and pronouncements" (Blee 2012: 135). I followed this insight comparing the 2003 and 2009 events (or lack thereof), drawing from a conception of "eventful temporality," which "assumes that events are normally 'path dependent,' that is, that what has happened at an earlier point in time will affect the possible outcomes of a sequence of events occurring at a later point in time" (Sewell Jr. 2005: 100). As Blee put it: "It is tempting to explain why a particular group acts or thinks in a particular way by using proximate causes—its current size or ideological proclivities—but activist groups also act in the shadow of their pasts, however distant, [or] forgotten" (Blee 2012: 41). In summary, the theoretical toolkit of social movement studies can be expanded by further incorporating longitudinal qualitative studies and negative case methodology to explain dynamics of demobilization.

NOTES

INTRODUCTION

1. The names of specific localities and people have been modified to ensure anonymity.
2. I use the term "peasant" following the self-identification of interviewees as *campesino/a*. On this disputed category see, among a vast literature, Akram-Lodhi and Kay (2009), Borras (2013), Otero (1999), Shanin (1990), and Van der Ploeg (2008). Marc Edelman (2013) provides an insightful and succinct discussion of the term. For debates about the category *campesino* in Argentina, see Archetti and Stølen (1975), Barbetta, Domínguez, and Sabatino (2012), Giarracca (1990), Manzanal (1990), and Posada (1993).
3. For this scene, see Robin (2008).
4. The Flavr-Savr tomato, engineered to have slower ripening. Calgene, the company developing the tomato, had a series of problems with its commercialization and withdrew it from the market in 1997. Monsanto Co. eventually acquired Calgene. For this early story of biotechnology, see Rabinow (1996).
5. For Brazil, see Jepson, Brannstrom, and De Souza (2008), Peláez and Schmidt (2004), Peschard (2012), and Scoones (2008). For Paraguay, see Galeano (2012) and Palau and Kretschmer (2004). For both countries, see Richards (2010).
6. See, for instance, Benbrook (2001) and Heinemann et al. (2013). The data is inconclusive and varies depending on the crop and the criteria for evaluation. For instance, Stone (2011) shows that Bt cotton in India may have higher yields and reduce the use of some pesticides, but in the long run, the appearance of other pests and systemic ecological problems offset these advantages. For these issues in Argentina, see Benbrook (2005).
7. Michel Foucault proposed the concept of "discursive formation" in reference to "a historically situated system of institutions and discursive practices" (Dreyfus and Rabinow 1983: 73).

8. For succinct discussion of the social embeddedness of agricultural biotechnology, see Kleinman (2005: 15–33).

9. Productivism refers to "a commitment to an intensive, industrially driven and expansionist agriculture with state support based primarily on output and increased productivity ... which became the paramount aim of rural policy following World War II" (Lowe et al. 1993, quoted in Wilson 2001: 78).

10. A study supported by the UN, FAO, and the World Bank, for instance, states that "data based on some years and some GM crops indicate highly variable 10–33% yield gains in some places and yield declines in others" (IAASTD 2009: 8).

11. For a classic and authoritative demonstration that the problem of hunger is not one of lack of food availability, see Sen (1981). For a discussion of this argument applied to GM crops, see among others Altieri and Rosset (1999) and Scoones (2002).

12. As stated in a UN report, "there has been a process of consolidation in the global agribusiness in recent years ... the outcome of which is a few major integrated companies, each controlling proprietary lines of agricultural chemicals, seeds, and biotech traits. A significant increase in the concentration of agrochemical industry has been observed with three leading companies accounting for roughly half of the total market" (UNCTAD 2006: iv).

13. Among a vast literature on food regimes, see Clapp and Fuchs (2009), Pechlaner (2012), Pechlaner and Otero (2008), and Wolf and Bonanno (2013). For the concept of food regime, see Friedmann (1993) and McMichael (2009); and for debates about this perspective, Araghi (2003) and Otero, Pechlaner, and Gürcan (2013), among others.

14. Take, for instance, the emphasis of food regime scholars on "historization and politization" but not on spatialization (McMichael 2009: 146, 151, 156).

15. On the lack of attention to the spatial manifestations and uneven geographies of global agriculture, see Goodman and Watts (1994), Le Heron and Roche (1995), Le Heron (2009), Moran et al. (1996), and Woods (2007). Goodman and Watts, for instance, take issue with the food regime literature in terms of positing "a sort of worldwide agricultural mimesis ... a suggestion which erases important spatial heterogeneities in national (and regional) agricultural systems," and argue for focusing on "place-specific practices" (1994: 12, 38). I heeded the first criticism in chapter 1, and paid close attention to the second in chapters 2 to 5.

16. See a list compiled by the Center for Food Safety here: www.centerforfoodsafety. org/issues/976/ge-food-labeling/state-labeling-initiatives#.

17. On co-optation and social movements, see the classic study of Selznick (1949), and also Coy and Hedeen (2005), Ho (2010), Jaffee (2012), McCarthy and Wolfson (1992); Murphree, Wright, and Ebaugh (1996), Schwartz (1976), and Trumpy (2008). On the institutional impact of social movements even long after they demobilize, see Andrews (2006).

18. A connected problem, the *lack* of collective action, has long preoccupied social scientists (Burawoy 1982, Gaventa 1980, Moore 1978, Scott 1985), yet my interest lies in dynamics of *demobilization* rather than the total absence of mobilization. For recent studies on the lack of mobilization and environmental problems, see Auyero and Swistun (2009), McAdam and Boudet (2012), and Wright and Boudet (2012).

19. For instance, see this definition by McAdam, Tarrow, and Tilly: "With respect to mobilization we must explain how people who at a given point in time are not making contentious claims start doing so—and, for that matter, how people who are making claims stop doing so. (We can call that reverse process *de*mobilization)" (2001: 34, original emphasis).

20. For an insightful discussion on the uses of global ethnography, see Erikson (2011). For a comparison between global ethnography and multisite ethnography, see Lapegna (2009).

CHAPTER 1

1. See "Acusan a Binner de 'xenófobo' por sus dichos sobre la pobreza," *La Capital de Rosario*, September 25, 2013. An audio of the radio interview can be found here: www. diarioregistrado.com/politica/79609-para-binner--la-pobreza-de-rosario-es-de-otras-provincias.html.

2. On the murky process of national authorities approving GM soybeans, see "El escandaloso expediente de la soja transgénica," *Página 12*, April 26, 2009 and "15 años de soja: la prueba del delito," *La Vaca*, March 24, 2011.

3. The source for the area planted with soybeans is the Ministry of Agriculture, data available at http://www.siia.gov.ar/series-mobile.

4. Calculated based on the 2012 report of CASAFE (Cámara de Sanidad Agropecuaria y Fertilizantes), the Argentine chamber of agrochemical companies, available at http://www.casafe.org/publicaciones/estadisticas/. I assume that glyphosate sales equal glyphosate use.

5. Nidera Co. originally patented GM soybeans seeds in Argentina (Delvenne, Vasen, and Vara 2013). In 1999, Monsanto sought to implement a system of "extended royalties," signing contracts in which farmers agreed to not reproduce seeds—arguably contradicting the Argentine law allowing farmers to reproduce the seeds obtained in their farms (Rodríguez 2010: 184). On this dispute, see also Newell (2009: 44–47).

6. In 1988 there were roughly 421,000 farms in Argentina, occupying 30.8 million hectares with agrarian activities (76 million acres). In 2002, 333,000 farms occupied 33.5 million hectares with agrarian activities (82.8 million acres) (based on the data of the National Institute of Statistics and Censuses, http://www.indec. gov.ar/nivel4_default.asp?id_tema_1=3&id_tema_2=8&id_tema_3=87).

Hence nearly 88,000 farms were pushed out of business in the 1990s. See further analyses of these figures in Teubal, Domínguez and Sabatino (2005).

7. As these authors explain, the Argentine landed elites maintained control of the state and thus the country followed a different, more unequal path of development.

8. See Archetti and Stølen (1975), Giarracca, Aparicio, and Gras (2001), Giarracca and Teubal (2005), Manzanal and Rofman (1989), Paz (2011), and Posada (1993).

9. On the concept of "environmental suffering," see Auyero and Swistun (2009)

10. On the MOCASE see, among others, Barbetta (2005), Barbetta and Lapegna (2002), Dargoltz (1997), and Durand (2008).

11. The original law (number 26160) was extended through law 26554. See Informe Ley 26160 at http://endepa.org.ar/?page_id=1085.

12. See "Una ley para mantener la vida campesina," *Página 12*, November 9, 2010.

13. See "Ni un muerto más por el agronegocio," *Página 12*, October 12, 2012, and "Por la tierra," *Página 12*, December 18, 2012.

14. See "Audiencia campesina con sabor a poco," in *Comunicación Ambiental*, September 19, 2013.

15. See "Argentina: Ataque armado a terreno comunal en Santiago del Estero," *Agencia de Noticias Biodiversidad*, June 13, 2012; "Avance sojero," *Página 12*, August 14, 2012; "Una familia campesina va a juicio por defender la salud y el ambiente," *Chaco Dia por Dia*, September 9, 2013; and "El modelo sumó otra víctima," *Rebelión*, October 12, 2012.

16. The official name of the law (number 26331) is Ley de Presupuestos Mínimos de Protección Ambiental de los Bosques Nativos.

17. For instance, the use of Dicamba increased 157%, of Imazethapyr 50%, and of 2.4D 10% in Argentina between 2001 and 2004; see Benbrook (2005). Cf. Qaim and Traxler (2005).

18. In 2012, Gatica received the Goldman Prize, awarded to grassroots environmental activists; see www.goldmanprize.org/recipient/sofia-gatica. Also see the blog of the Madres de Ituzaingó at http://madresdeituzaingo.blogspot.com/. A coverage of the trial can be found at www.juicioalafumigacion.com.ar/.

19. Based on the report of the Argentine chamber of agrochemical companies.

20. See also http://cepronat.org.ar/editorial.html for cases in the province of Santa Fe and http://darioaranda.wordpress.com/ for reports on agrochemical exposure throughout Argentina.

21. See http://www.grupodereflexionrural.com/campanapdf/index.php.

22. See "Para frenar los agrotóxicos," *Página 12*, September 22, 2010.

23. See "Lo que sucede en Argentina es casi un experimento masivo," *Página 12*, May 3 2009, and "Una cacería de brujas para la soja y el glifosato," *La Nación*, September 25, 2010. As part of the Wikileaks affair, it was revealed that the US embassy in Argentina lobbied the national and provincial governments defending the use of glyphosate; see "El glifosato es intocable," *Página 12*, March 9, 2011.

24. See "Un freno a los agroquímicos," *Página 12*, March 15, 2010; "Freno a la fumigación," *Página 12* June 14, 2010; and "Primero la salud, después los negocios," *Página 12*, March 18, 2011.

25. See, for instance, "La salud cercada de Avia Terai," *Página 12*, May 20, 2013 and "El uso de agrotóxicos," *Página 12*, August 20, 2013.

26. See their report http://www.reduas.com.ar/3rd-national-conference-of-physicians-of-crop-sprayed-towns/; and also "Encuentro de Pueblos Fumigados," *La Voz del Interior*, August 22, 2010; and "Un límite para las fumigaciones del campo," *Página 12*, August 31, 2010.

27. On the involvement of the Duhalde administration in these killings, see the book by the Frente Popular Darío Santillán (FPDS 2003). On the role of the media on the case, see the documentary by Patricio Escobar and Damián Finvarb "La crisis causó dos nuevas muertes," available at https://www.youtube.com/watch?v=Nfm-f2yJa0g.

28. To wit: Edgardo Depetri, a leader of the coalition Frente Transversal, became the head of the Sub-secretary of Relationships with the Civil Society and was, as of 2013, a Congress representative of the Frente para la Victoria, the Kirchnerista faction of Peronism. Similarly, Emilio Pérsico is the leader of the movement Movimiento Evita, and since 2012 he is Sub-secretary of Rural Development and Family Agriculture of the national Ministry of Agriculture.

29. I reconstruct these alliances based on two sources: for the FTV, my involvement in a research project of the Instituto de Desarrollo Económico y Social investigating popular movements; for the MNCI, my close relationship with a group of sociologists who became "organic intellectuals" of the MNCI and occupied positions at the PSA.

30. For a succinct overview of the *piquetero* movement, see Rossi (2013).

31. I had access to the fieldnotes of a researcher doing fieldwork on the FTV in 2003. The notes described that during a massive FTV rally during the electoral campaign, the main leader arrived carrying large bags filled with Kirchner's ballots. Holding a ballot, the leader addressed the crowd: "*Compañeros*, this guy is our candidate."

32. During the 1990s, D'Elía occupied a series of positions as local public official and representative of left-of-center parties, he ran for governor of Buenos Aires in 2003, and in 2011 he launched his own national political party.

33. Export taxes (called *retenciones* in Argentina) were eliminated during the 1990s and reinstated in 2002 under the interim government of President Eduardo Duhalde. Starting in 2002 at a rate of 10%, *retenciones* were increased later that year to 20%. During the Kirchner's government (2003–2007) export taxes for soybeans reached 24% and then were raised to 35% (Richardson 2009).

34. "Export taxes comprised 8 to 11% of the Kirchner government's total tax receipts, and around two-thirds of this—nearly US$2 billion in 2006—came from soy exports" (Richardson 2009: 242).

35. See also a special issue of the journal Lavboratorio, Vol. 10, no. 22, at www.lavbo-ratorio.sociales.uba.ar/.
36. See "Otras entidades, otras demandas," *Página 12*, July 27, 2008; and "Demandas del otro campo," *Página 12*, August 31, 2008.
37. See http://argentina.indymedia.org/news/2008/06/611660.php.
38. The continuity of PSA is determined annually. The upgrade translated into an automatic inclusion in the federal budget and a permanent incorporation of the SSDRAF into the state's bureaucratic structure.
39. See "El veneno que asoló el barrio de Ituzaingó," *Página 12*, January 12, 2009, and "Para que no se extienda la mancha venenosa," *Página 12*, January 15, 2009. See also the decree creating the commission at www.msal.gob.ar/agroquimicos/decreto-21-2009.php.

CHAPTER 2

1. See the National Agrarian Censuses of 1914, 1947, 1960, 1969, 1974, and 1988. Census data tends to underrepresent large properties and overrepresent small farms (Edelman and Seligson 1994); nevertheless, these figures suggest the unequal distribution of land in Formosa. The 2002 Agrarian Census shows a reduction in registered small properties, accounting for 57% of the farms.
2. See https://www3.epa.gov/airtoxics/hlthef/parathio.html.
3. For the Argentine Leagues see Bartolomé (1977), Ferrara (1973), and Roze (1992).
4. For instance, a document issued in 1971 after ULiCaF's second congress states: "Some of the things that we were able to get was to distract us and prevent our organization from growing. That's why, *compañeros*, we should always remember that our struggle isn't about winning small things, like candies silencing little kids [*como el caramelito que hace callar a las criaturas*]" (quoted in Ferrara 1973: 268).
5. The government offered a plot of 380,000 hectares (939,000 acres), but ULiCaF determined that only 14,000 were suitable for agriculture (Roze 1992: 99–100). In addition, peasants had to clear the land of forest and bushes.
6. According to Roze (1992: 103), local committees and grassroots members of ULiCaF were more radical than the leaders, who intervened after the occupations "to preserve the system."
7. The coup was the tipping point of the repression that started in 1975, when a weak constitutional government decreed the use of the military "to wipe out subversive elements." This repression, in turn, was triggered by the attack of a military base in Formosa in October 1975 organized by *Montoneros*, the youth and left-wing faction of Peronism that became increasingly militarized after 1975.

8. Public-owned cotton plants paid to farmers between 15 and 20% more for their cotton than private merchants (Rofman et al. 1987: 241).

9. The repression of the Peasant Leagues on the Argentine northeast, however, started before 1976. For instance, an activist of the Peasant Leagues in Corrientes, Norma Morello, was kidnapped and "disappeared" in 1971 and detained until 1972.

10. Rafael referred to Julio's father several times while Julio listened attentively to Rafael's opinion about politics, the Catholic Church, MAF, and rural NGOs. This offered Julio useful information about allies and adversaries of peasant movements: in subsequent MoCaFor meetings, I noticed that Julio's interventions were informed by these conversations.

11. I borrow the "roll back" and "roll out" expressions from geographers Jamie Peck and Adam Tickell in reference to the "twin process of financialization in the realm of economic policy and activation in the field of social policy" (2002: 391).

12. Reports and documents usually reflect the views of the World Bank, the agency funding the programs. Rural welfare projects in the northeast included the PROINDER (Development Project for Small Farmers, *Proyecto de Desarrollo de Pequeños Productores Agropecuarios*), the PRODERNEA (Project of Rural Development of Northeast Provinces *Proyecto de Desarrollo Rural de las Provincias del Noreste Argentino*), the Small Farm Program (*Programa Minifundio*), and the PSA (Social Agricultural Program, *Programa Social Agropecuario*).

13. Electronic Data Information Source, University of Florida, at http://edis.ifas.ufl.edu/pi104.

14. See PAN Pesticide Database, www.pesticideinfo.org.

15. Electronic Data Information Source, University of Florida, at http://edis.ifas.ufl.edu/pi105.

CHAPTER 3

1. Glyphosate is the *active ingredient* of Monsanto's Roundup Ready, making up around 40% of the herbicide. The combination with adjuvants may increase Roundup's toxicity (Bonn 2005, Cox and Surgan 2006). On the heated debate about Roundup's toxicity, see Séralini and collaborators (Séralini et al. 2013, Séralini et al. 2012).

2. The World Health Organization (WHO) considers glyphosate as "unlikely to be hazardous." It is listed as "unlikely" in the US EPA Carcinogens List and evaluated as "not acutely toxic to slightly toxic" for the US NTP Acute Toxicity Studies. 2,4D, in contrast, is assessed as "moderately hazardous" by the WHO, presents "unclassifiable, ambiguous data" in the US EPA Carcinogens List, and is considered "slightly to moderately toxic" in US NTP Acute Toxicity Studies; see www.pesticideinfo.org/. On health and glyphosate, see also Acquavella et al. (2006), Benachour et al. (2007), Benachour and Séralini (2009), De Roos et al. (2005), Richard et al. (2005), and Williams, Kroes, and Munro (2000). On 2,4D

and health, see Alexander et al. (2007), McDuffie et al. (2001), Stürtz et al. (2010), and Zahm et al. (1990).

3. This is the main claim behind the concept of "framing" (Benford and Snow 2000).

4. In the "status model" proposed by Nancy Fraser, the distributive dimension concerns the *economic structure* of society whereas recognition is connected to *status subordination*, with both dimensions interacting with each other (2003: 30–31).

5. The judge was later removed from her position. Several sources pointed to the case of Monte Azul as causing her removal, among other decisions contradicting the goals of the provincial government.

6. The note reads: "In my capacity as acting mayor of the Municipality of Moreno, I am pleased to inform you that the aerial fumigation will be momentarily suspended in our town and its surrounding areas. I request you to communicate this decision to those who are carrying out the tasks through the personnel under your supervision."

7. *La Mañana*, March 2, 2003, 27. An informant told me that the minister was getting daily calls from the businessmen pushing him to "do something" about the allegations of contamination.

8. *La Mañana*, March 6, 2003, 20.

9. *La Mañana*, March 4, 2003, 19.

10. *Opinion Ciudadana*, March 6, 2003, 11.

11. *Opinion Ciudadana*, March 7, 2003, 8.

12. *Opinión Ciudadana*, February 6, 2003, 16.

13. *La Mañana*, March 2, 2003, 27.

14. *La Mañana*, March 19, 2003, 13.

15. On biotechnology, science, and regulation see, among many others, Jasanoff (2005) and Kinchy (2012).

16. Adding to the customary slowness of Argentine courts, the case presents two further elements delaying its resolution. First, it is hard to prove the causal relationship between herbicide use and environmental and health problems and, furthermore, that the agrochemical drift was caused by CEFA. Second, a series of bureaucratic barriers: CEFA's lawyer questions every single document presented by the peasants' lawyer; the company's representatives have legal addresses in other provinces; and, as mentioned earlier, the original judge was removed.

17. For pioneer work on the tensions between leaders and members of social movements, see Schwartz, Rosenthal, and Schwartz (1981), and Schwartz (1976: 105–126 and 155–169).

18. On motherhood and environmental activism, see also Brown and Ferguson (1995), Culley and Angelique (2003), and Krauss (1993).

19. For a summary of *piqueteros*, see Rossi (2013) and, among many others, Svampa and Pereyra (2003) and Wolff (2007).

CHAPTER 4

1. As Ferguson and Gupta argue, states are "spatialized," usually in vertical terms (2002: 982).
2. For classic works on clientelism and reciprocity, see Eisentadt and Roniger (1984), Schmidt et al. (1977), and Wolf (1966). For contemporary Latin America from an ethnographic standpoint, see Alvarez Rivadulla (2012), Auyero (2000), Gay (1994), Lazar (2008), and Shefner (2001).
3. Quoted in the provincial newspaper *La Mañana*, June 15, 2004.
4. For a classic work on political opportunities, see McAdam (1982). See McAdam, Tarrow, and Tilly (2001) for a re-elaboration and Jasper and Goodwin (2011) for an assessment of the concept. On the demobilization of popular movements in contemporary Argentina, see Svampa and Pereyra (2004) and Wolff (2007).
5. See http://argentina.indymedia.org/news/2008/06/611660.php.
6. The continuation of the PSA was determined annually. The upgrade translated into an automatic inclusion in the federal budget and a permanent incorporation of the SSDRAF into the state's bureaucratic structure.
7. Oxford English Dictionary; http://oxforddictionaries.com/definition/american_english/co--opt?q=cooptation#co--opt__22.
8. For resistance among peasants, see the seminal studies of James C. Scott (1986, 1990, 2012). For discussions on the extensive literature on resistance, see Hollander and Einwohner (2004), Kerkvliet (2005), Seymour (2006), Sivaramakrishnan (2005), and White (1986).

CHAPTER 5

1. The list included soybean fields located next to the local elementary school, machinery used for fumigations that passed in front of the school and was cleaned in the water reservoirs of the area, no correct disposal of the containers of agrochemicals, and employees working in soybean fields without access to the protective garments necessary to avoid health problems.
2. All excerpts are obtained from the *Informe de Reconocimiento y Observación* (Report of Reconnaissance and Observation), issued by the CNIA.
3. Full report at http://www.agn.gov.ar/informes/acciones-de-control-de-agroquimicos. A summary can be found here: http://renace.net/?p=3105.
4. For the relationship between waiting and subordination in Argentina, see Auyero (2012).
5. Resources coming from the national government were going to be channeled through the roundtable composed by community and peasant organizations. Since PAIPPA is a government institution, peasants argue that it should not participate in the roundtable.

6. On the idealization of environmental struggles, see Rangan (2000) and Mawdsley (1998), among others.

7. For an insightful view on transgenic cotton, see Stone (2007, 2011) although his work in India focuses on Bt cotton and not RR cotton, the one promoted in Formosa. See also Tripp (2009) for arguments on transgenic cotton underpinning economic development.

CONCLUSION

1. See "Marcha en Córdoba contra una planta de Monsanto," *Página 12*, October 23, 2013, and "Tensión en el bloqueo a Monsanto en Malvinas Argentinas," *Cba24*, September 26, 2013.

2. The total of 29 GM crops commercialized in Argentina include: corn (21 varieties), soybeans (5), and cotton (3). Monsanto holds patents for 11 of these crops, and Syngenta for six. Information from the Argentine Office of Biotechnology, available here: http://www.minagri.gob.ar/site/agregado_de_valor/biotechnology/55-COMMERCIAL%20PERMITS/index.php.

3. Similarly, anthropologist Glenn D. Stone (2011) has shown that in Warangal, India, the adoption of transgenic cotton (genetically engineered to kill bollworms) initially reduced the use of pesticides but, in the long run, the appearance of new plagues (e.g., aphids) cast doubts on the environmental benefits of Bt cotton.

4. See "Dow AgroSciences, M.S. Technologies Submit for Approval First-Ever GM Soybean," *Agronews*, August 23, 2011; and "Bayer CropScience and MS Technologies Receive Approval for Balance GT Soybean Technology in US," *Agronews*, August 22, 2013.

5. For similar arguments in Mexico, see Hilgers (2009) and in Bolivia see Lazar (2008).

6. For a review of insider/outsider dynamics and the state, see Pettinicchio (2012).

7. See "El bloqueo que cumple un año," *Página 12*, September 19, 2014, reporting on the ongoing protests against Monsanto.

REFERENCES

Abu-Lughod, Lila. 1990. "The Romance of Resistance: Tracing Transformations of Power through Bedouin Women." *American Ethnologist* 17 (1): 41–55.

Acquavella, John F., Bruce H. Alexander, Jack S. Mandel, Christophe Gustin, Beth Baker, Pamela Chapman, and Marian Bleeke. 2006. "Glyphosate Biomonitoring for Farmers and Their Families: Results from the Farm Family Exposure Study." *Environmental Health Perspectives* 114 (11): 321–326.

Agnew, John. 1994. "The Territorial Trap: The Geographical Assumptions of International Relations Theory." *Review of International Political Economy* 1 (1): 53–80.

Ahearn, Laura M. 2001. "Language and Agency." *Annual Review of Anthropology* 30: 109–137.

Akram-Lodhi, Haroon, and Cristóbal Kay, eds. 2009. *Peasants and Globalization: Political Economy, Rural Transformation and the Agrarian Question*. London: Routledge.

Albro, Robert. 2007. "Indigenous Politics in Bolivia's Evo Era: Clientelism, Llunkerfo, and the Problem of Stigma." *Urban Anthropology & Studies of Cultural Systems & World Economic Development* 36 (3): 281–320.

Alexander, Bruce H., Jack S. Mandel, Beth A. Baker, Carol J. Burns, Michael J. Bartels, John F. Acquavella, and Christophe Gustin. 2007. "Biomonitoring of 2,4-Dichlorophenoxyacetic Acid Exposure and Dose in Farm Families." *Environmental Health Perspectives* 115 (3): 370–376.

Alexander, Jeffrey C., and Jason L. Mast. 2006. "Introduction. Symbolic Action in Theory and Practice: The Cultural Pragmatics of Symbolic Action." In *Social Performance: Symbolic Action, Cultural Pragmatics, and Ritual*, edited by Jeffrey C. Alexander, Bernhard Giesen, and Jason L. Mast, 1–28. New York: Cambridge University Press.

Altieri, M. A. 2005. "The Myth of Coexistence: Why Transgenic Crops Are Not Compatible with Agroecologically Based Systems of Production." *Bulletin of Science, Technology & Society* 25 (4): 361–371.

Altieri, Miguel A., and Peter Rosset. 1999. "Ten Reasons Why Biotechnology Will Not Ensure Food Security, Protect the Environment and Reduce Poverty in the Developing World." *AgBioForum* 2 (3&4): 155–162.

Alvarez Rivadulla, María José. 2012. "Clientelism or Something Else? Squatter Politics in Montevideo." *Latin American Politics and Society* 54 (1): 37–63.

Aminzade, Ron, and Doug McAdam. 2002. "Emotions and Contentious Politics." *Mobilization* 7 (2): 107–109.

Aminzade, Ronald. 1993. *Ballots and Barricades: Class Formation and Republican Politics in France, 1830–1871.* Princeton, NJ: Princeton University Press.

Andrée, Peter. 2011. "Civil Society and the Political Economy of GMO Failures in Canada: A Neo-Gramscian Analysis." *Environmental Politics* 20 (2): 173–191.

Andrews, Kenneth T. 2006. *Freedom is a Constant Struggle: The Mississippi Civil Rights Movement and Its Legacy.* Chicago: University of Chicago Press.

Araghi, Farshad. 2003. "Food Regimes and the Production of Value: Some Methodological Issues." *Journal of Peasant Studies* 30 (2): 41–70.

Arancibia, Florencia. 2013. "Challenging the Bioeconomy: The Dynamics of Collective Action in Argentina." *Technology in Society* 35 (2): 79–92.

Archetti, Eduardo P., and Kristi Anne Stølen. 1975. *Explotación Familiar y Acumulación de Capital en el Campo Argentino.* Buenos Aires: Siglo Veintiuno Editores.

Aronskind, Ricardo, and Gabriel Vommaro, eds. 2010. *Campos de Batalla: Las Rutas, los Medios y las Plazas en el Nuevo Conflicto Agrario.* Buenos Aires: Prometeo.

Austin, John L. 1962. *How To Do Things With Words.* London: Oxford University Press.

Austin, Kelly F. 2010. "Soybean Exports and Deforestation from a World-Systems Perspective: A Cross-National Investigation of Comparative Disadvantage." *Sociological Quarterly* 51 (3): 511–536.

Auyero, Javier. 2000. *Poor People's Politics: Peronist Survival Networks and the Legacy of Evita.* Durham, NC: Duke University Press.

Auyero, Javier. 2003. *Contentious Lives: Two Argentine Women, Two Protests, and the Quest for Recognition.* Durham, NC: Duke University Press.

Auyero, Javier. 2007. *Routine Politics and Violence in Argentina: The Gray Zone of State Power.* New York: Cambridge University Press.

Auyero, Javier. 2012. *Patients of the State: The Politics of Waiting in Argentina.* Durham, NC: Duke University Press.

Auyero, Javier, Pablo Lapegna, and Fernanda Page Poma. 2009. "Patronage Politics and Contentious Collective Action: A Recursive Relationship." *Latin American Politics and Society* 51 (3): 1–31.

Auyero, Javier, and Debora A. Swistun. 2009. *Flammable: Environmental Suffering in an Argentine Shantytown.* New York: Oxford University Press.

Azpiazu, Daniel, Eduardo Basualdo, and Miguel Khavisse. 1986. *El Nuevo Poder Económico en la Argentina de los Años 80.* Buenos Aires: Hyspamérica.

Baiocchi, Gianpaolo. 2003. "Emergent Public Spheres: Talking Politics in Participatory Governance." *American Sociological Review* 68 (1): 52–74.

Baiocchi, Gianpaolo. 2005. *Militants and Citizens: The Politics of Participatory Democracy in Porto Alegre*. Stanford, CA: Stanford University Press.

Baiocchi, Gianpaolo, Elizabeth A. Bennett, Alissa Cordner, Peter Taylor Klein, and Stephanie Savell. 2014. *The Civic Imagination: Making a Difference in American Political Life*. Boulder, CO: Paradigm.

Banaszak, Lee Ann. 2010. *The Women's Movement Inside and Outside the State*. New York: Cambridge University Press.

Bane, Mandi A. 2011. "Social Change in the Neoliberal Era: The Indigenous Movement in Saquisili, Ecuador." PhD dissertation, University of Michigan.

Barbetta, Pablo. 2005. "El Movimiento Campesino de Santiago del Estero: Luchas y Sentidos en torno a la Problemática de la Tierra." In *El Campo Argentino en la Encrucijada*, edited by Norma Giarracca and Miguel Teubal, 423–448. Buenos Aires: Alianza.

Barbetta, Pablo, Diego Domínguez, and Pablo Sabatino. 2012. "La Ausencia Campesina en la Argentina como Producción Científica y Enfoque de Iintervención." *Mundo Agrario* 13 (25). http://www.mundoagrario.unlp.edu.ar/article/view/MAv13n25a03.

Barbetta, Pablo, and Pablo Lapegna. 2002. "No hay Hombres sin Tierra ni Tierra sin Hombres: Luchas Campesinas, Ciudadanía y Globalización en Argentina y Paraguay." In *Ruralidades Latinoamericanas. Identidades y Luchas Sociales*, edited by Norma Giarracca and Bettina Levy, 305–355. Buenos Aires: Consejo Latinoamericano de Ciencias Sociales.

Bartolomé, Leopoldo J. 1977. "Populismo y Diferenciación Social Agraria: Las Ligas Agrarias en Misiones (Argentina)." *Cahiers du Monde Hispanique et Luso-Brásilien* 28 (1): 141–168.

Bebbington, Anthony, ed. 2012. *Social Conflict, Economic Development and the Extractive Industry: Evidence from South America*. New York: Routledge.

Becker, Howard S. 1993. "How I Learned What a Crock Was." *Journal of Contemporary Ethnography* 22 (1): 28–35.

Becker, Marc. 2013. "The Stormy Relations between Rafael Correa and Social Movements in Ecuador." *Latin American Perspectives* 40 (3): 43–62.

Bell, Shannon Elizabeth. 2013. *Our Roots Run Deep as Ironweed: Women and the Fight for Environmental Justice in the Appalachian Coalfields*. Urbana: University of Illinois Press.

Benachour, N., H. Sipahutar, S. Moslerni, C. Gasnier, C. Travert, and G. E. Seralini. 2007. "Time- and Dose-Dependent Effects of Roundup on Human Embryonic and Placental Cells." *Archives of Environmental Contamination and Toxicology* 53 (1): 126–133.

Benachour, Nora, and Gilles-Eric Séralini. 2009. "Glyphosate Formulations Induce Apoptosis and Necrosis in Human Umbilical, Embryonic, and Placental Cells." *Chemical Research in Toxicology* 22 (1): 97–105.

Benbrook, Charles. 2001. "Troubled Times Amid Commercial Success for Roundup Ready Soybeans: Glyphosate Efficacy Is Slipping and Unstable Transgene

Expression Erodes Plant Defenses and Yields." Sandpoint, ID: Northwest Science and Environmental Policy Center. Available at: www.iatp.org/documents/troubled-times-amid-commercial-success-for-roundup-ready-soybeans-introduction.

Benbrook, Charles. 2003. "Economic and Environmental Impacts of First Generation Genetically Modified Crops: Lessons from the United States." Winnipeg, Manitoba: International Institute for Sustainable Development. Available at: www.iisd.org/library/economic-and-environmental-impacts-first-generation-genetically-modified-crops-lessons.

Benbrook, Charles. 2005. Rust, Resistance, Run Down Soils, and Rising Costs–Problems Facing Soybean Producers in Argentina. Ag Bio Tech Technical Paper Number 8. Available at: http://www.biosafety info.net/article.php?aid=220.

Benford, Robert D. 1997. "An Insider's Critique of the Social Movement Framing Perspective." *Sociological Inquiry* 67 (4): 409–430.

Benford, Robert D., and David A. Snow. 2000. "Framing Processes and Social Movements: An Overview and Assessment." *Annual Review of Sociology* 26: 611–639.

Berger, John. 1992. *Pig Earth*. New York: Vintage.

Bilakovics, Steven. 2012. *Democracy Without Politics*. Cambridge, MA: Harvard University Press.

Binimelis, Rosa, Walter Pengue, and Iliana Monterroso. 2009. "'Transgenic Treadmill': Responses to the Emergence and Spread of Glyphosate-Resistant Johnsongrass in Argentina." *Geoforum* 40 (4): 623–633.

Bisang, Roberto. 2003. "Apertura Económica, Innovación y Estructura Productiva: La Aplicación de Biotecnología en la Producción Agrícola Pampeana Argentina." *Desarrollo Económico* 43 (171): 413–442.

Bisang, Roberto, Guillermo Anlló, and Mercedes Campi. 2008. "Una Revolución (no tan) Silenciosa. Claves para Repensar el Agro en Argentina." *Desarrollo Económico* 48 (190/191): 165–207.

Blee, Kathleen M. 2012. *Democracy in the Making: How Activist Groups Form*. New York: Oxford University Press.

Bonn, Dorothy. 2005. "Roundup Revelation." *Environmental Health Perspectives* 113 (6): A403–A404.

Borges, Jorge Luis. 1974. *In Praise of Darkness*. New York: Dutton.

Borland, Elizabeth, and Barbara Sutton. 2007. "Quotidian Disruption and Women's Activism in Times of Crisis, Argentina 2002–2003." *Gender & Society* 21 (5): 700–722.

Borras, Saturnino M, Jr. ed. 2013. *Critical Perspectives in Rural Development*. London: Routledge.

Bourdieu, Pierre. 1984. *Distinction: A Social Critique of the Judgement of Taste*. Cambridge, MA: Harvard Univ Press.

Bourdieu, Pierre. 1991. *Language and Symbolic Power*. Cambridge, MA: Harvard University Press.

Bourdieu, Pierre. 1999. "Understanding." In *The Weight of the World: Social Suffering in Contemporary Society*, edited by Pierre Bourdieu, 607–626. Stanford, CA: Stanford University Press.

Bravo, Ana Lucía, ed. 2010. *Los Señores de la Soja. La Agricultura Transgénica en América Latina*. Buenos Aires: Consejo Latinoamericano de Ciencias Sociales.

Brodersohn, Víctor, and Daniel Slutzky. 1975. Diagnóstico de la Estructura Social de la Región NEA. Buenos Aires: Consejo Federal de Inversiones.

Brooks, Sally. 2005. "Biotechnology and the Politics of Truth: From the Green Revolution to an Evergreen Revolution." *Sociologia Ruralis* 45 (4): 360–379.

Brown, Phil, and Faith I. T. Ferguson. 1995. "'Making A Big Stink': Women's Work, Women's Relationships, and Toxic Waste Activism." *Gender & Society* 9 (2): 145–172.

Brusco, Valeria, Marcelo Nazareno, and Susan C. Stokes. 2004. "Vote Buying in Argentina." *Latin American Research Review* 39 (2): 66–88.

Buechler, Steven M. 2000. *Social Movements in Advanced Capitalism*. New York: Oxford University Press.

Burawoy, Michael. 1982. *Manufacturing Consent: Changes in the Labor Process Under Monopoly Capitalism*. Chicago: University of Chicago Press.

Burawoy, Michael. 1998. "The Extended Case Method." *Sociological Theory* 16 (1): 4–33.

Burawoy, Michael. 2001. "Manufacturing the Global." *Ethnography* 2 (2): 147–159.

Burawoy, Michael. 2010. "From Polanyi to Pollyanna: The False Optimism of Global Labor Studies." *Global Labour Journal* 1 (2): 301–313.

Burdick, John S. 1995. "Uniting Theory and Practice in the Ethnography of Social Movements: Notes Toward a Hopeful Realism." *Dialectical Anthropology* 20 (3): 361–385.

Buttel, Frederick H. 2003. "The Global Politics of GEOs." In *Engineering Trouble: Biotechnology and its Discontents*, edited by Rachel A. Schurman and Dennis Doyle Takahashi Kelso, 152–173. Berkeley: University of California Press.

Canel, Eduardo. 2010. *Barrio Democracy in Latin America: Participatory Decentralization and Community Activism in Montevideo*. University Park: Pennsylvania State University Press.

Canel, Eduardo. 2012. "'Fragmented Clientelism' in Montevideo. Training Ground for Community Engagement with Participatory Decentralization?" In *Clientelism in Everyday Latin American Politics*, edited by Tina Hilgers, 137–158. New York: Palgrave Macmillan.

Carolan, Michael S. 2010. *Decentering Biotechnology: Assemblages Built and Assemblages Masked*. Burlington, VT: Ashgate.

Casabé, N., L. Piola, J. Fuchs, M. L. Oneto, L. Pamparato, S. Basack, R. Gimenez, R. Massaro, J. C. Papa, and E. Kesten. 2007. "Ecotoxicological Assessment of the Effects of Glyphosate and Chlorpyrifos in an Argentine Soya Field." *Journal of Soils and Sediments* 7 (4): 232–239.

Cátedra UNESCO de Sostenibilidad de la Universidad Politécnica de Cataluña (UPC), Educación para la Acción Crítica (EdPAC), Grupo de Cooperación del Campus de Terrassa (GCCT), Grupo de Investigación en Derechos Humanos y Sostenibilidad (GIDHS). 2009. Informe: Situación de los Derechos Humanos en el Noroeste Argentino en 2008. Barcelona: Cátedra Unesco de Sostenibilitat, Universitat Politécnica de Catalunya. Available at: https://investigacionddhh. wordpress.com/2010/06/18/informe-situacion-de-los-derechos-humanos-en-el-noroeste-argentino-en-2008/.

CELS. 2003. Plan Jefes y Jefas: ¿Derecho Social o Beneficio sin Derechos? Buenos Aires: Centro de Estudios Laborales y Sociales.

Cerdeira, Antonio L., and Stephen O. Duke. 2010. "Effects of Glyphosate-Resistant Crop Cultivation on Soil and Water Quality." *GM Crops* 1 (1): 16–24.

Cerdeira, Antonio L., Dionsio L. P. Gazziero, Stephen O. Duke, and Marcus B. Matallo. 2010. "Agricultural Impacts of Glyphosate-Resistant Soybean Cultivation in South America." *Journal of Agricultural and Food Chemistry* 59 (11): 5799–5807.

Cerrutti, M., and A. Grimson. 2004. "Buenos Aires, Neoliberalismo y Después. Cambios Socioeconómicos y Respuestas Populares." *Cuadernos del IDES* 5: 3–63.

Chamosa, Oscar. 2008. "Indigenous or Criollo: The Myth of White Argentina in Tucumán's Calchaquí Valley." *Hispanic American Historical Review* 88 (1): 71–106.

Clapp, Jennifer A., and Doris A. Fuchs, eds. 2009. *Corporate Power in Global Agrifood Governance*. Cambridge, MA: MIT Press.

Clemens, Elisabeth S., and Debra C. Minkoff. 2004. "Beyond the Iron Law: Rethinking the Place of Organizations in Social Movement Research." In *The Blackwell Companion to Social Movements*, edited by David A. Snow, Sarah A. Soule, and Hanspeter Kriesi, 155–170. Malden, MA: Blackwell.

Clua, A., M. Conti, and J. Beltrano. 2012. "The Effects of Glyphosate on the Growth of Birdsfoot Trefoil (Lotus Corniculatus) and its Interaction with Different Phosphorus Contents in Soil." *Journal of Agricultural Science* 4 (7): 208–218.

Cohen, Joel I., and Robert Paarlberg. 2004. "Unlocking Crop Biotechnology in Developing Countries—A Report from the Field." *World Development* 32 (9): 1563–1577.

Comerford, John Cunha. 1999. *Fazendo a luta: sociabilidade, falas e rituais na construção de organizações camponesas*. Rio de Janeiro: Relume-Dumara.

Cooper, Frederick. 2005. *Colonialism in Question: Theory, Knowledge, History*. Berkeley: University of California Press.

Cooper, Joseph, Leslie Lipper, and David Zilberman, eds. 2005. *Agricultural Biodiversity and Biotechnology in Economic Development*. New York: Springer.

Corbin, Juliet M., and Anselm Strauss. 1990. "Grounded Theory Research: Procedures, Canons, and Evaluative Criteria." *Qualitative Sociology* 13 (1): 3–21.

Cox, Caroline, and Michael Surgan. 2006. "Unidentified Inert Ingredients in Pesticides: Implications for Human and Environmental Health." *Environmental Health Perspectives* 114 (12): 1803–1806.

Coy, Patrick G., and Timothy Hedeen. 2005. "A Stage Model of Social Movement Co-Optation: Community Mediation in the United States." *The Sociological Quarterly* 46 (3): 405–435.

Culley, Marci R., and Holly L. Angelique. 2003. "Women's Gendered Experiences as Long-Term Three Mile Island Activists." *Gender & Society* 17 (3): 445–461.

Dargoltz, Raúl. 1997. "El Movimiento Campesino Santiagueño-MOCASE." *Taller* 2 (4): 154–178.

Dargoltz, Raúl. 2003. "Las Economías Regionales Argentinas y la Globalización. El Caso de Santiago del Estero y la Explotación del Quebracho Colorado." *Trabajo y Sociedad* 5 (6). Available at: http://www.unse.edu.ar/trabajoysociedad/Dargoltz.htm.

de Martinelli, Guillermo. 2008. "Pools de Siembra y Contratistas de Labores. Nuevos y viejos Actores Sociales en la Expansión Productiva Pampeana Reciente." In *Pasado y Presente en el Agro Argentino*, edited by Javier Balsa, Graciala Mateo, and María S. Ospital, 547–570. Buenos Aires: Lumiere.

De Roos, Anneclaire J., Aaron Blair, Jennifer A. Rusiecki, Jane A. Hoppin, Megan Svec, Mustafa Dosemeci, Dale P. Sandler, and Michael C. Alavanja. 2005. "Cancer Incidence among Glyphosate-Exposed Pesticide Applicators in the Agricultural Health Study." *Environmental Health Perspectives* 113 (1): 49–54.

De Sousa, Ivan Sergio Freire, and Rita de Cássia Milagres Teixeira Vieira. 2008. "Soybeans and Soyfoods in Brazil, with Notes on Argentina." In *The World of Soy*, edited by Christine Du Bois, Chee-Beng Tan, and Sidney Mintz, 234–256. Urbana: University of Illinois Press.

Delamata, Gabriela. 2004. "The Organizations of Unemployed Workers in Greater Buenos Aires." In *CLAS Working Papers* No. 8. Center for Latin American Studies, UC Berkeley. Available at: http://escholarship.org/uc/item/1wb6n7kw.

Delvenne, Pierre, Federico Vasen, and Ana Maria Vara. 2013. "The 'Soy-ization' of Argentina: The Dynamics of the 'Globalized' Privatization Regime in a Peripheral Context." *Technology in Society* 35 (2): 153–162.

Desmarais, Annette Aurélie. 2007. *La Vía Campesina: Globalization and the Power of Peasants*. Halifax: Fernwood Publishing.

Dinerstein, Ana C. 2003. "'Que se vayan todos!' Popular Insurrection and the Asambleas Barriales in Argentina." *Bulletin of Latin American Research* 22 (2): 187–200.

Domínguez, Diego Ignacio, and María De Estrada. 2013. "Asesinatos y Muertes de Campesinos en la Actualidad Argentina: La Violencia como Vector (Des)territorializador." *Astrolabio* 10: 489–529. Available at: http://revistas.unc.edu.ar/index.php/astrolabio/article/view/2816.

Domínguez, Diego, and Pablo Sabatino. 2010. "La Muerte que Viene en el Viento. La Problemática de la Contaminación por Efecto de la Agricultura Transgénica en Argentina y Paraguay." In *Los Señores de la Soja. La Agricultura Transgénica en América Latina*, edited by Ana Lucía Bravo, 31–121. Buenos Aires: Consejo Latinoamericano de Ciencias Sociales.

Dreyfus, Hubert L., and Paul Rabinow. 1983. *Michel Foucault, Beyond Structuralism and Hermeneutics*. 2nd ed. Chicago: University of Chicago Press.

Druille, Magdalena, Marta N. Cabello, Marina Omacini, and Rodolfo A. Golluscio. 2013. "Glyphosate Reduces Spore Viability and Root Colonization of Arbuscular Mycorrhizal Fungi." *Applied Soil Ecology* 64: 99–103.

Durand, Patricia Beatriz. 2008. "Representar y no Mandar: Dirigentes Campesinos en Santiago del Estero, Argentina." *Mundo Agrario* 8 (16): 1–12.

Earl, Jennifer, Andrew Martin, John D. McCarthy, and Sarah A. Soule. 2004. "The Use of Newspaper Data in the Study of Collective Action." *Annual Review of Sociology* 30: 65–80.

Eaton, Emily. 2009. "Getting Behind the Grain: The Politics of Genetic Modification on the Canadian Prairies." *Antipode* 41 (2): 256–281.

Edelman, Marc. 1999. *Peasants Against Globalization: Rural Social Movements in Costa Rica*. Stanford, CA: Stanford University Press.

Edelman, Marc. 2001. "Social Movements: Changing Paradigms and Forms of Politics." *Annual Reviews in Anthropology* 30: 285–317.

Edelman, Marc. 2013. "What Is a Peasant? What Are Peasantries? A Briefing Paper on Issues of Definition." New York: Hunter College and the Graduate Center, City University of New York.

Edelman, Marc, and Mitchell A. Seligson. 1994. "Land Inequality: A Comparison of Census Data and Property Records in Twentieth-Century Southern Costa Rica." *Hispanic American Historical Review* 74 (3): 445–491.

Edwards, Bob, and Sam Marullo. 1995. "Organizational Mortality in a Declining Social Movement: The Demise of Peace Movement Organizations in the End of the Cold War Era." *American Sociological Review* 60 (6): 908–927.

Eisenstadt, Shmuel Noah, and Luis Roniger. 1984. *Patrons, Clients and Friends*. New York: Cambridge University Press.

Eliasoph, Nina. 1998. *Avoiding Politics: How Americans Produce Apathy in Everyday Life*. Cambridge: Cambridge University Press.

Eliasoph, Nina, and Paul Lichterman. 2003. "Culture in Interaction." *American Journal of Sociology* 108 (4): 735–794.

Emerson, Robert M., Rachel I. Fretz, and Linda L. Shaw. 1995. *Writing Ethnographic Fieldnotes*. Chicago: University of Chicago Press.

Emigh, Rebecca J. 1997. "The Power of Negative Thinking: The Use of Negative Case Methodology in the Development of Sociological Theory." *Theory and Society* 26 (5): 649–684.

Emirbayer, Mustafa, and Chad Alan Goldberg. 2005. "Pragmatism, Bourdieu, and Collective Emotions in Contentious Politics." *Theory and Society* 34 (5): 469–518.

Erikson, Susan L. 2011. "Global Ethnography: Problems of Theory and Method." In *Reproduction, Globalization, and the State: New Theoretical and Ethnographic Perspectives*, edited by Carole H. Browner and Carolyn F. Sargent, 23–37. Durham, NC: Duke University Press.

Evans-Pritchard, E. E. 1951. *Social Anthropology*. London: Cohen & West.

Faccini, Delma. 2000. "Los cambios Tecnológicos y las Nuevas Especies de Malezas en Soja." *AgroMensajes (Universidad de Rosario)* 4 (5). Available at: http://www.fcagr.unr.edu.ar/Extension/Agromensajes/04/2AM4.htm.

Fantasia, Rick. 1988. *Cultures of Solidarity: Consciousness, Action, and Contemporary American Workers*. Berkeley: University of California Press.

Fantasia, Rick, and Judith Stepan-Norris. 2004. "The Labor Movement in Motion." In *The Blackwell Companion to Social Movements*, edited by David A. Snow, Sarah A. Soule, and Hanspeter Kriesi, 555–575. Malden, MA: Blackwell.

Farinetti, M. 2002. "La Conflictividad social después del Movimiento Obrero." *Nueva Sociedad* 182: 61–75. Available at: http://nuso.org/articulo/la-conflictividad-social-despues-del-movimiento-obrero/.

Ferguson, James. 2006. *Global Shadows: Africa in the Neoliberal World Order*. Durham, NC: Duke University Press.

Ferguson, James, and Akhil Gupta. 2002. "Spatializing States: Toward an Ethnography of Neoliberal Governmentality." *American Ethnologist* 29 (4): 981–1002.

Ferrara, Francisco. 1973. *Qué son las Ligas Agrarias: Historia y Documentos de las Organizaciones Campesinas del Nordeste Argentino*. Buenos Aires: Siglo Veintiuno.

Fisher, Carolyn F. 2012. "From Incentives to Ayudas: Historical, Social and Political Context of Development Projects with Small-Scale Coffee Farmers in Rural Nicaragua." PhD dissertation, City University of New York.

Fitting, Elizabeth. 2011. *The Struggle for Maize: Campesinos, Workers, and Transgenic Corn in the Mexican Countryside*. Durham, NC: Duke University Press.

Fligstein, Neil, and Doug McAdam. 2011. "Toward a General Theory of Strategic Action Fields." *Sociological Theory* 29 (1): 1–26.

Font, Mauricio A. 1990. "Export Agriculture and Development Path: Independent Farming in Comparative Perspective." *Journal of Historical Sociology* 3 (4): 329–361.

Fox, J. 1994. "The Difficult Transition from Clientelism To Citizenship: Lessons from Mexico." *World Politics* 46 (2): 151–184.

FPDS, Frente Popular Darío Santillán. 2003. *Darío y Maxi: Dignidad piquetera. El Gobierno de Duhalde y la Planificación Criminal de la Masacre del 26 de Junio en Avellaneda*. Buenos Aires: Editorial El Colectivo.

Fraser, Nancy. 2003. "Rethinking Recognition: Overcoming Displacement and Reification in Cultural Politics." In *Recognition Struggles and Social Movements: Contested Identities, Agency and Power*, edited by Barbara Hobson, 21–32. New York: Cambridge University Press.

Friedmann, Harriet. 1993. "The Political Economy of Food: A Global Crisis." *New Left Review* 197: 29–57.

Futrell, Robert. 1999. "Performative Governance: Impression Management, Teamwork, and Conflict Containment in City Commission Proceedings." *Journal of Contemporary Ethnography* 27 (4): 494–529.

Galeano, Luis A. 2012. "Paraguay and the Expansion of Brazilian and Argentinian Agribusiness Frontiers." *Canadian Journal of Development Studies/Revue Canadienne d'tudes du Développement* 33 (4): 458–470.

Gallo, Ezequiel. 1983. *La Pampa Gringa. La Colonización Agrícola de Santa Fe, 1870–1879*. Buenos Aires: Sudamericana.

Gamson, William A. 1975. *The Strategy of Social Protest*. Homewood, IL: Dorsey Press.

Gamson, William A. 1992. *Talking Politics*. Cambridge: Cambridge University Press.

García-Guadilla, Ma. Pilar. 2002. "Democracy, Decentralization, and Clientelism: New Relationships and Old Practices." *Latin American Perspectives* 29 (5): 90–109.

Gasparri, N. I., H. R. Grau, and J. Gutiérrez Angonese. 2013. "Linkages between Soybean and Neotropical Deforestation: Coupling and Transient Decoupling Dynamics in a Multi-Decadal Analysis." *Global Environmental Change* 23 (6): 1605–1614.

Gaventa, John. 1980. *Power and Powerlessness. Quiescence and Rebellion in an Appalachian Valley*. Urbana: University of Illinois Press.

Gay, Robert. 1994. *Popular Organization and Democracy in Rio De Janeiro: A Tale of Two Favelas*. Philadelphia: Temple University Press.

Giarracca, Norma. 1990. "El Campesinado en la Argentina: Un Debate Tardío." *Realidad Económica* 94: 54–65.

Giarracca, Norma, ed. 2001. *La Protesta Social en la Argentina: Transformaciones Económicas y Crisis Social en el Interior del País*. Buenos Aires: Alianza.

Giarracca, Norma, Susana Aparicio, and Carla Gras. 2001. "Multiocupación y Pluriactividad en el Agro Argentino: El Caso de los Cañeros Tucumanos." *Desarrollo Económico* 41 (162): 305–320.

Giarracca, Norma, and Miguel Teubal, eds. 2005. *El Campo Argentino en la Encrucijada. Estrategias y Resistencias Sociales, Ecos en la Ciudad*. Buenos Aires: Alianza.

Giarracca, Norma, and Miguel Teubal, eds. 2010. *Del Paro Agrario a las Elecciones de 2009: Tramas, Reflexiones y Debates*. Buenos Aires: Antropofagia.

Gibson, Edward L. 2012. *Boundary Control: Subnational Authoritarianism in Federal Democracies*. New York: Cambridge University Press.

Gille, Zsuzsa. 2000. "Cognitive Cartography in a European Wasteland: Multinationals and Greens Vie for Village Allegiance." In *Global Ethnography: Forces, Connections, and Imaginations in a Postmodern World*, edited by Michael Burawoy, 345–378. Berkeley: University of California Press.

Giraudy, Agustina. 2007. "The Distributive Politics of Emergency Employment Programs in Argentina (1993–2002)." *Latin American Research Review* 42 (2): 33–55.

Giraudy, Agustina. 2015. *Democrats and Autocrats: Pathways of Subnational Undemocratic Regime Continuity within Democratic Countries*. New York: Oxford University Press.

Girbal-Blacha, Noemí M. 2004. "Opciones para la Economía Agraria del Gran Chaco Argentino. El Algodón en Tiempos del Estado Intervencionista." In *El Campo Diverso: Enfoques y Perspectivas de la Argentina Agraria del Siglo XX*, edited by Guido Galafassi, 185–215. Bernal: Universidad Nacional de Quilmes.

Glover, Dominic. 2007. "Monsanto and Ssmallholder farmers: A Case Study in CSR." *Third World Quarterly* 28 (4): 851–867.

Glover, Dominic. 2010a. "Exploring the Resilience of Bt Cotton's 'Pro-Poor Success Story.'" *Development and Change* 41 (6): 955–981.

Glover, Dominic. 2010b. "The Corporate Shaping of GM Crops as a Technology for the Poor." *Journal of Peasant Studies* 37 (1): 67–90.

Goffman, Erving. 1959. *The Presentation of Self in Everyday Life*. Garden City, NY: Doubleday.

Goldfarb, Lucía, and Gemma van der Haar. 2016. "The Moving Frontiers of Genetically Modified Soy Production: Shifts in Land Control in the Argentinian Chaco." *Journal of Peasant Studies* 43 (2): 562–582.

Goldman, Marcio. 2001. "An Ethnographic Theory of Democracy. Politics from the Viewpoint of Ilhéus's Black Movement (Bahia, Brazil)." *Ethnos: Journal of Anthropology* 66 (2): 157–180.

Goldstone, Jack. 2003. "Introduction: Bridging Institutionalized and Non-Institutionalized Politics." In *States, Parties, and Social Movements*, edited by Jack A. Goldstone, 1–26. New York: Cambridge University Press.

Goodman, David, and Michael Redclift. 1991. *Refashioning Nature: Food, Ecology and Culture*. London: Routledge.

Goodman, David, and Michael Watts. 1994. "Reconfiguring the Rural or Fording the Divide?: Capitalist Restructuring and the Global Agro-Food System." *Journal of Peasant Studies* 22 (1): 1–49.

Goodwin, Jeff, and James M. Jasper. 2004a. "Introduction." In *Rethinking Social Movements: Structure, Meaning, and Emotion*, edited by Jeff Goodwin and James M. Jasper, vii–x. Lanham, MD: Rowman & Littlefield.

Goodwin, Jeff, and James M. Jasper, eds. 2004b. *Rethinking Social Movements: Structure, Meaning, and Emotion*. Lanham, MD: Rowman & Littlefield.

Goodwin, Jeff, James M. Jasper, and Francesca Polletta. 2001. *Passionate Politics: Emotions and Social Movements*. Chicago: University of Chicago Press.

Gordillo, Gastón. 2008. "The Clientelization of Ethnicity: Party Hegemony and Indigenous Political Subjectivities." *Journal of Latin American Cultural Studies* 17 (3): 335–348.

Gordillo, Gastón. 2014. *Rubble: The Afterlife of Destruction*. Durham, NC: Duke University Press.

Gordillo, Gastón, and Silvia Hirsch. 2003. "Indigenous Struggles and Contested Identities in Argentina: Histories of Invisibilization and Reemergence." *Journal of Latin American Anthropology* 8 (3): 4–30.

Gould, Deborah B. 2009. *Moving Politics: Emotion and ACT UP's Fight Against AIDS*. Chicago: University of Chicago Press.

Gowan, Theresa, and Seán Ó Riain. 2000. "At Home with the Global Ethnographer." In *Global Ethnography: Forces, Connections, and Imaginations in a Postmodern World*, edited by Michael Burawoy, ix–xv. Berkeley: University of California Press.

Gras, Carla. 2009. "Changing Patterns in Family Farming: The Case of the Pampa Region, Argentina." *Journal of Agrarian Change* 9 (3): 345–364.

Gras, Carla, and Valeria A. Hernández, eds. 2009. *La Argentina Rural: De la Agricultura Familiar a los Agronegocios*. Buenos Aires: Editorial Biblos.

Gras, Carla, and Victoria Hernandez, eds. 2013. *El Agro como Negocio. Producción, Sociedad y Territorios en la Globalización*. Buenos Aires: Biblos.

Greenpeace. 2006. Desmontes S.A. Quiénes están Detrás de la Destrucción de los últimos Bosques Nativos de la Argentina. Buenos Aires: Greenpeace.

GRR. 2009. Pueblos Fumigados. Informe sobre la Problemática del Uso de Plaguicidas en las Principales Provincias Sojeras de la Argentina. Buenos Aires: Grupo de Reflexión Rural.

Gupta, Akhil, and James Ferguson. 1997. "Discipline and Practice: 'The Field' as Site, Method, and Location in Anthropology." In *Anthropological Locations: Boundaries and Grounds of a Field Science*, edited by Akhil Gupta and James Ferguson, 1–46. Berkeley: University of California Press.

Guthman, Julie. 2003. "Eating Risk: The Politics of Labeling Genetically Engineered Foods." In *Engineering Trouble: Biotechnology and its Discontents*, edited by R. Schurman and D. D. Kelso, 130–151. Berkeley: University of California Press.

Haarstad, Håvard, ed. 2012. *New Political Spaces in Latin American Natural Resource Governance*. New York: Palgrave Macmillan.

Hale, Charles R., ed. 2008. *Engaging Contradictions: Theory, Politics, and Methods of Activist Scholarship*. Berkeley: University of California Press.

Hammersley, Martyn, and Paul Atkinson. 2007. *Ethnography: Principles in Practice*. New York: Routledge.

Harrison, Jill. 2004. "Invisible People, Invisible Places: Connecting Air Pollution and Pesticide Drift in California." In *Smoke and Mirrors: The Politics and Culture of Air Pollution*, edited by Melanie Du Puis, 288–304. New York: NYU Press.

Harrison, Jill Lindsey. 2011. *Pesticide Drift and the Pursuit of Environmental Justice*. Cambridge, MA: MIT Press.

Heaney, Michael T., and Fabio Rojas. 2011. "The Partisan Dynamics of Contention: Demobilization of the Antiwar Movement in the United States, 2007–2009." *Mobilization* 16 (1): 45–64.

Heinemann, Jack A., Melanie Massaro, Dorien S. Coray, Sarah Zanon Agapito-Tenfen, and Jiajun Dale Wen. 2013. "Sustainability and Innovation in Staple Crop Production in the US Midwest." *International Journal of Agricultural Sustainability* 12 (1): 71–88.

Heller, Chaia. 2013. *Food, Farms, and Solidarity: French Farmers Challenge Industrial Agriculture and Genetically Modified Crops*. Durham, NC: Duke University Press.

Hellman, Judith Adler. 1994. "Mexican Popular Movements, Clientelism, and the Process of Democratization." *Latin American Perspectives* 21 (2): 124–142.

Helmke, Gretchen, and Steven Levitsky, eds. 2006. *Informal Institutions and Democracy: Lessons from Latin America*. Baltimore, MD: Johns Hopkins University Press.

Hermanowicz, Joseph C. 2013. "The Longitudinal Qualitative Interview." *Qualitative Sociology* 36 (2): 189–208.

Hernández, Valeria A. 2007. "El Fenómeno Económico y Cultural del Boom de la Soja y el Empresariado Innovador." *Desarrollo Económico* 47 (187): 331–365.

Herod, Andrew. 2009. *Scale*. New York: Routledge.

Hetland, Gabriel, and Jeff Goodwin. 2013. "The Strange Disappearance of Capitalism from Social-Movement Studies." In *Marxism and Social Movements*, edited by Colin Barker, Laurence Cox, John Krinsky, and Alf Gunvald Nilsen, 83–102. Leiden: Brill.

Hilgers, Tina. 2009. "'Who Is Using Whom?' Clientelism from the Client's Perspective." *Journal of Iberian and Latin American Research* 15 (1): 51–75.

Hilgers, Tina, ed. 2012a. *Clientelism in Everyday Latin American Politics*. New York: Palgrave Macmillan.

Hilgers, Tina. 2012b. "Democratic Processes, Clientelistic Relationships, and the Material Goods Problem." In *Clientelism in Everyday Latin American Politics*, edited by Tina Hilgers, 3–22. New York: Palgrave Macmillan.

Ho, Ming-sho. 2010. "Co-opting Social Ties: How the Taiwanese Petrochemical Industry Neutralized Environmental Opposition." *Mobilization* 15 (4): 447–463.

Ho, Peter, Jennifer H. Zhao, and Dayuan Xue. 2009. "Access and Control of Agro-Biotechnology: Bt Cotton, Ecological Change and Risk in China." *Journal of Peasant Studies* 36 (2): 345–364.

Holland, Dorothy, Gretchen Fox, and Vinci Daro. 2008. "Social Movements and Collective Identity: A Decentered, Dialogic View." *Anthropological Quarterly* 81 (1): 95–125.

Holland, Janet. 2011. "Timescapes: Living a Qualitative Longitudinal Study." *Forum Qualitative Sozialforschung/Forum: Qualitative Social Research* 12 (3). Available at: <http://www.qualitative-research.net/index.php/fqs/article/view/1729>.

Hollander, Jocelyn A, and Rachel L Einwohner. 2004. "Conceptualizing Resistance." *Sociological Forum* 19 (4): 533–554.

IAASTD. 2009. "Agriculture at a Crossroads. Synthesis Report." Washington, DC: International Assessment of Agricultural Knowledge, Science and Technology For Development.

INTA. 2004. El avance de la soja en la Argentina y la sostenibilidad de los sistemas agrícolas. Reconquista, Santa Fe: Instituto Nacional de Tecnología Agropecuaria.

Jaffee, Daniel. 2012. "Weak Coffee: Certification and Co-Optation in the Fair Trade Movement." *Social Problems* 59 (1): 94–116.

James, Clive. 2012. "Global Status of Commercialized Transgenic Crops: 2012." *International Service for the Acquisition of Agri-biotech Applications Briefs* 44: 1–24. Available at http://www.isaaa.org/resources/publications/briefs/44/executivesummary/.

Jasanoff, Sheila. 2005. "In the Democracies of DNA: Ontological Uncertainty and Political Order in Three States." *New Genetics & Society* 24 (2): 139–155.

Jasper, James, and Jeff Goodwin. 2011. *Contention in Context: Political Opportunities and the Emergence of Protest*. Standford, CA: Stanford University Press.

Jasper, James M. 2004. "A Strategic Approach to Collective Action: Looking for Agency in Social-Movement Choices." *Mobilization* 9 (1): 1–16.

Jasper, James M. 2011. "Emotions and Social Movements: Twenty Years of Theory and Research." *Annual Review of Sociology* 37: 285–303.

Jasper, James M. 2006. *Getting Your Way: Strategic Dilemmas in the Real World*. Chicago: University of Chicago Press.

Jenkins, J. Craig, and Craig M. Eckert. 1986. "Channeling Black insurgency: Elite Patronage and Professional Social Movement Organizations in the Development of the Black Movement." *American Sociological Review* 51 (6): 812–829.

Jepson, Wendy E., Christian Brannstrom, and Renato Stancato De Souza. 2008. "Brazilian Biotechnology Governance: Consensus and Conflict Over Genetically Modified Crops." In *Food for the Few: Neoliberal Globalism and Biotechnology in Latin America*, edited by Gerardo Otero, 217–242. Austin: University of Texas Press.

Jergentz, S., H. Mugni, C. Bonetto, and R. Schulz. 2005. "Assessment of Insecticide Contamination in Runoff and Stream Water of Small Agricultural Streams in the Main Soybean Area of Argentina." *Chemosphere* 61 (6): 817–826.

Joensen, Lilian, Stella Semino, and Helena Paul. 2005. *Argentina: A Case Study on the Impact of Genetically Engineered Soya*. London: Gaia Foundation.

Jones, Mark P, and Wonjae Hwang. 2005. "Provincial Party Bosses: Keystone of the Argentine Congress." In *Argentine Democracy: The Politics of Institutional Weakness*, edited by Steven Levitsky and María Victoria Murillo, 115–138. University Park: Pennsylvania University Press.

Jozami, Eduardo, Pedro Paz, and Juan Villarreal. 1985. *Crisis de la Dictadura Argentina: Política Económica y Cambio Social, 1976–1983*. Buenos Aires: Siglo XXI.

Jung, Jai Kwan. 2010. "Disentangling Protest Cycles: An Event-History Analysis of New Social Movements in Western Europe." *Mobilization* 15 (1): 25–44.

Katz, Jack. 2004. "On the Rhetoric and Politics of Ethnographic Methodology." *Annals of the American Academy of Political and Social Science* 595 (1): 280–308.

Kerkvliet, Benedict J. Tria. 2005. *The Power of Everyday Politics: How Vietnamese Peasants Transformed National Policy*. Ithaca, NY: Cornell University Press.

Kinchy, Abby. 2012. *Seeds, Science, and Struggle: The Global Politics of Transgenic Crops*. Cambridge, MA: MIT Press.

Kleinman, Daniel Lee. 2005. *Science and Technology in Society: From Biotechnology to the Internet*. Malden, MA: Blackwell.

Klepek, James. 2012. "Against the Grain: Knowledge Alliances and Resistance to Agricultural Biotechnology in Guatemala." *Canadian Journal of Development Studies/Revue Canadienne d'tudes du Développement* 33 (3): 310–325.

Klintman, Mikael. 2002. "The Genetically Modified (GM) Food Labelling Controversy: Ideological and Epistemic Crossovers." *Social Studies of Science* 32 (1): 71–91.

Kloppenburg, Jack R. 2005. *First the Seed: The Political Economy of Plant Biotechnology, 1492–2000*. 2nd ed. Madison: University of Wisconsin Press.

Kooistra, Karst, Aad Termorshuizen, and Rhiannon Pyburn. 2006. "The Sustainability of Cotton: Consequences for Man and Environment." Report No. 223. Wageningen, The Netherlands: University and Research Center.

Krauss, Celene. 1993. "Women and Toxic Waste Protests: Race, Class and Gender as Resources of Resistance." *Qualitative Sociology* 16 (3): 247–262.

Kurzman, Charles. 1996. "Structural Opportunity and Perceived Opportunity in Social-Movement Theory: The Iranian Revolution of 1979." *American Sociological Review* 61 (1): 153–170.

Kurzman, Charles. 2008. "Introduction: Meaning-Making in Social Movements." *Anthropological Quarterly* 81 (1): 5–15.

Lang, John. 2013. "Genetically Modified Foods: Recent Developments." In *The Oxford Encyclopedia of Food and Drink in America*, edited by Andrew F. Smith, 90–98. New York: Oxford University Press.

Lapegna, Pablo. 2009. "Ethnographers of the World . . . United? Current Debates on the Ethnographic Study of 'Globalization.'" *Journal of World-Systems Research* 15 (1): 3–24.

Lazar, Sian. 2008. *El Alto, Rebel City: Self and Citizenship in Andean Bolivia*. Durham, NC: Duke University Press.

Lazar, Sian, and Monique Nuijten. 2013. "Citizenship, the Self, and Political Agency." *Critique of Anthropology* 33 (1): 3–7.

Le Heron, Richard. 2009. "Food and Agriculture in a Globalising World." In *Companion to Environmental Geography*, edited by Noel Castree, David Demeritt, Diana Liverman, and Bruce Rhoads, 552–566. Oxford: Blackwell.

Le Heron, Richard, and Michael Roche. 1995. "A 'Fresh' Place in Food's Space." *Area* 27 (1): 23–33.

Lee, Ching Kwan, and Yonghong Zhang. 2013. "The Power of Instability: Unraveling the Microfoundations of Bargained Authoritarianism in China." *American Journal of Sociology* 118 (6): 1475–1508.

Leguizamón, Amalia. 2014. "Modifying Argentina: GM Soy and Socio-Environmental Change." *Geoforum* 53: 149–160.

Levidow, Les. 1998. "Democratizing Technology—or Technologizing Democracy? Regulating Agricultural Biotechnology in Europe." *Technology in Society* 20 (2): 211–226.

Levidow, Les, and Karin Boschert. 2008. "Coexistence or Contradiction? GM Crops Versus Alternative Agricultures in Europe." *Geoforum* 39 (1): 174–190.

Levidow, Les, Joseph Murphy, and Susan Carr. 2007. "Recasting 'Substantial Equivalence': Transatlantic Governance of GM Food." *Science, Technology & Human Values* 32 (1): 26–64.

Levitsky, Steven. 2003. *Transforming Labor-Based Parties in Latin America: Argentine Peronism in Comparative Perspective.* New York: Cambridge University Press.

Levitsky, Steven, and María Victoria Murillo. 2008. "Argentina: From Kirchner to Kirchner." *Democracy* 19 (2): 16–30.

Levitsky, Steven, and Kenneth M. Roberts, eds. 2011. *The Resurgence of the Latin American Left.* Baltimore, MD: John Hopkins University Press.

Lichterman, Paul. 1998. "What Do Movements Mean? The Value of Participant-Observation." *Qualitative Sociology* 21 (4): 401–418.

Lipsky, Michael. 1970. *Protest in City Politics: Rent Strikes, Housing, and the Power of the Poor.* Chicago: Rand McNally.

Lodola, Germán. 2005. "Protesta Popular y Redes Clientelares en la Argentina: El Reparto Federal del Plan Trabajar (1996–2001)." *Desarrollo Económico* 44 (176): 515–536.

MAGyP. 2011. Producción de Oleaginosas por Cultivo. Total del país. Campañas 2005–06 a 2009–10. Buenos Aires: Ministerio de Agricultura, Ganadería y Pesca.

MAGyP. 2013. Producción, rea Sembrada y Cosechada, Cotizaciones Nacionales e Internacionales. Buenos Aires: Sistema Integrado de Información Agropecuaria—Ministerio de Agricultura, Ganadería y Pesca.

Maney, Gregory M., Rachel V. Kutz-Flamenbaum, Deana A. Rohlinger, and Jeff Goodwin, eds. 2012. *Strategies for Social Change.* Minneapolis: University of Minnesota Press.

Manzanal, Mabel. 1990. "El Campesinado en la Argentina: Un Debate Tardío o Políticas para el Sector: una Necesidad Impostergable." *Realidad Económica* 97: 137–152.

Manzanal, Mabel, and Alejandro Rofman. 1989. *Las Economías Regionales de la Argentina. Crisis y Políticas de Desarrollo.* Buenos Aires: Centro Editor de América Latina-Centro de Estudios Urbanos y Regionales.

Manzur, María Isabel, Georgina Catacora, María Isabel Cárcamo, Elizabeth Bravo, and Miguel Altieri. 2011. América Latina. La Transgénesis de un Continente. Fundación Heinrich Böll—Sociedad Científica Latinoamericana de Agroecología.

Marcus, George E. 1995. "Ethnography in/of the World System: The Emergence of Multi-Sited Ethnography." *Annual Review of Anthropology* 24: 95–117.

Martinez-Alier, Joan. 1995. "Political Ecology, Distributional Conflicts, and Economic Incomensurability." *New Left Review* 211: 70–88.

Massey, Doreen. 1994. *Space, Place, and Gender.* Minneapolis: University of Minnesota Press.

Massey, Doreen. 2005. *For Space*. Thousand Oaks, CA: Sage.

Mawdsley, Emma. 1998. "After Chipko: From Environment to Region in Uttaranchal." *Journal of Peasant Studies* 25 (4): 36–54.

McAdam, Doug. 1982. *Political Process and the Development of Black Insurgency, 1930–1970*. Chicago: University of Chicago Press.

McAdam, Doug, and Hilary Boudet. 2012. *Putting Social Movements in their Place: Explaining Opposition to Energy Projects in the United States, 2000–2005*. New York: Cambridge University Press.

McAdam, Doug, and Sidney Tarrow. 2010. "Ballots and Barricades: On the Reciprocal Relationship between Elections and Social Movements." *Perspectives on Politics* 8 (2): 529–542.

McAdam, Doug, Sidney Tarrow, and Charles Tilly. 2001. *Dynamics of Contention*. New York: Cambridge University Press.

McAdam, Doug, Sidney Tarrow, and Charles Tilly. 2008. "Methods for Measuring Mechanisms of Contention." *Qualitative Sociology* 31 (4): 307–331.

McAfee, Kathleen. 2003. "Neoliberalism on the Molecular Scale: Economic and Genetic Reductionism in Biotechnology Battles." *Geoforum* 34 (2): 203–219.

McCarthy, John D., and Mark Wolfson. 1992. "Consensus Movements, Conflict Movements, and the Cooptation of Civic and State Infrastructures." In *Frontiers in Social Movement Theory*, edited by Aldon D. Morris and Carol McClurg Mueller, 273–297. New Haven, CT: Yale University Press.

McDuffie, H. H., P. Pahwa, J. R. McLaughlin, J. J. Spinelli, S. Fincham, J. A. Dosman, D. Robson, L. F. Skinnider, and N. W. Choi. 2001. "Non-Hodgkin's Lymphoma and Specific Pesticide Exposures in Men." *Cancer Epidemiology Biomarkers & Prevention* 10 (11): 1155–1163.

McLeod, Julie, and Rachel Thomson. 2009. *Researching Social Change: Qualitative Approaches*. Thousand Oaks, CA: Sage.

McMichael, Philip. 2006. "Peasant Prospects in the Neoliberal Age." *New Political Economy* 11 (3): 407–418.

McMichael, Philip. 2009. "A Food Regime Genealogy." *Journal of Peasant Studies* 36 (1): 139–169.

Melucci, A. 1985. "The Symbolic Challenge of Contemporary Movements." *Social Research* 52 (4): 789–816.

Melucci, Alberto. 1996. *Challenging Codes: Collective Action in the Information Age*. Cambridge: Cambridge University Press.

Merton, Robert K., and Elinor Barber. 1976. "Sociological Ambivalence." In *Sociological Ambivalence and Other Essays*, edited by Robert K. Merton, 3–31. New York: Free Press.

Meyer, David S. 2007. *The Politics of Protest: Social Movements in America*. New York: Oxford University Press.

Michels, Robert. 1962. *Political Parties: A Sociological Study of the Oligarchical Tendencies of Modern Democracy*. Glencoe, IL: Free Press.

Mills, Charles Wright. 1940. "Situated Actions and Vocabularies of Motive." *American Sociological Review* 5 (6): 904–913.

Mills, Charles Wright. 1959. *The Sociological Imagination*. New York: Oxford University Press.

Mische, Ann. 2008. *Partisan Publics: Communication and Contention across Brazilian Youth Activist Networks*. Princeton, NJ: Princeton University Press.

Moore, Barrington. 1978. *Injustice: The Social Bases of Obedience and Revolt*. New York: Macmillan.

Moran, Warren, Greg Blunden, Martin Workman, and Adrian Bradly. 1996. "Family Farmers, Real Regulation, and the Experience of Food Regimes." *Journal of Rural Studies* 12 (3): 245–258.

Moscovich, Lorena. 2012. "From Top to Bottom (and Back to the Top Again): Federal Spending, Sub-National Coalitions, and Protests in Argentina, 2002–2006." *Journal of Politics* 4 (1): 35–72.

Motta, Renata. 2014. "Transnational Discursive Opportunities and Social Movement Risk Frames Opposing GMOs." *Social Movement Studies* 14 (5): 576–595.

Müller, Birgit. 2006. "Infringing and Trespassing Plants: Patented Seeds at Dispute in Canada's Courts." *Focaal* 48: 83–98.

Murphree, David W., Stuart A. Wright, and Helen Rose Ebaugh. 1996. "Toxic Waste Siting and Community Resistance: How Cooptation of Local Citizen Opposition Failed." *Sociological Perspectives* 39 (4): 447–463.

Newell, Peter. 2008. "Trade and Biotechnology in Latin America: Democratization, Contestation and the Politics of Mobilization." *Journal of Agrarian Change* 8 (2–3): 345–376.

Newell, Peter. 2009. "Bio-Hegemony: The Political Economy of Agricultural Biotechnology in Argentina." *Journal of Latin American Studies* 41 (1): 27–57.

O'Brien, Kevin J. 2003. "Neither Transgressive Nor Contained: Boundary-Spanning Contention in China." *Mobilization* 8 (1): 51–64.

O'Reilly, Karen. 2012. "Ethnographic Returning, Qualitative Longitudinal Research and the Reflexive Analysis of Social Practice." *Sociological Review* 60 (3): 518–536.

Ortner, Sherry B. 2006a. "Power and Projects: Reflections on Agency." In *Anthropology and Social Theory: Culture, Power and the Acting Subject*, 129–153. Durham, NC: Duke University Press.

Ortner, Sherry B. 2006b. "Resistance and the Problem of Ethnographic Refusal." In *Anthropology and Social Theory: Culture, Power and the Acting Subject*, 42–62. Durham, NC: Duke University Press.

Otero, Gerardo. 1999. *Farewell to the Peasantry? Political Class Formation in Rural Mexico*. Boulder, CO: Westview Press.

Otero, Gerardo, ed. 2008a. *Food for the Few: Neoliberal Globalism and Biotechnology in Latin America*. Austin: University of Texas Press.

Otero, Gerardo. 2008b. "Neoliberal Globalism and the Biotechnology Revolution: Economic and Historical Context." In *Food for the Few: Neoliberal*

Globalism and Biotechnology in Latin America, edited by Gerardo Otero, 1–29. Austin: University of Texas Press.

Otero, Gerardo. 2012. "The Neoliberal Food Regime in Latin America: State, Agribusiness Transnational Corporations and Biotechnology." *Canadian Journal of Development Studies/Revue Canadienne d'tudes du Développement* 33 (3): 282–294.

Otero, Gerardo, Gabriela Pechlaner, and Efe Can Gürcan. 2013. "The Political Economy of 'Food Security' and Trade: Uneven and Combined Dependency." *Rural Sociology* 78 (3): 263–289.

Otis, Eileen. 2012. *Markets and Bodies: Women, Service Work, and the Making of Inequality in China*. Standford, CA: Stanford University Press.

Paarlberg, Robert L. 2009. *Starved for Science: How Biotechnology Is Being Kept Out of Africa*. Cambridge, MA: Harvard University Press.

Paganelli, A., V. Gnazzo, H. Acosta, S. L. López, and A. E. Carrasco. 2010. "Glyphosate-Based Herbicides Produce Teratogenic Effects on Vertebrates By Impairing Retinoic Acid Signaling." *Chemical Research in Toxicology* 23 (10): 1586–1595.

Palau, Marielle, and Regina Kretschmer. 2004. "La 'Guerra de la Soja' y el Avance del Neoliberalismo en el Campo Paraguayo." *Revista Observatorio Social de América Latina* 13: 26–33.

Papa, Juan Carlos. 2002. "Malezas Tolerantes y Resistentes a Herbicidas." In *Actas del Seminario Sustentabilidad de la Producción Agrícola*. Rafaela, Santa Fe: Instituto Nacional de Tecnología Agropecuaria.

Park, Yun-Joo, and Patricia Richards. 2007. "Negotiating Neoliberal Multiculturalism: Mapuche Workers in the Chilean State." *Social Forces* 85 (3): 1319–1339.

Patel, Raj. 2012. "The Long Green Revolution." *Journal of Peasant Studies* 40 (1): 1–63.

Paz, Raúl. 2011. "Agricultura Familiar en el Agro Argentino: una Contribución al Debate sobre el Futuro del Campesinado." *European Review of Latin American and Caribbean Studies* 91: 49–70.

Pearson, Thomas W. 2012. "Transgenic-Free Territories in Costa Rica: Networks, Place, and the Politics of Life." *American Ethnologist* 39 (1): 90–105.

Pechlaner, Gabriela. 2012. *Corporate Crops: Biotechnology, Agriculture, and the Struggle for Control*. Austin: University of Texas Press.

Pechlaner, Gabriela, and Gerardo Otero. 2008. "The Third Food Regime: Neoliberal Globalism and Agricultural Biotechnology in North America." *Sociologia Ruralis* 48 (4): 351–371.

Peck, Jamie, and Adam Tickell. 2002. "Neoliberalizing Space." *Antipode* 34 (3): 380–404.

Peláez, Victor, and Wilson Schmidt. 2004. "Social Struggles and the Regulation of Transgenic Crops in Brazil." In *Agribusiness and Society: Corporate Responses to Environmentalism, Market Opportunities and Public Regulation*, edited by Kees Jansen and Sietze Vellema, 232–260. London: Zed Books.

Penfold-Becerra, Michael. 2007. "Clientelism and Social Funds: Evidence from Chávez's Misiones." *Latin American Politics and Society* 49 (4): 63–84.

Pengue, Walter A. 2004a. "El Modelo de Agricultura Industrial Intensivo." *Revista Saber Cómo* 16. Available at: https://www.inti.gob.ar/sabercomo/sc16/inti41.php.

Pengue, Walter A. 2004b. "La Ingeniería Genética y la Intensificación de la Agricultura Argentina: Algunos Comentarios Críticos." In *Los Transgénicos en América Latina y el Caribe: Un Debate Abierto*, edited by Alicia Bárcena, Jorge Katz, César Morales, and Marianne Schaper, 167–190. Santiago de Chile: Comisión Económica para América Latina y el Caribe.

Pengue, Walter A. 2005. "Transgenic Crops in Argentina: The Ecological and Social Debt." *Bulletin of Science Technology & Society* 25 (4): 314–322.

Perez, G. L., A. Torremorell, H. Mugni, P. Rodríguez, M. S. Vera, M. Nascimento, L. Allende, J. Bustingorry, R. Escaray, and M. Ferraro. 2007. "Effects of the Herbicide Roundup on Freshwater Microbial Communities: A Mesocosm Study." *Ecological Applications* 17 (8): 2310–2322.

Peschard, Karine. 2012. "Unexpected Discontent: Exploring New Developments in Brazil's Transgenics Controversy." *Canadian Journal of Development Studies/ Revue Canadienne d'tudes du Développement* 33 (3): 326–337.

Pingali, Prabhu, and Terri Raney. 2005. "From the Green Revolution to the Gene Revolution: How Will The Poor Fare?" In *Working Papers*: Agricultural and Development Economics Division of the Food and Agriculture Organization of the United Nations (FAO-ESA), Rome (Italy).

Piven, Frances Fox, and Richard A. Cloward. 1979. *Poor People's Movements: Why They Succeed, How They Fail*. New York: Vintage.

Poitras, Manuel. 2008. "Social Movements and Techno-Democracy: Reclaiming the Genetic Commons." In *Food for the Few: Neoliberal Globalism and the Biotechnology Revolution in Latin America*, edited by Gerardo Otero, 267–287. Austin: University of Texas Press.

Polletta, Francesca. 2008. "Culture and Movements." *Annals of the American Academy of Political and Social Science* 619 (1): 78–96.

Posada, Marcelo G., ed. 1993. *Sociología Rural Argentina: Estudios en Torno al Campesinado*. Buenos Aires: Centro Editor de América Latina.

Posada, Marcelo G., and Mariano Martínez de Ibarreta. 1998. "Capital Financiero y Producción Agrícola: Los "Pools" de Siembra en la Región Pampeana." *Realidad Económica* 153: 112–135.

Prudham, Scott. 2007. "The Fictions of Autonomous Invention: Accumulation by Dispossession, Commodification and Life Patents in Canada." *Antipode* 39 (3): 406–442.

Puricelli, E., and D. Tuesca. 2005. "Weed Density and Diversity Under Glyphosate-Resistant Crop Sequences." *Crop Protection* 24 (6): 533–542.

Qaim, Matin, and Greg Traxler. 2005. "Roundup Ready Soybeans in Argentina: Farm Level and Aggregate Welfare Effects." *Agricultural Economics* 32 (1): 73–86.

Quijada, Mónica. 2000. *Homogeneidad y Nación, con un Estudio de Caso: Argentina, Siglos XIX y XX*. Spain: Editorial CSIC.

Quirós, Julieta. 2006. *Cruzando la Sarmiento: Una Etnografía sobre Piqueteros en la Trama Social del Sur del Gran Buenos Aires*. Buenos Aires: Antropofagia.

Rabinow, Paul. 1996. *Making PCR: A Story of Biotechnology*. Chicago: University of Chicago Press.

Radnitz, Scott. 2010. *Weapons of the Wealthy: Predatory Regimes and Elite-Led Protests in Central Asia*. Ithaca, NY: Cornell University Press.

Rangan, Haripriya. 2000. *Of Myths and Movements: Rewriting Chipko into Himalayan History*. London: Verso Books.

REDAF. 2010. Conflictos sobre Tenencia de Tierra y Ambientales en la Región del Chaco Argentino. Reconquista, Santa Fe: Red Agroforestal Chaco Argentina (REDAF) - Observatorio de Tierras, Recursos Naturales y Medioambiente.

Richard, Sophie, Safa Moslemi, Herbert Sipahutar, Nora Benachour, and Gilles-Eric Seralini. 2005. "Differential Effects of Glyphosate and Roundup on Human Placental Cells and Aromatase." *Environmental Health Perspectives* 113 (6): 716–720.

Richards, Donald G. 2010. "Contradictions of the 'New Green Revolution': A View from South America's Southern Cone." *Globalizations* 7 (4): 563–576.

Richards, Patricia. 2013. *Race and the Chilean Miracle: Neoliberalism, Democracy, and Indigenous Rights*. Pittsburgh: University of Pittsburgh Press.

Richardson, Neal. 2009. "Export-Oriented Populism: Commodities and Coalitions in Argentina." *Studies in Comparative International Development* 44 (3): 228–255.

Roberts, John Michael, and Teela Sanders. 2005. "Before, During and After: Realism, Reflexivity and Ethnography." *Sociological Review* 53 (2): 294–313.

Robin, Marie-Monique. 2008. *The World According to Monsanto*. National Film Board of Canada, Thalie Productions.

Robnett, Belinda. 1997. *How Long? How Long? African-American Women in the Struggle for Civil Rights*. New York: Oxford University Press.

Rodríguez, Javier Leonel. 2010. "Consecuencias Económicas de la Difusión de la Soja Genéticamente Modificada en Argentina, 1996–2006." In *Los Señores de la Soja. La Agricultura Transgénica en América Latina*, edited by Ana Lucía Bravo, 155–259. Buenos Aires: Consejo Latinoamericano de Ciencias Sociales.

Roff, Robin Jane. 2007. "Shopping for Change? Neoliberalizing Activism and the Limits to Eating Non-GMO." *Agriculture and Human Values* 24 (4): 511–522.

Rofman, Alejandro, Aída Quintar, Nora Marqués, and Mabel Manzanal. 1987. *Políticas Estatales y Desarrollo Regional. La Experiencia del Gobierno Militar en la Región del NEA (1976–1981)*. Buenos Aires: Centro de Estudios Urbanos y Regionales.

Roniger, Luis, and Ayse Günes-Ayata. 1994. *Democracy, Clientelism, and Civil Society*. Boulder, CO: Lynne Rienner Publishers.

Roseberry, William. 1994. "Hegemony and the Language of Contention." In *Everyday Forms of State Formation: Revolution and the Negotiation of Rule in*

Modern Mexico, edited by Joseph Gilbert and Daniel Nugent, 355–366. Durham, NC: Duke University Press.

Ross, Eric B. 2003. "Malthusianism, Capitalist Agriculture, and the Fate of Peasants in the Making of the Modern World Food System." *Review of Radical Political Economics* 35 (4): 437–461.

Rossi, Federico M. 2013. "Piqueteros (Workers/Unemployment Movement in Argentina)." In *The Wiley-Blackwell Encyclopedia of Social and Political Movements*, edited by David A. Snow, Donatella della Porta, Bert Klandermans, and Doug McAdam, 929–932. Malden, MA: Blackwell.

Roy, Devparna. 2013. "To Bt or not to Bt? State, Civil Society, and Firms Debate Transgenic Seeds in Democratic India." In *The Neoliberal Regime in the Agri-Food Sector*, edited by Steven Wolf and Alessandro Bonanno, 153–169. London: Routledge.

Roze, Jorge Próspero. 1992. *Conflictos Agrarios en la Argentina: El Proceso Liguista*. Buenos Aires: Centro Editor de América Latina.

Rubin, Jeffrey. 1998. "Ambiguity and Contradiction in a Radical Popular Movement." In *Cultures of Politics/Politics of Cultures. Revisioning Latin American Social Movements*, edited by Arturo Escobar, Sonia E. Alvarez, and Evelina Dagnino, 141–164. Boulder, CO: Westview.

Sábato, Jorge. 1988. *La Clase Dominante en la Argentina Moderna*. Buenos Aires: Centro de Investigaciones Sociales sobre el Estado y la Administración/Grupo Editor Latinoamericano.

Saldaña, Johnny. 2003. *Longitudinal Qualitative Research: Analyzing Change Through Time*. Walnut Creek, CA: Altamira Press.

Sapkus, Sergio. 2002. "Campesinado y Protesta Rural en el Nordeste Argentino. El Movimiento Campesino de Formosa (1995–2000)." Masters thesis, National University of Misiones.

Sawyers, Traci M., and David S. Meyer. 1999. "Missed Opportunities: Social Movement Abeyance and Public Policy." *Social Problems* 46 (2): 187–206.

Schlosberg, David. 2007. *Defining Environmental Justice: Theories, Movements, and Nature*. New York: Oxford University Press.

Schmidt, Steffen W., Laura Guasti, Carl H. Landé, and James C. Scott. 1977. *Friends, Followers, and Factions: A Reader in Political Clientelism*. Berkeley: University of California Press.

Schurman, Rachel, and William A. Munro. 2010. *Fighting for the Future of Food: Activists versus Agribusiness in the Struggle Over Biotechnology*. Minneapolis: University of Minnesota Press.

Schwartz, Michael. 1976. *Radical Protest and Social Structure: The Southern Farmers' Alliance and Cotton Tenancy, 1880–1890*. Chicago: University of Chicago Press.

Schwartz, Michael, Naomi Rosenthal, and Laura Schwartz. 1981. "Leader-Member Conflict in Protest Organizations: The Case of the Southern Farmers' Alliance." *Social Problems* 29 (1): 22–36.

Scoones, Ian. 2002. "Can Agricultural Biotechnology be Pro-Poor?" *IDS Bulletin* 33 (4): 114–119.

Scoones, Ian. 2008. "Mobilizing Against GM Crops in India, South Africa and Brazil." *Journal of Agrarian Change* 8 (2–3): 315–344.

Scott, James C. 1976. *The Moral Economy of the Peasant: Rebellion and Subsistence in Southeast Asia.* New Haven, CT: Yale University Press.

Scott, James C. 1985. *Weapons of the Weak: Everyday Forms of Peasant Resistance.* New Haven, CT: Yale University Press.

Scott, James C. 1990. *Domination and the Arts of Resistance: Hidden Transcripts.* New Haven, CT: Yale University Press.

Scott, James C. 2005. "Afterword to 'Moral Economies, State Spaces, and Categorical Violence.'" *American Anthropologist* 107 (3): 395–402.

Scott, James C. 2012. *Decoding Subaltern Politics: Ideology, Disguise, and Resistance in Agrarian Politics.* London: Routledge.

Scott, Jim. 1986. "Everyday Forms of Peasant Resistance." *Journal of Peasant Studies* 13 (2): 5–35.

Selznick, P. 1949. *TVA and the Grass Roots: A Study in the Sociology of Formal Organization.* Berkeley: University of California Press.

Sen, Amartya. 1981. *Poverty and Famines: An Essay on Entitlement and Deprivation.* New York: Oxford University Press.

Séralini, G. E., E. Clair, R. Mesnage, S. Gress, N. Defarge, M. Malatesta, D. Hennequin, and J. S. de Vendômois. 2012. "Long Term Toxicity of a Roundup Herbicide and a Roundup-Tolerant Genetically Modified Maize." *Food and Chemical Toxicology* 50 (11): 4221–4231.

Séralini, Gilles-Eric, Robin Mesnage, Nicolas Defarge, Steeve Gress, Didier Hennequin, Emilie Clair, Manuela Malatesta, and Joël Spiroux de Vendômois. 2013. "Answers to Critics: Why There Is a Long Term Toxicity Due to a Roundup-Tolerant Genetically Modified Maize and to a Roundup Herbicide." *Food and Chemical Toxicology* (53): 476–483.

Servetto, Alicia. 2002. "El Peronismo en el Poder: La Primera y Fallida Experiencia de Gobierno en Formosa, 1973." *Cuadernos de Historia, Serie Economía y Sociedad* 5: 161–187. Available at: http://revistas.unc.edu.ar/index.php/cuadernosdehistoriaeys/article/view/9909.

Sewell, William H. Jr. 2005. *Logics of History: Social Theory and Social Transformation.* Chicago: University of Chicago Press.

Seymour, Susan. 2006. "Resistance." *Anthropological Theory* 6 (3): 303–321.

Shakow, Miriam. 2011. "The Peril and Promise of Noodles and Beer: Condemnation of Patronage and Hybrid Political Frameworks in 'Post-Neoliberal' Cochabamba, Bolivia." *PoLAR: Political and Legal Anthropology Review* 34 (2): 315–336.

Shanin, Teodor. 1990. *Defining Peasants: Essays Concerning Rural Societies, Expolary Economies, and the Learning From Them in the Contemporary World.* Cambridge, MA: Basil Blackwell.

Shefner, Jon. 2001. "Coalitions and Clientelism in Mexico." *Theory and Society* 30 (5): 593–628.

Shefner, Jon. 2008. *The Illusion of Civil Society: Democratization and Community Mobilization in Low-Income Mexico.* University Park: Pennsylvania State University Press.

Shiva, Vandana. 2000. *Stolen Harvest: The Hijacking of the Global Food Supply.* London: Zed Books.

Silva, Eduardo. 2009. *Challenging Neoliberalism in Latin America, Cambridge Studies in Contentious Politics.* New York: Cambridge University Press.

Sitrin, Marina. 2006. *Horizontalism: Voices of Popular Power in Argentina.* Oakland, CA: AK Press.

Sivaramakrishnan, K. 2005. "Some Intellectual Genealogies for the Concept of Everyday Resistance." *American Anthropologist* 107 (3): 346–355.

Slutzky, Daniel. 1973. Tenencia y distribución de la tierra en la región NEA. Buenos Aires: Consejo Federal de Inversiones.

Small, Mario Luis. 2009. "'How Many Cases Do I Need?' On Science and the Logic of Case Selection in Field-Based Research." *Ethnography* 10 (1): 5–38.

Smilde, David. 2008. "The Social Structure of Hugo Chávez." *Contexts* 7 (1): 38–43.

Smith, Neil. 2008. *Uneven Development: Nature, Capital, and the Production of Space.* Athens: University of Georgia Press.

Snow, David A., Calvin Morrill, and Leon Anderson. 2003. "Elaborating Analytic Ethnography: Linking Fieldwork and Theory." *Ethnography* 4 (2): 181–200.

Snow, David A., E. Burke Rochford Jr., Steven K. Worden, and Robert D. Benford. 1986. "Frame Alignment Processes, Micromobilization, and Movement Participation." *American Sociological Review* 51 (4): 464–481.

Steinberg, Marc W. 1998. "Tilting the Frame: Considerations on Collective Action Framing From a Discursive Turn." *Theory and Society* 27 (6): 845–872.

Steinberg, Marc W. 1999a. *Fighting Words: Working-Class Formation, Collective Action, and Discourse in Early Nineteenth-Century England.* Ithaca, NY: Cornell University Press.

Steinberg, Marc W. 1999b. "The Talk and Back Talk of Collective Action: A Dialogic Analysis of Repertoires of Discourse among Nineteenth-Century English Cotton Spinners." *American Journal of Sociology* 105 (3): 736–780.

Stone, Glenn Davis. 2005. "A Science of the Gray: Malthus, Marx, and the Ethics of Studying Crop Biotechnology." In *Embedding Ethics: Shifting Boundaries of the Anthropological Profession*, edited by Lynn Meskell and Peter Pels, 197–217. Oxford: Berg Publishers.

Stone, Glenn Davis. 2007. "Agricultural Deskilling and the Spread of Genetically Modified Cotton in Warangal." *Current Anthropology* 48 (1): 67–103.

Stone, Glenn Davis. 2010. "The Anthropology of Genetically Modified Crops." *Annual Review of Anthropology* 39: 381–400.

Stone, Glenn Davis. 2011. "Field Versus Farm in Warangal: Bt Cotton, Higher Yields, and Larger Questions." *World Development* 39 (3): 387–398.

Stürtz, N., G. A. Jahn, R. P. Deis, V. Rettori, R. O. Duffard, and A. M. Evangelista de Duffard. 2010. "Effect of 2, 4-Dichlorophenoxyacetic Acid on Milk Transfer to the Litter and Prolactin Release in Lactating Rats." *Toxicology* 271 (1–2): 13–20.

Summers-Effler, Erika. 2010. *Laughing Saints and Righteous Heroes: Emotional Rhythms in Social Movement Groups*. Chicago: University of Chicago Press.

Svampa, Maristella, and Sebastián Pereyra. 2003. *Entre la Ruta y el Barrio. La Experiencia de las Organizaciones Piqueteras*. Buenos Aires: Biblos.

Svampa, Maristella, and Sebastián Pereyra. 2004. "La Experiencia Piquetera: Dimensiones y Desafíos de las Organizaciones de Desocupados en Argentina." *Revista da Sociedade Brasileira de Economia Política* 15: 88–110.

Swidler, Ann. 1986. "Culture in Action: Symbols and Strategies." *American Sociological Review* 51 (2): 273–286.

Tarrow, Sidney. 2005. *Power in Movement: Social Movements and Contentious Politics*. 3rd ed. New York: Cambridge University Press.

Tarrow, Sidney. 2012. *Strangers at the Gates: Movements and States in Contentious Politics*. New York: Cambridge University Press.

Tarrow, Sidney. 2013. *The Language of Contention. Revolutions in Words, 1688–2012*. New York: Cambridge University Press.

Taylor, Diana. 1997. *Disappearing Acts: Spectacles of Gender and Nationalism in Argentina's "Dirty War."* Durham, NC: Duke University Press.

Taylor, Lucy. 2004. "Client-Ship and Citizenship in Latin America." *Bulletin of Latin American Research* 23 (2): 213–227.

Taylor, Verta. 1989. "Social Movement Continuity: The Women's Movement in Abeyance." *American Sociological Review* 54 (5): 761–775.

Teubal, Miguel, Diego Domínguez, and Pablo Sabatino. 2005. "Transformaciones Agrarias en la Argentina. Agricultura Industrial y Sistema Agroalimentario." In *El Campo Argentino en la Encrucijada. Estrategias y Resistencias Sociales, Ecos en la Ciudad*, edited by Norma Giarracca and Miguel Teubal, 37–78. Buenos Aires: Alianza Editorial.

Thompson, Edward P. 1991 [1963]. *The Making of the English Working Class*. New York: Penguin Books.

Thompson, Edward P., ed. 1993. "The Moral Economy Reviewed." In *Customs in Common: Studies in Traditional Popular Culture*, 259–351. New York: The New Press.

Tilly, Charles. 1978. *From Mobilization to Revolution*. Reading, MA: Addison-Wesley.

Tilly, Charles. 1991. "Domination, Resistance, Compliance . . . Discourse." *Sociological Forum* 6 (3): 593–602.

Tilly, Charles. 2006a. *Regimes and Repertoires*. Chicago: University of Chicago Press.

Tilly, Charles. 2006b. *Why? What Happens When People Give Reasons . . . and Why*. Princeton, NJ: Princeton University Press.

Tilly, Charles. 2008. *Credit and Blame*. Princeton, NJ: Princeton University Press.

Trigo, Eduardo J., and Eugenio J. Cap. 2003. "The Impact of the Introduction of Transgenic Crops in Argentinean Agriculture." *AgBioForum* 6 (3): 87–94.

Tripp, Robert, ed. 2009. *Biotechnology and Agricultural Development: Transgenic Cotton, Rural Institutions and Resource-Poor Farmers*. New York: Routledge.

Trumpy, Alexa J. 2008. "Subject to Negotiation: The Mechanisms Behind Co-Optation and Corporate Reform." *Social Problems* 55 (4): 480–500.

Tsing, Anna. 2000. "The Global Situation." *Cultural Anthropology* 15 (3): 327–360.

Tsing, Anna L. 2005. *Friction: An Ethnography of Global Connection*. Princeton, NJ: Princeton University Press.

Tuan, Yi-Fu. 2001. *Space and Place: The Perspective of Experience*. Minneapolis: University of Minnesota Press.

United Nations, Human Rights Council. 2012. *Report of the Special Rapporteur on the Rights of Indigenous Peoples, Mission to Argentina*, A/HRC/21/47/Add.2 (July 4). Available at: http://www.ohchr.org/EN/Issues/IPeoples/SRIndigenousPeoples/Pages/AnnualReports.aspx.

United Nations, United Nations Conference on Trade and Development (UNCTAD). 2006. *Tracking the Trend Towards Market Concentration: The Case of the Agricultural Input Industry*, UNCTAD/DITC/COM/2005/16. Available at http://unctad.org/en/Pages/Publications.aspx.

Van der Ploeg, Jan Douwe. 2008. *The New Peasantries: Struggles for Autonomy and Sustainability in an Era of Empire and Globalization*. London: Earthscan.

Van Zwanenberg, Patrick, and Valeria Arza. 2013. "Biotechnology and its Configurations: GM Cotton Production on Large and Small Farms in Argentina." *Technology in Society* 35 (2): 105–117.

Vanderford, Marsha L. 1989. "Vilification and Social Movements: A Case Study of Pro-Life and Pro-Choice Rhetoric." *Quarterly Journal of Speech* 75 (2): 166–182.

Villalon, Roberta. 2007. "Neoliberalism, Corruption, and Legacies of Contention: Argentina's Social Movements, 1993–2006." *Latin American Perspectives* 34 (2): 139–156.

Vitta, J. I., D. Tuesca, and E. Puricelli. 2004. "Widespread Use of Glyphosate Tolerant Soybean and Weed Community Richness in Argentina." *Agriculture, Ecosystems & Environment* 103 (3): 621–624.

Voss, Kim. 1996. "The Collapse of a Social Movement: The Interplay of Mobilizing Structures, Framing, and Political Opportunities in the Knights of Labor." In *Comparative Perspectives on Social Movements: Political Opportunities, Mobilizing Structures and Cultural Framings*, edited by Doug McAdam, John D. McCarthy, and Mayer N. Zald, 227–258. Cambridge: Cambridge University Press.

Voss, Kim, and Michelle Williams. 2012. "The Local in the Global: Rethinking Social Movements in the New Millennium." *Democratization* 19 (2): 352–377.

Wainwright, Joel, and Kristin Mercer. 2009. "The Dilemma of Decontamination: A Gramscian Analysis of the Mexican Transgenic Maize Dispute." *Geoforum* 40 (3): 345–354.

Walder, Andrew G. 2009. "Political Sociology and Social Movements." *Annual Review of Sociology* 35 (1): 393–412.

Weitz-Shapiro, Rebecca. 2014. *Curbing Clientelism in Argentina. Politics, Poverty, and Social Policy.* New York: Cambridge University Press.

White, Christine Pelzer. 1986. "Everyday Resistance, Socialist Revolution and Rural Development: The Vietnamese Case." *Journal of Peasant Studies* 13 (2): 49–63.

Williams, Gary M., Robert Kroes, and Ian C. Munro. 2000. "Safety Evaluation and Risk Assessment of the Herbicide Roundup and Its Active Ingredient, Glyphosate, for Humans." *Regulatory Toxicology and Pharmacology* 31 (2): 117–165.

Williams, Raymond. 1983. *Keywords: A Vocabulary of Culture and Society.* New York: Oxford University Press.

Wilson, Geoff A. 2001. "From Productivism to Post-Productivism … and Back Again? Exploring the (Un)changed Natural and Mental Landscapes of European Agriculture." *Transactions of the Institute of British Geographers* 26 (1): 77–102.

Wittgenstein, Ludwig. 1949. *Tractatus Logico-Philosophicus.* London: Routledge & Kegan Paul.

Wolf, Eric R. 1966. "Kinship, Friendship, and Patron–Client Relations in Complex Societies." In *The Social Anthropology of Complex Societies*, edited by Michael Banton, 1–22. London: Routledge.

Wolf, Steven, and Alessandro Bonanno. 2013. *The Neoliberal Regime in the Agri-Food Sector: Crisis, Resilience, and Restructuring.* London: Routledge.

Wolff, Jonas. 2007. "(De-) Mobilising the Marginalised: A Comparison of the Argentine Piqueteros and Ecuador's Indigenous Movement." *Journal of Latin American Studies* 39 (1): 1–29.

Wolford, Wendy. 2007. "From Confusion to Common Sense: Using Political Ethnography to Understand Social Mobilization in the Brazilian Northeast." In *New Perspectives in Political Ethnography*, edited by Lauren Joseph, Matthew Mahler, and Javier Auyero, 14–36. New York: Springer.

Wolford, Wendy. 2009. "Everyday Forms of Political Expression." *Journal of Peasant Studies* 36 (2): 411–414.

Wolford, Wendy. 2010. *This Land Is Ours Now: Social Mobilization and the Meanings of Land in Brazil.* Durham, NC: Duke University Press.

Woods, Michael. 2007. "Engaging the Global Countryside: Globalization, Hybridity and the Reconstitution of Rural Place." *Progress in Human Geography* 31 (4): 485–507.

Wright, Angus L. 2005. *The Death of Ramón González: The Modern Agricultural Dilemma.* Austin: University of Texas Press.

Wright, Rachel A., and Hilary Schaffer Boudet. 2012. "To Act Or Not To Act: Context, Capability, and Community Response to Environmental Risk." *American Journal of Sociology* 118 (3): 728–777.

Yankelevich, Andrea. 2006. *GAIN Report. Argentina Biotechnology Annual 2005.* Buenos Aires: USDA Foreign Agricultural Service.

Zahm, S. H., D. D. Weisenburger, P. A. Babbitt, R. C. Saal, J. B. Vaught, K. P. Cantor, and A. Blair. 1990. "A Case-Control Study of Non-Hodgkin's Lymphoma and the Herbicide 2, 4-Dichlorophenoxyacetic Acid (2, 4-D) in Eastern Nebraska." *Epidemiology* 1 (5): 349–356.

INDEX

abeyance structures, 13

Abu-Lughod, Lila, 134, 150, 166, 172

accommodation: agency and, 168; of agrochemical exposure and GM crops, 149–54

ACINA. See Asamblea Campesina Indígena del Norte Argentino

activists: killings of, 37–39; peasant, 20; political network use by, 16

aerial crop dusting, bill to ban, 43

aerial fumigation, 79, 80

agency: accommodation and negotiation in, 168; clientelism and, 16; collective action and, 168; demobilization and, 16, 19, 20, 166–68; mobilization and, 19, 168

Agnew, John, 11

agrarian politics, 165

agribusiness, 8, 22; Argentine, 31–34; consolidation in, 180n12; in Formosa, 77–80; imposition of, 108; large-scale firms, 33; mobilization of, 49–50; scale of, 35–36

agricultural biotechnology: neoliberal policies and, 29; TNCs and, 31

agricultural investment funds, 31–33

agricultural market, concentration of, 8

agriculture: neoliberalization of, 11, 19, 35, 164; Pampas models of, 36

agrochemical companies, 8

agrochemical drift, 186n16; as accident, 105, 111; in California, 112; crop destruction from, 79, 84, 86; damage in Monte Azul from, 88; economic impacts of, 106–7; in Formosa, 79–80; fumigation planes causing, 80; GM cotton as defense against, 156–57; reports of, 43; as social problem, 112; in 2009, 2, 21, 23, 133, 137, 140, 167; in 2003, 1, 84, 102–3, 126, 163, 166–67

agrochemicals, 1, 2; accommodating exposure to, 149–54; damage from, 90; dependence on, 162; injuries from, 138; lack of consensus on exposure to, 146; national campaign against, 43–44; organophosphate, 55; responses to exposures to, 139–42; rising use in Argentina of, 41–42; soy boom and exposure to, 41–45

agrotoxics, 153

Argentina: agrarian and environmental politics of GM crops in, 165; agrochemical use increasing in, 41–42; authorization of glyphosate-resistant soybeans in, 27; center and north, 26f; demobilization in, 2; GM